D0365589

By the same author

REPORT MY SIGNALS

BALL OF FIRE
The Fifth Indian Division 1939–46

THE TRIPLE STREAM
Four Centuries of English, French and German Literature, 1531–1930

GENERAL GRAHAM, LORD LYNEDOCH

WELLINGTON AT WAR, 1794–1815

IMPHAL
(*with Lt.-Gen. Sir Geoffrey Evans*)

THE HUNDRED DAYS

1812

Eyewitness Accounts of Napoleon's Defeat in Russia

COMPILED, EDITED, AND
TRANSLATED BY

Antony Brett-James

ST. MARTIN'S PRESS
New York
1966

To my friends
JOCK and LETTICE DAWSON

First published in the United States of America 1966

Library of Congress Catalog Card Number 66-15638
Manufactured in the United States of America

First printing

Contents

Illustrations

Maps

Introduction

WHEN General the Duke de Fezensac came to publish his recollections of the campaign in Russia, he wrote above the opening chapter a quotation from Vergil's *Aeneid*:

> O ashes of Troy, and you, shades of my companions: I take you as witnesses that in your disaster I recoiled neither before the shafts of the enemy nor before any kind of danger, and that, if my destiny had willed it so, I should have been worthy to die at your side.
>
> (II. 431–4)

It is a terrible story which unfolds in the eyewitness accounts set down day by day or years afterwards; and whether the men and women who became involved in the disastrous events were on the side of the victors or the vanquished, whether they marched with Napoleon's Grand Army through mud and dust towards the heart of Russia or watched with anxiety the fires and plundering which devastated Moscow, or pursued the retreating, starving, sick soldiers across the Berezina and a long snow-laden landscape, they experienced suffering and fear and watched humanity in the raw. And as one lives beside them through the appalling scenes of pursuit and retreat, one recalls Thomas Campbell's lines about a battle which had been fought a dozen Decembers earlier, at Hohenlinden, where the untrodden snow became stained with blood:

> Few, few shall part, where many meet!
> The snow shall be their winding-sheet,
> And every turf beneath their feet
> Shall be a soldier's sepulchre.

* * *

All dates are given in the New Style of the Gregorian Calendar, which in 1582 came into force for Roman Catholic countries only. Though England adopted the new dating method in 1752, Russia continued to use the old Julian Calendar until the end of the First World War. All French participants in the campaign of 1812 used the New Style, and so did most of the Germans, but the majority of those fighting on the Russian side gave dates in the Old Style or else wrote down both, e.g. 10/22 October. The battle fought on 7 September has been named throughout after the village of Borodino, though almost all French narratives use the name of the River Moskowa (more correctly Moskva) which flows across the battlefield. I should add that names of Polish origin, for example Poniatowski and Wilkowiski, have not been spelt in conformity with equivalent Russian names.

I should like to thank the Editor of *La Revue de Paris*, for permission to translate and to include in this volume parts of 'Napoléon en Lithuanie 1812, d'après documents inédits', a translation of Butkevicius's recollections by René Martel, from the issue of 15 August 1932. English translations have also been made of extracts from the following publications: *Le Général Compans (1769–1845), d'après ses notes de campagne et sa correspondence de 1812–1813*, by M. Ternoux-Compans (Paris 1912); *Mémoires du Général de Caulaincourt, Duc de Vicence*, Vols. 1 and 2; *Mémoires du Général Comte François Dumonceau*, edited by Jean Puraye, published by Editions Brepols, Brussels; 'Journal du Général Rossetti: La Campagne de Russie', from *La Revue de France*, 15 March 1932, and 1 March 1933; letters by Colonel François Parguez and Bacler d'Albe from *Lettres Interceptées par les Russes durant la Campagne de 1812*, edited by L. Hennet and E. Martin, published by *La Sabretache* in 1913; *Journal d'un Chirurgien de la Grande Armée, 1802–1813*, edited by Eugène Tattet; and *Mémoires du Général Griois, 1792–1822*, edited by Arthur Chuquet.

My special thanks are due to Mr. William Lough, M.B.E., whose generous offer to translate a score of Russian passages I accepted with gratitude; to the Hon. Mrs. Liliana Archibald, who besides drawing my attention to various errors and ambiguities, took immense pains over helping me to achieve consistency in the transliteration of Russian names; and to Brigadier Peter Young, D.S.O., M.C., F.S.A., whose guidance on numerous points of military detail and translation has been of great value. I am also indebted to Mr. Zigmund Chojecki, who very kindly found answers to a number of queries; to Mr. Philip Whitting, G.M., whose comments have saved me from some confusions and infelicities as well as enhancing the usefulness of the maps; and to Mr. F. I. S. McKendrick, my helpful and encouraging publisher. I gladly avail myself of this opportunity publicly to express my warm appreciation of their friendly interest and aid, and of my mother's assistance, skilled after long experience, with the arduous work of compiling an index.

A. B.-J.

Mill Hill and Camberley

How it came to War

IN the five years before 1812 several events chilled the friendship which had been expressed between Napoleon and the Tsar of All The Russias at the Peace of Tilsit in July 1807, and again one year later at the Congress of Erfurt. Deep mutual distrust and antagonistic ambitions made the friendship a brittle one.

When, at Erfurt, Napoleon suggested the possibility of his marrying the Tsar's sister Catherine, Alexander was evasive, and the Grand Duchess married instead the King of Württemberg. Later, when Napoleon put in a formal offer for the hand of the Tsar's younger sister, Anna, even though she was only fourteen, the Empress Mother was bitterly opposed to such an alliance, and to Napoleon himself. Since she considered Tilsit to be a pact with the devil, she was unlikely to consent to one of her daughters entering into a marriage pact with the same devil. Napoleon regarded the delay in replying to his offer as a personal slight, yet even before the anticipated refusal was received from St. Petersburg, he was negotiating with Metternich for the hand of the Emperor of Austria's eldest daughter, Marie-Louise. This offer was accepted immediately, and Napoleon had to go back somewhat unceremoniously on proposals to Russia of his own making. The Tsar might appear angry, but the Russian Court was secretly relieved at the removal of so delicate a question. However, France's subsequent *rapprochement* with Austria was unwelcome in Russia, and Napoleon admitted that his Austrian marriage had set Alexander and himself at variance.

The Duchy of Oldenburg caused another small rift in the alliance. When, at the end of 1810, Napoleon annexed the German coast, the ruler of this state was offered the alternatives of staying where he was in spite of French customs restrictions or of receiving Erfurt in exchange. The former was chosen, but in January 1811 France annexed Oldenburg as well, thereby breaking the Treaty of Tilsit which guaranteed Oldenburg to the peaceful possession of its lawful sovereign. The Tsar's displeasure was exacerbated by the fact that this expulsion occurred just when the marriage of his sister and the Duke's son was taking place.

Whereas the occupation of north Germany was designed to intensify Napoleon's Continental System, his retention of the fortresses along the Oder was important to Napoleon because it upheld his influence in German eyes and his position in Prussia. It also gave him an army corps on the northern flank of Austria in case she attacked him while his troops were far from France. His defeat of Austria at Wagram in 1809 altered this situation. The Tsar thought the placing of Napoleon's army three hundred leagues in advance of his frontiers incompatible with the spirit of the alliance. For Russia's own safety Alexander wanted the evacuation of Prussia, as well as to allow that country to recover full independence. Napoleon, however, would have none of this request, despite the urging of Caulaincourt, his Ambassador at St. Petersburg, and of others, who pointed out that Europe was more in need of reassurance than of terrorization.

Then there was Poland. Until 1795 the Kingdom of Poland had stood between Prussia and the dominions of the Tsar. At the outbreak of the French Revolution, in accordance with the 1772 partition, it had extended westwards almost to the Oder, including towns like Posen (Poznan), while eastwards it had reached beyond Vilna and Minsk to within a short distance of Smolensk in the north and of Kiev further south. Then, at the partition of 1793, Russia had annexed eastern Poland, including Minsk, Podolia, and Volynia, while Prussia had grabbed Posen, Kalish, Thorn, and Danzig. Two years later Poland was extinguished as an independent kingdom when Prussia gained Warsaw and surrounding districts, Austria took Cracow and much of Galicia, and the Russians straightened their frontier between Minsk and Grodno.

Things had remained thus until 1807, in which year Napoleon created a small Polish state under the name of the Grand Duchy of Warsaw. It contained the greater part of Austrian Poland and the whole of Prussia's share forfeited after Jena and Tilsit, and was placed under the rule of the King of Saxony as Grand Duke. Napoleon's creation did not satisfy Polish patriots, who looked to the Emperor of the French to restore their independence. Alexander had concurred at the time, but was suspicious that the Grand Duchy might prove a step towards the restoration of the Polish kingdom. Russia might in that case be obliged to cede provinces which she had taken earlier.

When, at the crushing Peace of Schönbrunn of October 1809, Austria yielded parts of eastern Galicia (one and a half million inhabitants) to enlarge the Grand Duchy, Alexander, even though he had received some territorial compensation, requested a guarantee that Napoleon would not revive an independent Poland. As a result, a convention with Russia was signed in St. Petersburg by Caulaincourt, the French Ambassador, stating that the Kingdom of Poland would never be re-established. Napoleon refused to ratify this agreement, so the Tsar secretly sounded the feelings of the Poles to ascertain whether he stood a chance of winning them over to Russia's side. He even offered to restore the kingdom, provided that he himself bore the title of Polish king. His overtures failed, the Poles sticking faithfully to Napoleon, who had once assured them that they could always count on his 'all-powerful protection' and had won the support of enough Poles to form a contingent of 30,000 men for his army.

Privately he denied any wish to be the Don Quixote of Poland, and told the Russian Ambassador in Paris that he did not intend to restore Poland. In the event, both sovereigns left the question in abeyance, each hoping to win Poland's support but reluctant to commit himself to definite steps.

One question which could not be overlooked, and which was the principal cause of friction between France and Russia during these years, was Napoleon's Continental System aimed against maritime Britain. Its effectiveness depended upon total enforcement, and Napoleon became obsessed with what was almost as much a yard-stick of his personal power as a method of economic warfare. To leave an inlet for goods in northern Europe undermined measures enforced elsewhere, and those who found ways round the System were challenging his power as well as aiding his principal foe. 'Without Russia,' he declared, 'the Continental System is an absurdity'; and if Russia was not prepared to maintain the blockade, then his remedy would be coercion.

Russia viewed the matter with different eyes. Internal discontent and opposition to Government policy had resulted from commercial troubles, a falling rate of exchange, and a disquieting depreciation of Russian paper money, and these in turn had been caused by a constant drain of capital abroad to pay for imported goods at a time when Russia was prevented by Napoleon's demands from exporting her own products. Russian agriculture and her timber trade had been sustaining grave losses. It was to remedy the financial balance that on 31 December 1810 an edict virtually prohibited the entry into Russia of luxury articles, wines, and silks, most of which came from France.

Not content with demanding the exclusion of British ships and goods, Napoleon accused Russia of infringing the Continental System by the admission of neutral ships to her ports, and claimed that the so-called neutral vessels in fact carried British goods. He was not pleased when Caulaincourt reminded him in June 1811 that licensed ships sailing directly from England had been allowed to enter French harbours on payment of a fifty per cent tax, and that French ships had returned with cargoes from England. If the Emperor allowed such secret modifications to the blockade, then he could hardly expect the Russians to do otherwise than follow suit. The Tsar's Ministers had kept to their side of the bargain by confiscating the cargoes of more than sixty vessels which had called at English ports, but had then decided to admit any neutral ship which could prove that she was genuinely neutral and had not touched at England. The Tsar refused to adopt the arbitrary measure urged upon him by Napoleon of confiscating the cargoes of neutral ships in the Baltic — at one time more than six hundred waited there, unable to enter German harbours and hoping to be allowed into Russian waters.

Napoleon believed that after a few quick, decisive victories he could persuade Alexander back into the Continental System in all its rigour. 'A single blow delivered at the heart of the Russian Empire, at Moscow the Great, at Moscow the Holy, will instantly put this whole blind, apathetic mass at my mercy. I know Alexander. I once had influence over him, and it will come back.' This was the view he expressed in March 1812. It reveals his under-estimation of the Tsar's firmness and the resistance of the Russian serfs, who made up ninety per cent of the population. Oppressed they might be, and hating their exploiters, but Holy Mother Russia must be defended against foreigners who came with fire and sword. Napoleon also failed to grasp that the Tsar, even though he was prepared to withdraw his protest against the annexation of Oldenburg and to introduce special concessions for French goods, was not ready for a second Tilsit. Alexander was well aware of the indignation aroused in Russia by that treaty, and sensed that the upper classes would not tolerate either a repetition of such humiliation or obedience to Napoleon at the price of commercial ruin. Prussians like Stein were urging the Tsar to make war with France; English agents were urging his merchants to declare for commercial freedom from the yoke of blockade; and his Ministers were stressing the threat of economic disaster. And the Tsar himself? Back in 1809 he had written to his sister Catherine: 'Bonaparte believes that I am nothing but a fool. He who laughs last laughs best! I put all my hope in God.' Though often inconsistent and vacillating, Alexander had proved to be far more astute, tenacious, and intractable than Napoleon had suspected from his showing at Tilsit.

On the diplomatic front Napoleon secured the concurrence of both Prussia and Austria, but failed to gain the active support of either Sweden or Turkey. On 24 March 1812 Russia and Sweden signed a treaty of alliance, a direct outcome of Napoleon's invasion of Swedish Pomerania after Prince Bernadotte's refusal to exclude entirely colonial goods to which the Continental System applied. As for Turkey, the conclusion of Russia's long-drawn-out war by the signature, on 28 May, of the Peace of Bucharest removed the danger from the Tsar's southern frontier and released an army which, under Admiral Chichagov, would play its part in defeating Napoleon's invasion. France had tried to dissuade Turkey from making peace with Russia, and had failed, as had an attempt by the British Navy to force the Dardanelles in 1807 and compel Turkey to declare war on France.

In April 1812 Napoleon sent peace overtures to London, promising to quit Spain if Britain would acknowledge his brother Joseph as King there and withdraw Wellington's army from the Peninsula. This offer, which would have freed Napoleon to devote almost all his resources to conquering Russia, was promptly rejected, so he tried to subdue the Tsar while Spain and Portugal still drained his military strength, and to dominate Europe while his control was being challenged from Moscow to Cadiz. He should have remembered the words he had written to Talleyrand in 1797: 'It is only with prudence, wisdom, and great skill that obstacles are surmounted. From triumph to a fall there is only one step.' But he could not rest. Nor could he accept a policy of moderation to allow France to recuperate from war-weariness, depression, and the crop-failure of 1811, and to safeguard his many conquests. It was time to stop, but he could not see it. One more quick success — and maybe he would require no more.[1]

Instead we have Admiral Decrès prophesying at Dresden in June 1812, just before the Grand Army marched towards Russia: 'He will not return from this war; or if he does return, it will be without his army.'

[1] His views were not consistent. For example, on 13 June he said to the young Count de Flahault: 'This war is not going to be a matter of a single campaign. I shall pursue the Russians as far as the Dvina and the Dnieper. I shall form a sort of bridgehead between these two rivers and behind them I shall establish 120,000 French troops.'

The Grand Army Prepares

WHILE Napoleon was making extensive diplomatic preparations for the war against Russia, he was also occupied with assembling the Grand Army and all the supplies, horses, cattle, guns, waggons, ammunition, and other materials essential to the conduct of a major campaign.

Early in 1811 Marshal Davout's corps in northern Germany and the French garrisons in Prussia had been strengthened. In a letter to the Marshal on 24 March Napoleon wrote: 'I do not want war with Russia, but I want to occupy offensive positions, and for that purpose I wish to make troop movements such as would cause war to break out if they occurred at a later date.' In August that year Napoleon outlined to his Ministers in general terms the plan for invading Russia, and by December he was ordering the Imperial Guard to be made ready for active service, and the princes of the Confederation of the Rhine to be informed of the need to remount their cavalry and prepare their contingents. A week before Christmas he was requesting the most detailed accounts available in French of Charles XII's campaign in Poland and Russia a century before; in Moscow nine months later Napoleon was to spend many hours reading Voltaire's history of the Swedish King.

As early as 8 January 1812, a Polish cavalry regiment in Valencia heard news of the impending campaign and two days later left Spain for the north. On February the *Armée d'Italie* set off across the Brenner Pass to Innsbruck and thence to Regensburg. From France troops crossed the Rhine at Köln, Bonn, Koblenz, and above all at Mainz, where Imperial Headquarters stayed until the last day of February. While Ney's corps headed for Erfurt and Leipzig, Oudinot's marched from Münster to Magdeburg, and thence via Berlin to Frankfurt-an-der-Oder, and Davout's also moved eastwards to that river, but along the coastal route, prior to holding a line on the Vistula with his left wing at Danzig, his centre at Thorn, and his right linking with Prince Poniatowski's Poles around Warsaw. Behind were the Bavarians at Posen and, in Kalish, the Saxons and King Jérôme's Westphalians. Further back still, forming a support line along the Oder, were cantoned the corps of Ney, Oudinot, and Eugène de Beauharnais, Viceroy of

Italy and Napoleon's stepson. There was also the Imperial Guard, numbering close on 36,000 men.

Whereas in Saxony the assembling troops received an excellent welcome, those in Prussia were often met by silent, hostile people. Attacks on individual soldiers were not infrequent, and one major who had cause to reflect on events in Spain observed: 'Here we lack only mountains to make guerrillas.' Much of this hostility was justified, because from Bohemia to the Hanseatic shores the motley army virtually invaded towns, villages, and isolated houses, too often frightening the inhabitants as its members imposed upon them, requisitioned their horses, their cattle, their waggons, their supplies. The name of 'Frenchman' became execrated, and so did that of some of the allies, not least by Prussians who resented the passage or quartering of troops and the burdensome levy of wheat, rye, rice, meat, hay, straw, dried vegetables, brandy and beer (two million bottles of each), and 15,000 horses, to which their king had agreed.

The cosmopolitan nature of the Grand Army is shown by a list of the countries which furnished regiments or squadrons: Anhalt, Austria, Baden, Bavaria, Berg, Croatia, Dalmatia, Denmark, France, Hesse-Darmstadt, Holland, Illyria, Italy, Lippe, Mecklenburg, Poland, Portugal, Prussia, Saxony, Spain, Switzerland, Westphalia, and Württemberg. Many of the troops had no idea of their destination, some believing it to be India, others convinced they would embark on the Baltic and invade England.

Napoleon himself, accompanied by the Empress Marie-Louise and their household, left Saint-Cloud on 9 May, crossed the Rhine at Mainz, and was ceremonially met by the King and Queen of Saxony just outside Dresden on the 15th. For the next fortnight, amid *Te Deums*, receptions, levées, gala performances at the theatre, gun salutes, boar-hunts, illuminations, torchlight processions, and firework displays, Napoleon aimed at intimidating his opponents and impressing Europe with his prestige as he dominated this glittering assembly of rulers great and small. Not only did German vassal princes arrive to pay homage. The Emperor and Empress of Austria came, and were treated with gratifying courtesy. So did the King and the Crown Prince of Prussia.

Having dominated the scene and conferred with statesmen and diplomats as well as monarchs, the Emperor of the French left Dresden on 29 May to join the Grand Army and confer instead with his marshals, generals, and administrative staff.

Figures of the Grand Army's strength vary sharply from one account to another, ranging from 430,000 to 610,000; but it seems likely that between June and November about 530,000 troops crossed the Niemen, with more than a thousand guns, some

30,000 carts and waggons, over 150,000 horses, and several thousand officials, grooms, *cantinières*, and the like.

The Russians were disposed in an arc behind the Niemen. General Wittgenstein's corps, on the right wing, was centred on Rossieny, a hundred miles north-west of Vilna and facing the Tilsit–Riga road. The left wing (two corps) of the First Army of the West, commanded by General Barclay de Tolly, was around Lida, sixty miles south of Vilna and opposite Grodno, where Platov's Cossacks guarded the frontier. In the centre three other corps held the line of the Niemen above and below Kovno. Further back three more army corps stood between Vilkomir and Smorgon. Barclay's force totalled about 125,000 troops and 584 guns.

Further to the south the Second Army of the West, under Prince Bagration and numbering 47,000 men and 168 guns, held positions around Volkovisk. A third Russian army was assembling under the command of General Alexander Tormassov in Volynia, and would build up to a strength of more than 40,000.

A nun named Antonina, who had been a serf before joining the Girls' Convent, saw a comet in 1811.[1]

One evening, when we were going to a commemoration service in the Church of the Beheading of St. John, I suddenly spotted on the far side of the church what looked like a shower of glittering flames. I gave a cry, and almost dropped my lantern. The mother abbess came to me and said: 'What are you doing? What is the matter?' Then she took several paces forward, also saw the meteor, and remained watching it for a long while. I asked her: '*Matondike*, what star is that?' She replied: 'It is not a star, but a comet.' I asked again: 'But what is a comet? I have never heard that word before.' The abbess then said: 'They are signs in the sky sent to us by God before any calamity.' Every night this comet blazed in the sky, and we all asked one another: 'What misfortunes will it bring upon us?'

[1] This comet was seen in many parts of Europe, ranging from Portugal in September to Glasgow University the following January.

On 1 March, just before leaving Paris for Metz, Dresden, Glogau, and Thorn, Captain Louis-Florimond Fantin des Odoards, a veteran of Ulm, Austerlitz, Friedland, and Spain, and now with the Grenadiers of the Old Guard, wrote in his journal:

It is going to begin, this new campaign which will greatly increase the glory of France. The formidable preparations are made, and our eagles will soon take wing towards countries of which our fathers scarcely know the names. . . . The Russian Army is not to be despised, no doubt: a large population attacked at home is not easily subjugated. Spain proves that, but what is there that the great Napoleon cannot achieve?

Besides, we cannot avoid going to visit the favourite of the Peter who deserved the name 'Great'. St. Petersburg will see us within its walls just as Vienna, Berlin, Rome, Madrid, and so many other capitals have done. Then we shall see.

In these circumstances I share the thoughts of the whole Army. It has never shown itself more impatient to run after fresh triumphs. Its august leader has so accustomed it to fatigue, danger, and glory that a state of repose has become hateful. With such men we can conquer the world.

Paul de Bourgoing, a second lieutenant in the Young Guard, recalls the warlike ardour which inspired the French people in 1812.

The period of discouragement and lassitude had not yet come, when the nation complained about the cruel demands of a war which kept on starting up again. The conscripts went happily away, and many voluntary enlistments swelled the ranks of a vast army.

Nothing can convey the enthusiasm with which the young men prepared for this distant expedition. I was nineteen at the time. We were so confident of success that, according to our calculations of promotion and ambition, we regretfully considered this campaign as the last in which the Emperor would take his chance in battle to become master of the world.

'What a pity,' said my contemporaries, my fellow second lieutenants, 'what a pity that we are arriving so late, after so many splendid victories, at the end of everything!'

'Don't worry,' replied the worthy Captain Théry, the oldest of our officers in the Grenadiers of the Old Guard. 'Don't worry, we have not reached the end yet. The Emperor will give us work to do. *There will be work for everyone.*'

On 6 March Guillaume Peyrusse, a paymaster with the Army at La Ferté-sur-Jouarre, wrote to his father in Carcassonne:

The intentions of His Majesty are impenetrable. In Paris people circulate all sorts of stories about what he plans to do. They send him to Egypt, to Constantinople, to India, etc. I would go to the ends of the world. I have a good carriage, good horses, some waggons on which I have a fair stock of provisions which I shall not touch except in an emergency. I am well, and Heaven can see to the rest.

General Auguste Bigarré, aide-de-camp to King Joseph in Madrid, was in Paris during March and April and moved a good deal in high society.

In the Paris salons the sole topic of conversation was the great expedition being mounted against Russia. . . . The fear of being sent to India once Russia had been conquered kept several young sprigs back in Paris, but the majority of the fashionable young military men required no tweak of the ear to persuade them to set off in pursuit of fresh laurels in as yet virgin territory for French arms.

During April one saw leaving the capital a huge crowd of generals, officers of all ranks, and military employees in all the administrative services. It has never been possible to calculate just what left Paris in the way of vehicles, horses, and supplies of all sorts. Throughout March and April the route from the city to Mainz and from Mainz to Dresden was so cluttered with troops and vehicles, with men and women who announced that they were off to Russia, that the people of Mainz and Cassel believed that the French were deserting their country. The coachbuilder Gros Jean alone made more than three hundred carriages in his workshops for the King of Naples [Murat], the Viceroy of Italy [Prince Eugène de Beauharnais], and the principal generals. Over ten thousand wills were drawn up by the notaries of Paris. A number of pretty women, some of them married, others not, accompanied their husbands or lovers as far as the Rhine.

Ludwig Wilhelm Gottlob Schlosser, a country clergyman in Saxony, saw a good deal of Napoleon's troops in his village near Leipzig.

On 19 March strong contingents of French troops began to arrive, and went on doing so without a break until 7 April. As most of Europe had suffered a bad harvest the previous year, and in our district we had gathered in little over one-third of the usual yield of hay, corn, and straw, the feeding of so many hundreds of men and horses became a heavy burden. The poor people handed over their seed-oats and bought hay at between one and two thalers a hundredweight. . . .

The French, down to the lowliest drummer, were very fastidious. These poor French devils were not satisfied with less than soup, meat and vegetables, roast, and salad for their midday meal, and there was no sign of their famous frugality. The officers were completely devoid of it! Some of them had to have pike and ham cooked in red wine. They drank great jugs of the richest cream, and cinnamon essence with it.

One consolation amid all our troubles was the news that the Government proposed to grant compensation, which for our village would amount to several thousand thalers. But only nine hundred were paid out. Our King was counting on a contribution in arrears from Prussia.

Among the troops quartered among us at the time were three companies of Portuguese.[1] They could not speak German, we had no Portuguese, and I had to do the job of quartermaster, so it was hard to make ourselves understood, though with a hotchpotch of French, Italian, and Latin words we managed in rather a makeshift way. These poor fellows, torn from their homeland and driven to the raw North, behaved much better than the French did, and they showed themselves to be co-operative and good-natured. If

[1] The Portuguese wore light-brown uniforms with scarlet facings. Two Portuguese regiments served in Ney's 3rd Corps.

one gave them some sausage, eggs, or whatever else it might be when they left, they would accept the smaller half and return the larger portion with thanks, whereas the French lived and kept house just as though nobody else knew how to do either. They exemplified their saying: '*Après nous le déluge.*'[1] They praised my profession as the most fortunate one, because in Portugal the best produce from garden, field, and kitchen was brought to the priest, and they inquired whether we had the same custom. I replied that we were paid a fixed salary, but neither received, wanted, nor would accept such gifts.

François Dumonceau, who though born in Brussels had lived mostly in Holland and had attended the artillery school in Groningen, took part in the campaign as a captain in the 2nd Regiment of Chevau-légers lanciers *of the Imperial Guard.*

At this time [April] the whole of Germany was covered with columns on the march towards the north, and although these were carefully echelonned so as to avoid any congestion, the countryside was nevertheless trampled down by reiterated and often excessive demands. All these troops, whether allies (from Bavaria, Württemberg, Baden, Westphalia, and elsewhere) or the French, were imbued with a fighting spirit which, now that they found themselves once more on a war footing, made them frequently too imperious in their relations with the owners of military billets. As a result many abuses occurred. However, Marshals Davout and Oudinot,[2] whose corps were ahead of us, tried to remedy the situation by a regulation which fixed the composition of each meal, for officers as well as for other ranks; among other things, this regulation allowed the officers half a bottle of wine a day. We found this regulation printed, posted, and strictly observed everywhere. At the slightest dispute, the local inhabitants took advantage of the regulation; and this helped to guarantee a measure of justice or moderation in our mutual relationships.

Furthermore, the population of the region we were passing

[1] The expression '*Après moi, le déluge*' was attributed to Louis XV (1710–74).

[2] Louis-Nicolas Davout, Duke of Auerstädt, Prince of Eckmühl (1770–1823), commanded the 1st Corps. Charles-Nicolas Oudinot, Duke of Reggio (1767–1847), had the 2nd Corps.

through seemed to have become temporarily resigned. Our hosts received us with urbanity, without too much apparent resentment, despite all the inconveniences we caused them. They certainly complained about the continual troop movements, and about the consequent expense, but these complaints did not amount to reproaches against us. They considered us less as accomplices than as victims of these ceaseless wars and made out that, according to rumours going about, once the Russians had been defeated Napoleon's ambition would drag us across Asia towards India.

In April Colonel Jean-Nicolas Noël of the artillery wrote down a frank and realistic appraisal of what lay in store.

War has not been declared, and many hope that it will not take place. Why then all these preparations and this concentration of troops on the Vistula? One could wish that the Emperor would impose a limit on his ambition at long last and would concern himself more effectively with the welfare of France, which is exhausted by these continual wars. What can a war with Russia lead to? In the event of success what will we take from her? If we suffer a reverse, all the false friends who march with us only because they are compelled or forced to do so will turn against us. That is what all the officers around me are saying.

Lieutenant Karl von Suckow, a Mecklenburger serving in the Chasseurs à pied *of the Württemberg Guard, recalls an occasion at Schorndorf, near Stuttgart, before the campaign opened.*

I remember, as if it were yesterday, a dinner we gave our brigade commander, General [Ernst] von Hügel, in the large room of the Golden Stag. He had come to inspect our battalion. During the meal our conversation was naturally concerned mostly with the imminent campaign.

The General warned us to have no illusions on the matter and to prepare ourselves resolutely to meet every eventuality. One young lieutenant did not share this point of view. He believed that everything would go well, and he was even thoughtless enough to exclaim:

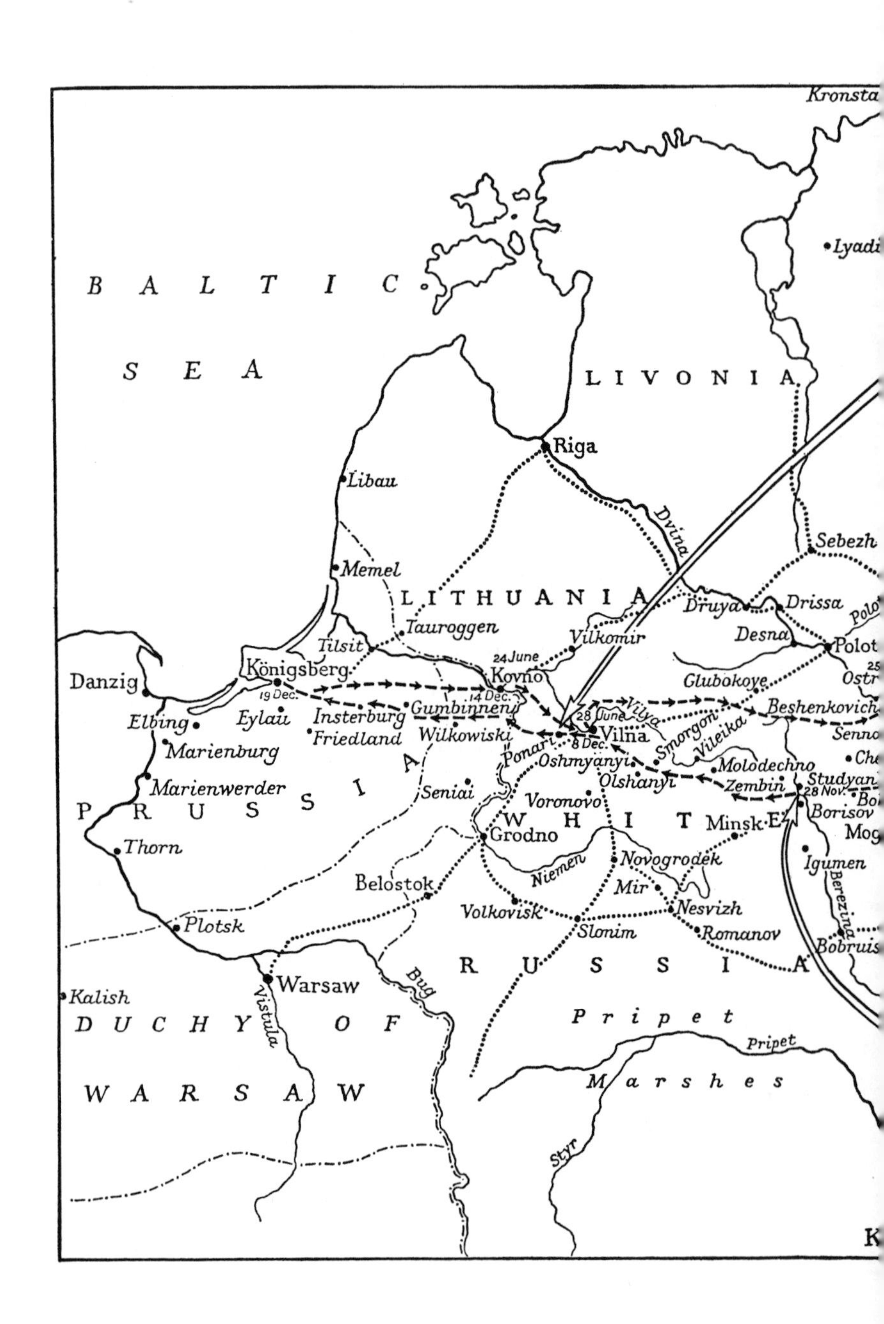

BALTIC
SEA
LIVONIA
LITHUANIA
PRUSSIA
WHITE
RUSSIA
DUCHY OF
WARSAW
Pripet
Marshes
Riga
Libau
Memel
Dvina
Tauroggen
Tilsit
Königsberg
19 Dec.
Danzig
Elbing
Eylau
Insterburg
Gumbinnen
Friedland
Wilkowiski
Marienburg
Marienwerder
Thorn
Plotsk
Kalish
Warsaw
Vistula
Bug
Belostok
Seniai
Grodno
Kovno
24 June
14 Dec.
Vilkomir
Vilna
28 June
8 Dec.
Ponari
Oshmyanyi
Olshanyi
Voronovo
Smorgoni
Vileika
Vilya
Molodechno
Zembin
Studyan
28 Nov.
Borisov
Minsk
Novogrodek
Niemen
Mir
Nesvizh
Volkovisk
Slonim
Romanov
Igumen
Berezina
Druya
Drissa
Desna
Glubokoye
Beshenkovich
Sebezh
Pripet
Styr

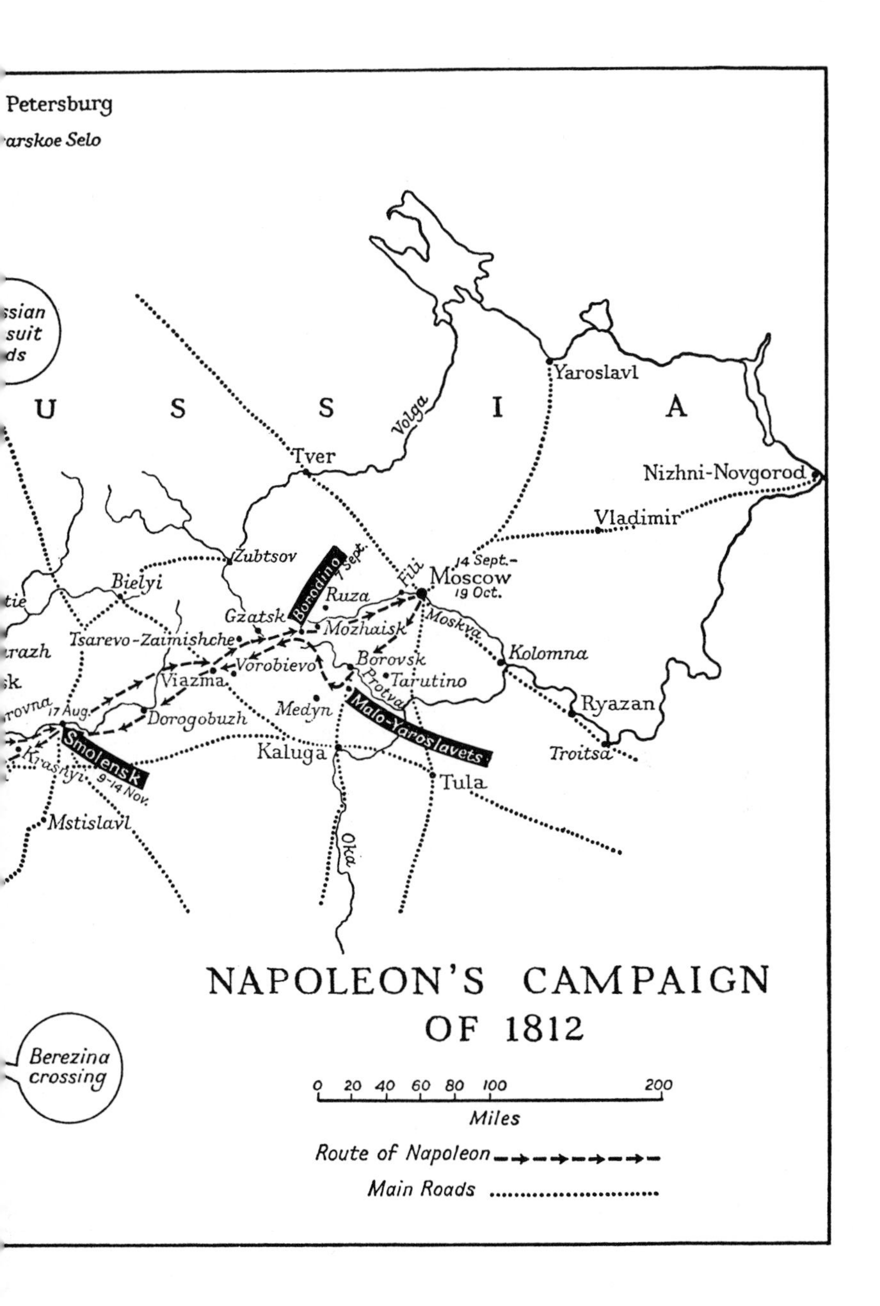

NAPOLEON'S CAMPAIGN OF 1812

'Pooh! A war against Russia! The prospect worries me no more than eating a slice of bread and butter!'

At these words the General replied in a grave tone of voice:

'All right, Lieutenant. When the occasion arises, I shall not fail to remind you of the slice of bread and butter.'

He kept his promise.

Nine-year-old Wilhelm von Kügelgen, who had been born in St. Petersburg, was living with his family in Dresden when Napoleon's Grand Army passed through the capital of Saxony on its way to Russia.

I can still see the long dark columns of the Old Guard with their proud eagles, tall bearskins, and martial faces hovering like gloomy dream pictures; first the warlike sound of drums and pipes, then the ghostly figures of the pioneers with glinting axes and long black beards, and behind them the endless columns of transport.

They went past under our windows like this every day, man by man, brigade by brigade. I saw nearly all the arms of the service in the Grand Army: the tall carabiniers with plumed helmets and golden cuirasses, the light *chasseurs*, lancers, hussars, *voltigeurs*, all the types of infantry and artillery with good horse-drawn vehicles, and finally long columns of pontoon-bridging and military equipment. It was an excellent army, such as the world had never seen before, well supplied and equipped with every necessity; even winter shoes had been thought of, and green-tinted glasses against the glare of the snow. . . .

The German, Spanish, and Italian troops, obeying the tyrant's command, looked warlike and proud. They had taken part in his victories, shared the honours of his army, and were to share in the final catastrophe.

At the beginning of May Napoleon appeared in person[1] and, surrounded by numerous other vassal princes, received visits from his allies, the Emperor Francis and King Frederick William. The latter I met while walking on the Brühl Terrace[2] and immediately

[1] He and the Empress arrived on 16 May.

[2] The terrace, some four hundred yards long and planted with trees, extended along the south bank of the Elbe. The garden had belonged to Count Brühl, a former Minister, who died in 1763.

took to him because he looked so worthy and so sad, and Senff[1] told me he was a good royal gentleman.

There was a great deal to be seen in Dresden at this time. The presence of so many armies filled the town with martial pomp; bells pealed and cannons boomed in welcome to the princes, grand parades and manœuvres entertained them, and at night the town shone under the magical glare of a thousand lamps. I don't know if it was on this or another Napoleonic occasion[2] that a broad rainbow made up of gay paper lanterns arched the sky high above the Elbe which reflected every colour of the spectrum — it was the finest light effect one could ever hope to see at night. Fireworks crackled in the air. . . .

Every house was full of soldiers who talked, laughed, and swore in nearly every European language. Even we, although only tenants, had a general billeted on us, and he and his suite occupied almost half our rooms, and my hard-pressed mother was considerably startled when one fine morning an aide-de-camp on the staff of the King of Naples, who was lodged nearby, added his presence to the household.

While arrangements were being made to accommodate him, the following conversation took place between him and my mother.

'If Madame would like to see the Emperor,' said the stranger, 'she has only to go to the window, and he will pass the house almost at once.'

'If my guest will allow it, I shall withdraw to the kitchen,' replied my mother, 'because I have little inclination to see the man who is in the process of crushing a poor nation which has done him no harm.'

The officer laughed and said it could only lead to something from which one must avert one's eyes again. Then he added confidentially:

'Believe me, Madame, I share your taste, and could well envy you such a kitchen.'

This admission was rather unexpected from an officer of the Grand Army, and my mother broke off the conversation. When we got to know him better we discovered that the officer we had taken

[1] Senff was Kügelgen's teacher.
[2] It was on 19 May, to celebrate the arrival of the Emperor and Empress of Austria.

for a Frenchman was in fact Italian, and as such perhaps had some justification in wishing the benefactor of his motherland out of the way.

The artist Adrian Ludwig Richter (1803–84) was nearly nine when the French soldiers arrived in Dresden. He and his father, an engraver and draughtsman, lived on one floor of a house near the Amalienstrasse, while his mother and the other two children had gone to look after the grandfather, who had just lost his wife.

There was no end to the billeting of troops. The two of us had one room only for our own use. The others were always full of soldiers. The floors were covered with straw, on which they slept. Weapons, items of uniform, ration loaves, cartridges, and who knows what else lay around higgledy-piggledy. For a time we had thirteen men in our moderate-sized apartment, because my kind-hearted father had also taken in the men who had been allotted to two widows living above us. These women had shut their door and pestered my father to make room for the men, promising to help him look after them as best they could. And this they did.

Amid all these hardships, the disrupted family life, and the severe shortages of money and provisions, our kitchen often presented a comic scene. Father would be standing by the range, stirring an enormous pan of rice or potato mash. The elderly and obliging widows split firewood, put pepper in the mortar for pounding, rubbed hard rolls on the grater, washed plates, fetched water, laughed and joked, while the soldiers took their muskets to pieces, cleaning and oiling, or else polished their straps; and all the time they tried to carry on a conversation by means of miming and nonsense, because none of us spoke French, and the soldiers could not understand German. It was all extremely amusing to watch and listen to.

The Austrian Foreign Minister, Klemens Wenzel Lothar, Count Metternich, met Napoleon at Dresden and had the Emperor's campaign plans explained to him during a long interview.

'My undertaking is one of those where the solution is to be found in patience. Victory will go to the most patient. I shall open the campaign by crossing the Niemen, and it will be concluded at Smolensk and Minsk. There I shall stop and fortify those two points. At Vilna, where the main headquarters will spend next winter, I shall busy myself with organizing Lithuania, which is impatient to be freed from the yoke of Russia. I shall wait and see which of us tires first: I of feeding my army at Russia's expense, or Alexander of maintaining my army at the expense of his country. Perhaps I myself shall spend the most inclement months of the winter in Paris.'

To my question what he would do in the event of Tsar Alexander not making peace because of the occupation of Lithuania, Napoleon replied: 'In that case I shall advance next year to the centre of the empire, and I shall be patient in 1813 as I shall have been in 1812! As I have already told you, the affair is a question of time.'

Napoleon sent one of his aides-de-camp, Louis, Count de Narbonne, who had been Minister of War to Louis XVI and, years later, French Minister in Bavaria, to the Tsar's headquarters in Vilna. This account of their meeting is taken from the memoirs of Narbonne's son-in-law, Count de Rambuteau, who was Chamberlain to the Emperor.

The Tsar received him very well and in the course of their conversation said: 'What does the Emperor want? Does he want to get me on his side, to compel me to adopt measures which will ruin my people? And because I refuse, he means to make war on me, in the belief that after two or three battles and the occupation of several provinces I shall sue for peace, on terms dictated by himself. He is mistaken.' Then, taking a huge map of his states, he slowly unfolded it on the table and went on: '*Monsieur le Comte*, I am convinced that Napoleon is the greatest general in Europe, his armies are the best trained, his lieutenants the most courageous and experienced. But space is a barrier. If, after several defeats, I withdraw, sweeping the inhabitants along with me; if I let time, deserts, and climate defend Russia for me, then perhaps I shall have the last word on the most formidable army of modern times.'

This conversation struck Monsieur de Narbonne so forcibly that he reported it to the Emperor [in Dresden] exactly as I have given it here. It seemed to make some impression on Napoleon, but the die was cast. He wanted to march at the head of all the nations of Europe except two — England and Russia — and to triumph over the one by crushing the other.

Captain Louis Bro, with the 5th Squadron of the Chasseurs à cheval *of the Guard, arrived in Posen on 25 May.*

Posen was the centre of a vast camp. Murat was putting the finishing touches to the organization of his superb and numerous cavalry. The infantry corps, commanded by marshals, crossed the River Wartha singing martial airs. Order and discipline reigned throughout. The Emperor, who came from Glogau in a single journey, arrived at sunset.[1] He had given orders forbidding any compliments being paid to him. Imperial Headquarters had been established in a Jesuit monastery, the members of which gave the Sovereign a fervent welcome. So as not to disturb his sleep, the head of the monastery decided to cancel night-time chanting in the chapel.

At ten o'clock that evening I went into the quarters reserved for Marshal Berthier, intending to visit Leduc, his private secretary. The poor fellow was working by the light of a kind of lantern in a large cell hung with what seemed to be very fine pictures. The Prince of Neuchâtel, who knew me, called out: 'You have arrived at a very convenient moment, Captain Bro. Your handwriting is good. You will write twenty letters for me. Sit down there, beside your cousin.'

Outside, in the courtyard, a bell rang every hour. By midnight the work was finished. The Chief of Staff took the papers, a door was opened for him, and he went in to the Emperor who was seated in front of a large fire, his face flushed by the heat and wearing a very hard expression, as though he were displeased about something. Once the letters had been signed, sealed, and dispatched, the Marshal dismissed me, saying: 'Now you can go to the tavern or to bed. I shall bear in mind that you have served me as a temporary secretary.'

Leduc took me out. In the cloister court we met a procession of

[1] Napoleon left Dresden on 29 May, spent one night at Glogau, and two at Posen.

men robed in black who were quietly intoning in Latin. The clank of my sword on the paving-stones startled several of them.

Captain Heinrich von Brandt, of the 2nd Regiment of the Vistula, a Polish officer who had fought in Spain, affords a glimpse of Napoleon at Thorn on the night of 3–4 June.

At about one o'clock in the morning the officers on duty were not a little surprised to hear him pacing up and down his room for quite a long time, singing loudly this verse from the Hymn of Méhul[1] (*Le Chant du départ*):

Et du nord au midi la trompette guerrière
A sonné l'heure des combats!
Tremblez, ennemis de la France, etc.

This unusual evocation of memories of the Revolution seemed to be inspired by a premonition of the huge difficulties and dangers the new campaign held in store. It made a deep impression on those who were listening. I was told this incident by one of them, Colonel Malzewski, who was then on the staff and who later assumed command of our regiment after the capture of Smolensk.

Captain Girod de l'Ain, who was aide-de-camp to General Dessaix commanding the 4th Division, had not only fought at Friedland in 1807 but had spent three years campaigning in the Peninsula, and contrasted the Grand Army with the army in Spain which he had just left.

What struck me most was the immense number of vehicles and baggage of all kinds which the former took with it. Each division had in its wake a column occupying about two leagues.[2] It is true that a large part of this baggage comprised vehicles laden with provisions, which every corps had orders to requisition as it crossed Prussia and Poland, and these vehicles, with their horses

[1] Étienne-Nicolas Méhul (1763–1817), French composer who wrote the music for the well-known patriotic song, to words written in 1794 by André Chénier's brother, Marie-Joseph.

[2] A league was about three miles.

and drivers, were not dismissed, if ever they were, until the reserves of provisions were progressively used up. These, of course, were not touched until the resources of each locality had been exhausted. But the generals and senior staff officers all had waggons and carriages drawn by two horses, and even two-wheeled cabriolets or post-chaises. Add to these the trains of the large artillery parks, the pontoon bridges, the ambulances, etc., etc., and you can judge what such an army looked like by comparison with that in Spain which, besides its guns and their ammunition waggons, took with it only a few pack-mules.

Another officer who had served in Spain, Colonel François, Count Roguet, of the Foot Grenadiers of the Old Guard, travelled 1,200 miles in sixteen weeks to join the Grand Army and take command of the 2nd Division of the Young Guard.

The generals and senior officers of the division were young, tough, energetic, experienced — soldiers in the true sense of the word. They inspired complete confidence. Some of them looked on Russia as a first step and believed they were going as far as Persia, and had made preparations accordingly. Without thinking of any such adventurous destination, I had a carriage, two waggons, books, a great many maps, twelve horses, six servants. The officers were equipped in proportion, and this was to prove one of our embarrassments.

Sergeant Joseph Schrafel relates that when the 5th Bavarian Line Regiment left Memel, his wife Walburga managed to accompany it.

All vehicles, apart from guns and ammunition waggons, had to travel separately, either in front of or behind the troops. My wife used to set off every time with the baggage and other carts an hour before we left. One day when we reached the place where the division was to assemble, I saw something in the distance, swimming around in a lake, but I could not make out what it was. As we got nearer, however, the soldiers shouted to me: 'Sergeant! Your wife is out there in the lake, in great danger.' You can imagine the shock I felt. I ran as hard as I could to the lake and saw

Tsar Alexander I in 1818, from the painting by Sir Thomas Lawrence in the Waterloo Chamber at Windsor Castle

General Barclay de Tolly, from the painting by George Dawe

General Prince Bagration, from the painting by Tropinin

a great many people standing on the bank and watching, but not one of them ventured in. Eventually, before I could reach the bank, I saw a soldier throw off his weapons, coat, and shoes, plunge into the water, swim out to the cart, seize the bridle, and by the time I arrived on the scene he had pulled the horses to dry land at the same spot where it had gone in. My wife stood dripping on the shore. Her rescuer was a Frenchman who was on his own and following his unit, and Providence had sent him there, so to speak, for that purpose, because he was the only man of all those on the spot who could swim. I wanted to give him a crown thaler, but he handed back the present as if offended and said in broken French: 'Not so, my friend! That is not good. Is your wife rescued, so you would also rescue my wife if she fall into the water.'

The good Frenchman was wrong. I should have had to dispense with fetching his wife out of the water, because I could not swim. I discovered later that General Wrede[1] also wanted to reward him for this action, but even from him the noble fellow would accept nothing. What distressed me most was that I could not converse with him, because neither knew the other's language. I don't even know his name, and have never heard of him again.

My wife had found herself in extreme danger through no fault of her own. It was a very hot day, and when the horses, who were suffering from thirst, spotted the water, they tore their reins out of her grasp and plunged with the cart from the high bank down into the lake.

A Lithuanian named Butkevicius, who worked as a parish priest for many years and died in 1871 at an advanced age, was a schoolboy at the time of Napoleon's invasion, living at Wilkowiski.

A few weeks before the French arrived, an order came to requisition all bread, all alcohol, and all the provisions in the area. At the same time it was announced in the *Warsaw Journal* — the subprefect received the only copy in the district — that the Army of Westphalia had arrived in Warsaw and that preparations were being made in Germany for receiving the Grand Army. A few

[1] Karl Philipp Wrede (1767–1838) commanded the 20th Bavarian Division in Saint-Cyr's corps.

days later strong detachments of French cavalry appeared near Seniai,[1] where I was attending the *lycée*. The commander of all the cavalry was General Grouchy,[2] and the corps lodged in Seniai was under the command of a Bavarian general, Prince Wrede. The latter, who was displeased to see that the inhabitants of the town had failed to welcome his arrival within their walls with sufficient enthusiasm, levied a war contribution of 24,000 francs, and gave warning that fire and bloodshed would ensue if this sum were not paid on the following day. The sub-prefect went to see General Grouchy to have this inhuman order withdrawn, and he won his case. But Prince Wrede took revenge on the inhabitants by having the thatch pulled from roofs and given to the horses and by devastating the crops instead of being content with the contributions of hay which had been specified by the local authorities. The Prince sent two dragoon regiments, which had spent the night there, out of the town, made them bivouac in the fields, and ordered them to plunder the kitchen-gardens and gardens. Some trees were even stripped of their branches and mutilated, but not one of them withered. Furthermore, the corn, flattened or trampled down by the cavalry, grew again, and the people reaped a good harvest that year. Although I cannot call this event a miracle, I do consider it to be a rare and remarkable event.

Captain François Dumonceau mentions the difficulties of feeding the immense army that was assembling west of the Niemen early in June.

Care had certainly been taken to accumulate huge stocks of provisions in various localities nearby so as to ensure the supplies desirable, but the means of transport, however great these were, did not always suffice to bring up what was necessary in the wake of the army at the right time. Then the mills, required for grinding such a vast quantity of grain, and the ovens for baking such numbers of loaves, were often lacking. This led to cases of scarcity among the troops, with all that usually ensues in the way of depredations on the local inhabitants. In vain the Emperor issued re-

[1] Forty miles to the south.
[2] Emmanuel de Grouchy (1766–1847) had the 3rd Cavalry Corps.

proaches and recommendations. In vain was there feverish activity everywhere. In vain did companies of masons and bakers, specially organized for the purpose, go ahead at each stage of the march to build ovens and bake bread. The distribution of food still left much to be desired, and the misery continued.

As for the horses, they had long since been reduced to eating green forage or corn cut in the fields, as and when needed, and only very occasionally did they receive a small ration of oats or barley.

All this made one think of other embarrassments which could be foreseen, and the forecasts brought up other equipment measures which were ordered during the three days' rest we enjoyed in Königsberg. Thus each company was provided with a large axe for cutting down big timber or for slaughtering cattle; this was entrusted to the quartermaster-sergeant. Eight small hatchets were issued to the troop corporals for cutting wood, sharpening picket points, and building huts or bivouac shelters. Finally, each horseman received a sickle for cutting standing crops as forage. These various articles had to be fastened on to the portmanteau by means of the straps provided. We were ordered to keep ourselves in a constant state of readiness for an immediate start.

Meanwhile, our guard detachment at the royal castle was changed every day at noon, and escorted the Emperor during his daily excursions. These always occurred at about one or two o'clock in the afternoon. . . . The Emperor was preceded by two lancers whom he followed at a distance of ten to fifteen yards, riding alone, the Duke of Istria[1] a little behind him to the left, and then, farther back, the rest of the suite and the escort. From time to time he would speak to the Duke, who hurriedly approached, took off his hat and remained uncovered throughout the conversation, not replacing his hat until he withdrew. All the way along a crowd would dash up to watch the Emperor pass, and well beforehand the windows would be full of spectators. Women predominated, and each would greet him respectfully and in silence. Now and then he acknowledged them by raising his hat, though without appearing to pay any attention: his usual expression — impassive, phlegmatic, and solemn — never altered.

[1] Marshal Jean-Baptiste Bessières (1766–1813), commanding the Cavalry of the Imperial Guard.

Colonel Alfred-Armand-Robert de Saint-Chamans, in command of the 7th Regiment of Chasseurs, *disliked the French Army's usual policy of living off the country rather than paying its way.*

We had received orders, on our own responsibility to take all we could find in the way of grain, brandy, and cattle from every billet we might occupy between the Rivers Vistula and Niemen. This was a very rich and fertile country, but the requisitions and removals we made were, alas, very heavy, and each corps, when it reached the Niemen, brought in its wake rich herds of cattle and immense parks of vehicles laden with provisions.

However, the carrying-out of these orders had been most repugnant to all officers, and one must admit that, after spending several days in the home of a village noble or a wealthy farmer, and having been received there as well as we would have been in France, often better, it was extremely cruel of us to take away their teams of horses, their grain, and their cattle, as if in gratitude for the excellent way in which they had treated us. These poor people besought us to mitigate the harshness of this order which was reducing them from wealth to penury. And I believe that every officer tried, as I did, to soften their lot; yet even with adjustments, we still did them great harm.

This was how we treated an ally, whose troops had joined us to fight the Russian armies. On seeing this bad behaviour and disorder, I was prejudiced in advance against the campaign we were about to undertake. I had just come from Andalusia where I had been in a position to judge that we had only been able to maintain ourselves hitherto thanks to excellent discipline and good military administration. In the army that was to enter Russia I saw totally different elements. The military administration in particular was filled with men who had never seen war and who proclaimed loudly that they had come on the campaign in order to make their fortunes. They seemed to think that once outside France they had only to stoop down and grab, but all these notions of making a fortune, as well as the people who had been excited at the prospect, were to remain on the road from Moscow to Königsberg.

The memoirs of Lieutenant von Suckow, in the Chasseurs à pied *of the King of Württemberg's Guard, contain numerous complaints about French behaviour towards allies in respect of rations.*

On arrival in Posen, one of the most beautiful towns in Poland, we realized yet again the defective organization of the supply services and the complete lack of provisions. Furthermore, we now had to deal far more often with the employees of the Imperial administration, and this was not always pleasant. From now on our rations depended entirely on the magazines. One needs to have served with the French to understand fully the arrogance with which the 'weevils' — a nickname given by our soldiers to the commissaries and others — treated their German allies. When rations were distributed, each loaf, each pound of meat had to be fought for. In this respect the French always treated us as little boys. It was quite another matter on the battlefield, when Napoleon's orders had to be carried out.

Butkevicius tells us that on 21 June the people of Wilkowiski turned out to see Napoleon arrive from Königsberg and Gumbinnen.

At sunset we saw a cloud of dust along the road and trumpets heralded the Emperor's approach. A few moments later he appeared, seated in a waggon which he was driving himself. Trumpeters rode ahead, and Napoleon had an escort of cavalry officers and N.C.O.s. . . . He headed straight for the castle where a lodging had been prepared for him. Despite its coating of dust, the Emperor's face showed signs of fatigue, excitement, and displeasure caused by bad news he had received on the way. His ill humour changed to anger when he learnt in Wilkowiski that not only the army but even the Guard was short of provisions. He did not sleep that night, and everywhere people were organizing ovens to bake bread. The army remained four extra days in Wilkowiski, and war was declared on Russia four days later than expected. The troops had to rest after their long march, and in the meantime the supplies were completed. . . .

Napoleon's study had been installed in a rustic pavilion surrounded by tall poplars. Numerous maps were spread out on his desk. At another table sat Marshal Berthier,[1] Chief of Staff of the Grand Army. Although the weather was very hot, Napoleon kept on his dark greatcoat and his little hat which he wore while talking to the generals and marshals, whereas these all stood uncovered to listen. He often walked round the office, and looked at the plans and maps as he gave out his orders. Throughout his stay in Wilkowiski he was certainly in a very bad mood, because he dictated letters in a terrible tone of voice. Every day I spent several hours in the courtyard, watching at close range the Emperor Napoleon of whom I had heard so much since childhood, and trying to engrave his features on my memory.

[1] Pierre-Alexandre Berthier, Prince of Neuchâtel (1753–1815).

Across the Niemen

AFTER Napoleon had reconnoitred the Niemen on 23 June, a pontoon and a pile bridge were thrown across that river after dark, a little upstream from Kovno, which was served only by a ferry. Next morning the main part of the Grand Army began to cross, watched by the Emperor who played with a riding-whip and hummed the tune '*Malbrouk s'en va-t-en guerre.*' While these divisions and squadrons headed straight across Lithuania on their way to Vilna, two other columns crossed the Niemen — at Tilsit, eighty miles to the west, and at Grodno, a similar distance south. Of these columns the first, under Marshal Macdonald's command, set off on the extreme left flank for Riga, while the second, comprising three corps under the inexperienced King of Westphalia, Jérôme Bonaparte, was to advance eastwards in close pursuit of Bagration's Second Army. Still further to the south the Austrians, commanded by Prince Schwarzenberg and supported by General Reynier's Saxons, entered Volynia to face a detached and barely-formed Russian Army.

The plan was to try and see whether the main French Army, driving Barclay before it, could advance some distance before Bagration became alarmed, by which time it would be too late and he would find Napoleon between him and Barclay. To achieve this end it was vital for Jérôme, by holding back for one or two days, to discourage Bagration from retreating at the same time as Barclay. Though imperfectly executed, as will be seen, these several moves did prevent the two Russian armies from effecting a junction anywhere west of Smolensk.

Davout and Jérôme were to encircle Bagration from north and south, converge in his rear, and perhaps force the Russians into the almost trackless Pripet Marshes, an area calculated to disrupt almost any force. Jérôme, under orders to march nearly 180 miles to Minsk and towards Nesvizh to the south-west, was delayed by bad weather and other problems, and the Russians managed to evade the trap by a swift retreat from Volkovisk through Slonim and Novogrodek. On 4 July Bagration bridged the flooded Niemen and then heard from Cossack leaders that Davout and 30,000 troops were heading for Minsk and that Jérôme was belatedly on the march with more than 50,000. He made a dash for Mir, only to learn that Davout had already entered Minsk and thus lay across the route he must take in order to join Barclay. Accordingly he undertook a perilous march across the enemy's front, heading for Bobruisk and thence to the Dnieper at Mogilev. Napoleon, furious at what he considered Jérôme's slowness and loss of a priceless opportunity, placed his brother under Marshal Davout's command, whereupon the King of Westphalia, understandably hurt, retired to his court in Cassel.

And what of the main army advancing under Napoleon's eye? It was encountering no real opposition, only a thin chain of Russian cavalry posts which withdrew steadily. The Emperor, hoping for a battle near Vilna, forced the pace, but within fifty miles poor roads, sultry heat, and torrential thunderstorms had lowered morale, killed off 10,000 horses, and caused the provision trains to lag far behind. Their vehicles stuck in the mud or foundered in ruts left by the guns. Much has been written about the horrors of the eventual retreat from Moscow, too little about the long, painful advance to the ancient capital.

The soldiers, swollen with insect bites which plagued them day and night, suffered from bad water or thirst — '*Niema panie*' ('There is none, sir') became a gloomy catchphrase. The heat was intense and the dust suffocating, or else the rains fell so hard that the men tramped in deep mud and failed to light their cooking-fires. Horses died by the hundred, mostly from eating green rye, and one officer counted the corpses of 1,240 in the space of five leagues between Kovno and Vilna. Lack of horses led in turn to guns and waggons being left behind. At every march hunger, diarrhoea, and dysentery laid men low. Many found the shortness of the nights fatiguing; others were overcome by depression, even to the point of suicide. The villages blazed. The few inhabitants remaining on the line of march were unfriendly, even hostile with oaths and brandished pikes. Many a bridge built to carry light local carts collapsed under the weight of guns and ammunition waggons. Wherever possible, such local carts were used, but the loads they could carry were a great deal smaller, and transport shortcomings soon became apparent even to the most sanguine members of the army. Widespread surprise was voiced at the good order of Barclay's retreat, because it seemed as though not a Russian vehicle had been abandoned, not a horse had died, not a straggler been left who might be induced to indicate the way — which was important, as the enemy rearguard had cut down and removed all the verst posts marking distances to Smolensk and Moscow.

On the Russian side the Tsar left Vilna on 26 June, and two days later Barclay de Tolly, mustering about 127,000 men and

9,000 Cossacks in his First Army of the West, began to retire north-eastwards on Drissa, more than 130 miles away. The Grand Army did not enter a city *en fête*. The walls had been placarded with long Russian proclamations which the French and German troops could not read. Expecting to be treated as allies and to benefit from good order as well as independence, the people soon had to barricade themselves indoors while Napoleon's soldiers looted shops, taverns, and depots. Amid such disorder, national ardour quickly froze. The Emperor, who used his stay in the capital to set up a provisional Government and turn Lithuania's military resources to his own advantage, did not take trouble enough to conciliate the inhabitants. When, at the end of June, the Polish Diet meeting in Warsaw proclaimed the restoration of their kingdom and set about the unification of Lithuania and Poland, Napoleon was reluctant to forfeit the possibility of a reconciliation with the Tsar by giving his approval to the decisions of the Diet, and he advised the Polish deputation who welcomed him in Vilna to be cautious about committing themselves *vis-à-vis* Alexander.

During this time Barclay and Wittgenstein had, with little trouble or fighting, retreated from Vilna and Vilkomir to the River Dvina, and by 11 July the whole of the Russian right and centre had been established either at the entrenched camp of Drissa or thirty miles downstream at Druya. The Tsar had hoped, in the light of advice from his Prussian mentor, Colonel Pfull, that Barclay would be able to make a stand at Drissa, but the defences were by no means complete, and little hope was entertained of repulsing a greatly superior force, because Pfull's plan required the main army to await Napoleon in the defensive camp while the other army, Bagration's, harassed his flank or rear. And Bagration was far away. In any case, the camp did not cover the road to St. Petersburg and lay too far north of any route to Moscow that Napoleon was likely to use. Accordingly a new plan was evolved: Wittgenstein would remain along the Dvina with 25,000 men to guard the St. Petersburg road; Barclay's army, now little over 80,000 strong, would continue the retreat another hundred miles through Polotsk to Vitebsk, capital of White Russia and equidistant from Moscow and St. Petersburg; and Bagration's Second Army of the West would march north via Mogilev to join forces with Barclay at Vitebsk.

When Barclay reached this town a week after leaving Drissa on the 16th, he decided to offer battle, but then withdrew further towards Smolensk because Bagration had still not managed to join him. Indeed, the latter had been extremely hard pressed. Marshal Davout, having decided that to march on Bobruisk was likely to be futile because the Russians would get there first, had directed his divisions on Mogilev instead, further north and 110 miles east of Minsk. His men advanced through Igumen, crossed the Berezina on 15 July, and five days later captured Mogilev against little opposition. Next they barred Bagration's path into this town, in which they had captured much-needed stocks of flour, biscuits, and other provisions. Bagration failed to break through from the south and was obliged to cross the Dnieper and march as far as Mstislavl before turning north to Smolensk. He arrived there on 2 August, a day later than Barclay, his army having covered over 540 miles — a notable feat of endurance given the nature of the ground.

And so, despite errors, difficulties of communication, poor intelligence, contradictory orders, and disunity at command level, the two main Russian armies had extricated themselves from a situation of danger and effected a junction, even though further into Russia than expected.

As far back as Polotsk on 18 July the Tsar had decided, or been persuaded, to leave the army and travel to Moscow in order to hearten his people there. Nine days he spent in the city, attending assemblies of merchants and nobility, who offered him their property and their lives. Contributions of serfs and roubles were made, as well as promises of militia regiments to be raised at private expense, though arming these men would be a problem, since very few muskets were left and pikes had to serve instead. Alexander, gratified by the eagerness of all classes to fight Napoleon to the death, declared that this was a national war and that he would not conclude peace so long as a single armed enemy soldier remained on Russian soil — a statement which aroused widespread enthusiasm.

Meanwhile Polotsk itself had been the scene of a battle. Marshal Oudinot had occupied the place on 26 July and then advanced north on Sebezh, hoping to cut Wittgenstein's communications with St. Petersburg, but his information on Russian movements was scanty and on the 31st of the month it was Oudinot who found himself attacked by Wittgenstein. The former, unduly cautious, ordered a withdrawal and was obliged to fight again next day as his 2nd Corps made their way back across the Drissa. A furious Napoleon ordered Oudinot to resume the offensive, this time with the support of Saint-Cyr's weak 6th Corps of 12,000 Bavarians, sent from Beshenkovichi west of Vitebsk. On 17–18 August — just when the struggle for Smolensk was in progress — a battle was fought near Polotsk. Oudinot, who had some 35,000 troops to match 24,000 Russians, was severely wounded on the first evening, and it was left to Saint-Cyr to attack Wittgenstein next afternoon. Both sides lost heavily, but the Russians were beaten and obliged to retreat, Saint-Cyr becoming the belated recipient of a marshal's bâton.

At Vitebsk Napoleon had ordered a halt, with his forces on a frontage of some 130 miles. The Grand Army appeared to have won numerous advantages: territory, towns, stores and prisoners taken, and losses inflicted upon the retreating enemy. But had so much really been gained by hurrying across vast tracts of central Russia? French losses had been even more serious than if they had fought several costly battles. Sheer exhaustion of men and horses alike compelled the Emperor to grant the army a fortnight's rest and an opportunity for stragglers to rally, commanders to check insubordination and ill discipline, commissaries to amass food reserves, and supply trains to catch up the forward divisions.

Then, no sooner had bridges been put across the Dnieper near Orsha, than Ney, Davout, and Eugène, together with two cavalry corps, advanced on 14 August along the south bank of the river towards Smolensk. At Krasnyi they encountered Neverovsky's division which was guarding Barclay's left flank. Though outnumbered by five to one, the Russian general withdrew skilfully, resisting so stubbornly that he lost five-sixths of his force before reaching Smolensk.

Captain Abraham Rosselet, who served with the 1st Swiss Regiment throughout the campaign, gives a description of the theatre of war.

Lithuania is a large country which formerly belonged to Poland. Parts of this province are excellent and fertile, particularly in respect of grain and forage. It produces no wine, it abounds in game, and has rivers teeming with fish. Most of it is a plain, watered by the Dnieper, Dvina, Niemen, Pripet, and Bug Rivers. The Lithuanians, like the Poles, are robust, of medium height, brave, have a fairly military turn of mind, are great eaters and drinkers, and in general speak Latin and Croat-Slovene. White Russia includes Novogrodek, Minsk, Mstislavl, Vitebsk, and Polotsk. It stretches to beyond the Dvina and Polota. The inhabitants are in part serfs who are sold along with the land, and those in Lithuania are even more wretched than the Poles. However, readers will find it difficult to believe that, in spite of being slaves, they look happy and gay because they know nothing else.

Since the serfs are very lazy, the landowners, so as to compel them to work, give them only what is strictly necessary to keep them alive, and the coarsest foodstuffs in grains, vegetables, etc. Their dwellings are built of pieces of wood placed one on top of the other and without a framework. The openings or chinks are blocked up with moss. In order to let daylight into these houses, people cut a sort of porthole which opens and closes by means of slots or grooves. One finds no furniture and seldom a bed, however poor.

. . . In Poland, as in Lithuania, the villages are dreadfully dirty. The peasants' houses contain one room or type of stable large enough to accommodate the family and the animals. A quarter of the room is taken up by a large stove which serves as a bed, in which mother, father, daughter, and son-in-law sleep together on straw, and in which everything goes on much as in a rabbit warren.

In the castles you find more or less everything necessary for man and society to live, even a library and politeness — in fact everything which can give ease and amenities to a distinguished family who, living isolated in a village or hamlet, cannot, because of the very bad state of the roads, visit their neighbours except in summer-time or when there is a very hard frost.

Save in the towns, there is neither butcher nor baker. It is the nobleman who has in his house everything needed for keeping body and soul together. A bullock that is killed provides fresh meat for several days and salt meat for a longer or shorter time, depending on the number of people in the family. Bread counts for little in these people's diet, and their dishes are made of paste and flour, particularly in winter.

. . . For three-quarters of the year the inhabitants wear sheepskins, turning the fur to the inside when the weather is at its coldest. In the hot season, which lasts barely two months, the men's clothes are made of grey linen and consist of wide trousers and a sort of shirt and blouse. The women wear a kind of pelisse shaped like a shirt fastened at the neck and also made of sheepskin or grey linen.

On their feet both sexes wear a type of clog. These people possess very little body linen. As a result the French soldier did not find there, as he had done in Germany, any changes of linen or shoes, handing in the old in exchange for the new. At the most each person has three shirts.

. . . In the winter evenings these people use for lighting thick logs, which they burn one after another.

The horses, which are called *konia*, are small but excellent, very nimble, and they eat anything they are given, even bad straw.

In the castles you meet bailiffs or stewards who have received some education, speak several languages, and are usually retired soldiers.

Whenever he talks to his master or to a bailiff or indeed to any man better dressed than himself, the peasant bows down to the ground. The Jews handle *all trade* almost on their own, and do everything: innkeepers, merchants, tailors, cobblers. Indeed they practise every profession.

In each village one finds that the Jew's house is the inn, but what an inn! You find only small beer, bad brandy, and a kind of dough which they call bread. These houses resemble their occupants — disgustingly dirty!

The roads are neither metalled nor paved, and are hardly distinguishable through the forests. When a thaw comes, the roads turn into swamps and mud and become almost impassable. Men are often drowned there. When these roads get too bad, equal lengths of wood are laid across them, laid close together and side by side. But what a thoroughfare, especially for the horses!

General Armand de Caulaincourt, Grand Equerry, relates that Napoleon joined Marshal Davout's headquarters near the Niemen early on 23 June.

Day was breaking, and he at once reconnoitred the river banks and the neighbourhood. He did not return until the evening, when he spent two hours dictating orders and then mounted his horse once more to make a reconnaissance by moonlight closer to the river and decide on the place for crossing. He left everybody, without exception, at a distance so as to avoid attracting the attention of any Russian outposts which might be across the Niemen. The Emperor rode to and fro along the bank, accompanied by General Haxo[1] of the Engineers. In the morning he had been compelled to wear a Polish soldier's cloak in order to be less conspicuous.

[1] François-Nicolas-Benoît Haxo (1774–1838).

When the reconnaissance was over he rejoined his staff, and once again examined the various points which the troops could occupy. As he galloped through the wheat a hare started out between his horse's legs, and made him swerve a little. The Emperor, who had a very bad seat, rolled to the ground but stood up so quickly that he was on his feet before I could reach him and lend a hand. He mounted again without a word. As the ground was very soft, he only bruised his hip slightly. It occurred to me at once that this was a bad omen, and I was certainly not alone in thinking so, because the Prince of Neuchâtel [Berthier] instantly grasped my hand and said: 'We should do better not to cross the Niemen. This fall is a bad augury.'

The Emperor, who had remained silent to begin with and whose thoughts were undoubtedly no more cheerful than our own, presently pretended to joke with the Prince and myself about his fall, but he could not hide his bad temper and forebodings. In other circumstances he would have blamed the horse which had caused this stupid mishap, and would not have spared the Grand Equerry. Now, however, he affected serenity and did his best to dispel the gloomy thoughts which he sensed we were all thinking, for people are superstitious despite themselves in such serious moments and on the eve of such great events. Everyone talked about his accident, and some of the Headquarters staff remarked that the Romans, who believed in omens, would not have undertaken the river-crossing. The Emperor, usually so cheerful, so active when his troops were carrying out great operations, was solemn and preoccupied throughout the day.

Lieutenant J. L. Henckens, a Dutchman with the 6th Regiment of Chasseurs à cheval, *states that, after crossing the Niemen, Grouchy's corps bivouacked in fields of rye.*

As a result of eating green rye, the horses foundered, and we lost hundreds in this way before ever we reached Minsk. Fortunately the depot sent us some remounts, otherwise we should very soon have presented a sorry picture.

In Russia one is closer to the Pole than in other countries of Europe, or at least in those we had come from [Italy and Germany], and we found the very short nights exhausting — a factor which later added to our fatigue on the retreat. It all contributed to make our situation an unenviable one, though we had to put up with it. This reminded me of what I had said to a rather simple German who asked me what the four N's on my sabretache stood for. I replied: '*Nur Nicht Nach Norden.*'[1]

On 29 June General Jean-Dominique Compans,[2] commanding the 5th Infantry Division in Davout's corps, wrote to his wife, whom he had married only a year before. He dated his letter 'Four leagues from Vilna, on the Kovno road, in a hamlet which is not marked on our best maps and the name of which I cannot discover, because my interpreter is out on duty.'

There, my dear Louise, is a pretty strange date. I shall often be compelled to use this method of letting you know where I am writing from, because we are not well off for maps of Russia. Every day I am made aware of the inadequacy of those we have, so I have bought a compass to guide me. Although I am not used to this instrument, it seems as if I should be able to find Chile with its aid. I am not unhopeful that it will enable me to find St. Petersburg or Moscow. . . .

The countryside through which we are moving is quite attractive, but the inhabitants and their houses are very ugly and extremely dirty. The castles built of stone are as rare as are towns with three thousand inhabitants in France. The houses built of wood are much more common, but can only be distinguished from peasants' dwellings by one or two chimneys which one never finds in the latter — a type of hut and quite impossible for us to live in. As a result I have not gone inside except as a last resort. When the weather is fine, I sleep on straw under a shelter of branches and manage very well. When the weather is bad, I sleep in a carriage, but when morning comes I feel the effects of not being able to stretch my legs. However, none of this prevents me from enjoying excellent health, strength, and vigour.

[1] They stood for 'Napoleon'. Henckens's version meant literally 'Only not to the North', or more freely, 'Preserve us at least from going to the North'.

[2] Compans (1769–1845), destined for the priesthood, had joined the Army in 1791 and after service in Italy, at Toulon, and in the Pyrenees, had commanded a brigade against Suvorov in Italy in 1799. He had taken part in the battles of Austerlitz and Essling, and served as chief of staff to Marshal Soult.

I eat in the open air four or five times a day and my digestion works admirably: indeed, my stomach and I are in perfect harmony, and it couldn't function better. Every day I drink my bottle of Bordeaux wine, a little glass of rum, and several glasses of beer when I have any that is good, which does happen occasionally. Now and then I take a cup of coffee. We are not short of beef and mutton. Duval[1] is still at his post, and produces quite good campaign cooking. From time to time we get a chicken or a goose, but unfortunately in this country these stupid creatures would rather be captured than purchased, and the takers are far more numerous than the buyers. Before leaving Elbing I laid in a store of hams, smoked tongues, sausage, and rice. These help to vary the menu, but of all this food my favourite dish is rice cooked in a good tablet soup *à la Duval.* No green vegetables in this country; they take flight whenever our soldiers appear. Nevertheless, we have found a few which had been hidden in their knapsacks. I have had occasion to punish soldiers in my division who have been caught in this way: in my view one should be more on one's guard than this in war-time.

Michel Oginski, a Polish politician who was a member of the St. Petersburg Senate and had been entrusted with several missions by the Tsar, was delayed by ill health from accompanying Alexander to Vilna, and did not leave the capital until 18 June.

On reaching Rumszyski, forty miles from Vilna, at nightfall on the 21st I was very surprised to see large fires on the far side of the Niemen, in the Duchy of Warsaw, and to meet several strong Cossack patrols on this side of the river. I learnt from the local postmaster that for the past three days fires had been visible on the left bank of the Niemen, and that the French Army was expected to enter Lithuania from one day to the next. I could not get over my amazement.

On leaving my carriage in Vilna I wrote to Count Tolstoy,[2] the Grand Marshal, asking him to inform the Tsar of my arrival. He replied that if I were not too tired after my journey, the Tsar would be pleased to see me that same evening at the ball which his

[1] Compans's *valet de chambre,* who was to die in Russia.

[2] Count Peter Tolstoy had been Russian Ambassador to France in 1807.

Marshal Ney, from the painting by Maurin

Marshal Davout, from the painting by Gautherot at Versailles

Marshal Oudinot, from the painting by Robert Lefèvre at Versailles

General Eblé

Marshal Murat, King of Naples, from the painting by Baron François Gérard at Versailles

aides-de-camp were giving at Zakret;[1] and if I was unable to go, His Majesty ordered me to present myself next morning at nine o'clock.

This news of a ball astounded me after all I had seen and heard in Rumszyski. I went eagerly to Zakret and was no less surprised to find unalloyed gaiety prevailing at the very large gathering than I had been twenty-four hours earlier to learn that the French Army was such a short distance away from where the Tsar was staying.

His Majesty received me with great kindness, expressed his satisfaction at my arrival, and spoke to me about a variety of matters at intervals during the evening without betraying the slightest change of mood. Yet I discovered afterwards that he was aware that the French had just crossed the Niemen.

Next day the Tsar sent word that he could not see me at nine o'clock, because he had to dispatch several couriers, but he commanded me to dine with him.

On 23 June the Tsar appeared to be his usual calm self and in his normal mood all the time we were at table, but after dinner, when he summoned me to his study, I noticed he was dreamy and preoccupied. He told me he had been very satisfied by his stay in Vilna and by the behaviour of the inhabitants of Lithuania. I had not, he added, misled him with my assurances of their zeal and their attachment to his person. They had all come forward with enthusiasm and volunteered to provide whatever was required for maintaining the Army; and by way of repayment he had given them a proof of his confidence by nominating a committee composed of nationals charged with the task of dividing out what each landowner was to supply, so as not to subject them to vexations at the hands of those responsible for collecting supplies for the Army.

. . . Just as I was about to leave the Tsar, he received a report from the outposts of the Army and appeared to be upset by what he read. Looking out of the window and seeing a downpour with hailstones and a most violent thunderstorm, he turned to me and exclaimed: 'My poor wretched soldiers who are now on the march!'

That was how I first heard that the French had crossed the

[1] A country house, some two miles from Vilna, belonging at the time to General Bennigsen, who had been living there in retirement.

Niemen. The Tsar, in telling me this, added that the ice was broken; that he had not to reproach himself for having provoked the war; that he would do whatever his duty required of him; and that he had full trust in Providence, which could not but bless a good cause.

I asked his permission to spend a little time on my estates in Lithuania and White Russia before returning to St. Petersburg. 'I hope very much,' said the Tsar, 'that before going to St. Petersburg you will come and see me at headquarters in Drissa.'

When I woke next morning I learnt that the Tsar had left Vilna three hours after midnight, and one was made aware of this fact by the general bustle throughout the town.

Nobody who had not witnessed the scene could have any idea what it was like. Every arrangement for the evacuation of Vilna by the military was carried out in the best possible order, but what a picture! Here one saw lines of vehicles overtaking one another in their efforts to get out of the town; there one noticed carts blocking the way and, once they had got clear of the gates, bustling along to give warning of the enemy's approach. At every square and cross-roads groups of people stood discussing what they should do. Every face was animated, either by terror at the retreat of the Russian Army or by pleasure at seeing it replaced by the Poles who formed Napoleon's advance-guard.

Those who wanted to hasten their departure were further alarmed by the difficulty of procuring horses. There were none to be hired, because nearly all of them had been requisitioned to carry the Army's baggage, and people had no scruples about un-harnessing horses from private carriages which were about to leave Vilna. Amid all this confusion, I recall that one lady had her horses taken up to her rooms on the first floor to prevent anyone seizing them.

Major Baron Woldemar von Löwenstern, who had fought on the French side in the Austerlitz campaign of 1805, was now serving on the staff at Russian Headquarters and spent the last days of June in Vilna.

The tumult, the noise, and the anxiety were extreme. All horses were commandeered in the streets. Disorder was at its height. The inhabitants took refuge inside their houses and barricaded themselves in. At the gates of Vilna preparations were made to offer a stout resistance. The Commander-in-Chief[1] sent the troops at his disposal into a camp near the town. He made frequent reconnaissances and he alone did not belie his character. He remained calm throughout, but uncommunicative.

All the news we had from our advance-guard left us in no doubt that the enemy were concentrating with a view to forcing the Vilna position. At two o'clock in the morning all the aides-de-camp were summoned to the Commander-in-Chief and we were sent off in all directions, time after time.

The question did not seem to have been decided yet as to whether we were to oppose the enemy or retreat. Eventually General Barclay de Tolly called me into his office and instructed me to write to His Majesty the Tsar and lay before him the reasons why he was going to abandon Vilna without firing a shot. In fact, Vilna did not offer any advantageous positions. The decision to abandon the capital of Lithuania to the enemy was crushing, but the enemy would not derive too much benefit from the place, because the Commander-in-Chief had taken care to have all magazines, bridges, etc., destroyed.

On 28 June, at one o'clock in the afternoon, Headquarters left the town.

. . . The great plan for the retreat of our Army appeared to stem from the moment we abandoned Vilna. Hitherto no one had really had the courage to contemplate it, still less to present it to the Tsar as a plan of operations. Any man who had ventured to suggest abandoning Vilna would have been regarded as a traitor; but once we had left the place, everybody looked on the operation not only as very urgent but even as perfectly natural.

The Countess de Choiseul-Gouffier, one of the maids of honour to the Tsarina, was in Vilna when the French arrived on 28 June.

Not only did the Russian troops evacuate Vilna, but Russian individuals who had lived there for a great many years hastened to

[1] Mikhail, Prince Barclay de Tolly (1761–1818), a Russian general descended from a Scottish family which had settled in Livonia during the seventeenth century. As Minister of War since 1810 he had done much to reorganize the Russian Army.

leave with their wives and children and everything they possessed. All the horses in the town and those privately owned were requisitioned in these circumstances of dire necessity — all, that is, except those belonging to my father, who had not even taken the precaution of hiding them, as some people had done, placing their horses in the loft where the police never thought of looking for them.

There was an interval of two days only between the departure of Tsar Alexander and the entry of the French, yet we were so agitated and worried that the time seemed interminable. There was not the sound of a horse to be heard in the streets, but people ran about passing on alarming and nearly always false news. Some were saying that a battle would be fought under the town walls, and I was advised to flee to the mountains because cannon-balls would knock down the bells on to our house. Other people, pale and frightened, ran up to announce that the Russians were setting fire to the town as they were withdrawing; others, again, claimed that they had seen Tsar Alexander dashing through the streets, without any uniform, in an effort to reassure the inhabitants, promising not to abandon them. The Governor-General, Korsakov by name, assured my father[1] as he was leaving that there was nothing to fear. . . .

On the night of 27–28 June the Russian troops filed past in good order, and in a most impressive silence. No, this was certainly not a flight as has been stated. At eight o'clock in the morning a detachment of French cavalry hurried into the town, galloping to defend the bridge which had been set on fire by the Russians.

I can find no words to describe my emotion when I saw some Polish troops! Poles who were galloping at full speed, sabres drawn yet laughing, waving their lance pennants which were in the national colours. I was wearing these for the first time! I stood at an open window, and they saluted me as they passed. The sight of these real compatriots set my heart racing. I felt that I was Polish by birth, that I was going to become Polish again. Tears of joy and enthusiasm streamed down my face. This was a delicious moment, but it was not to last long.

[1] Colonel Tisenhaus soon became one of the members of a commission set up by Napoleon to govern Vilna and district.

A Polish artillery officer on Napoleon's staff, Count Roman Soltyk by name, describes this entry.

The 6th Lancers, leading the column, arrived at the gate of the town. Major Suchorzewski, who could scarcely contain his exuberant courage, asked his colonel for permission to go forward; and having obtained leave to do so, he put himself at the head of a squadron of his regiment to go through the Vilna barrier. The Russian troops had already evacuated the place, and there remained only a part of the rearguard, who were busy following the stragglers and baggage which had remained behind. As a result, it could not stop the handful of brave men who galloped through the town, knocking down enemy detachments as they went and pursuing the fugitives as far as a wood half a league from Vilna, on the Sventsiany[1] road, by which they retreated. This bold move resulted in 500 prisoners and the capture of a good deal of baggage. . . .

Our entry was a triumph. The streets and public places were full of people. All the windows were adorned with wildly enthusiastic ladies; valuable carpets hung in front of several houses; every hand appeared to be waving a handkerchief; and repeated shouts of joy rang out.

I had a perfect view of the preparations for this solemn and improvised reception, because I was sent by the Emperor, half an hour before he made his entry, to fetch the Rector of the University, Sniadecki by name, a celebrated astronomer and a most enlightened patriot. His name and reputation were known to the Emperor, who wished to talk to him.

So I galloped through the streets towards the University. . . . I reached the gates, left my horse in the charge of several students, who competed to offer me their services, and hurried upstairs to the Rector, whose rooms people were quick to point out. I told Sniadecki the purpose of my visit, and as soon as he knew who had sent me, he invited me to rest for a few minutes while he put on more suitable attire. He was wearing the Academy uniform, but he wanted to put on silk stockings instead of his boots. I told him that my mission would be prejudiced and that it admitted of no delay. As he was insistent, I said to him: 'Rector, it does not matter. The

[1] Twenty miles to the north-east.

Emperor attaches no importance to exterior things which only impress the common people. Science is the dress of the wise. Let us be off.' He acquiesced with good grace.

Captain Fantin des Odoards, with the Grenadiers of the Old Guard, wrote cynically in his journal:

On the eve of my departure from Vilna I had the pleasure of watching a very interesting spectacle. A number of Deputies, who had come from the various regions of ancient Poland, renewed at the altar an oath they had already taken in Warsaw to obtain independence for their country, which had become the prey of foreigners. The tremendous enthusiasm of all present was particularly noticeable among the women who attended this ceremony. They all wore on their breasts a large rosette in the Lithuanian colours — crimson and blue. An entertainment given on this occasion afforded me a better opportunity of judging the fair sex of Vilna. At the religious service I had already formed a favourable opinion of their charms, but when I saw them animated by dancing, pleasure, and patriotism, and noticed how white and rounded were the objects that rose and fell under the national colours during the gentle embraces of the waltz, I was filled with quite another sort of admiration. These ladies' costumes were fairly similar to those worn by our French women, but among the men one saw many heads shaved in the Chinese style and long tunics drawn in tightly at the waist by a belt — old-fashioned styles to which circumstances had lent a renewed popularity.

A few days ago, in this same Catholic church where the Lithuanians have just taken an oath breaking the bond which united them to Russia, the Tsar Alexander attended a *Te Deum* sung in honour of his arrival, and on that occasion Vilna resounded with parties and similar demonstrations. The fair ladies had danced with, and cast amorous glances at, the Russian officers, in just the same way as, last week, they danced and simpered with us. Nothing was missing, except the crimson and blue ribbons. Sovereigns! Put not your trust in nations, and above all not in the Polish nation!

General Baron Henri de Jomini served in the Swiss Guards at Versailles before rising to be chief of staff to Marshal Ney and, in 1804, attracting Napoleon's attention by his book Traité des grandes opérations militaires. *In Russia he served at the Emperor's headquarters and states that, a few days before Napoleon left Vilna, he dined with the Emperor and two Polish deputies, Wibicki and Count Alexander Potocki. Jomini writes in the third person when referring to himself.*

During the meal the Emperor asked Wibicki: 'How far is it from Vilna to Moscow?' (Napoleon knew this better than anyone, as he studied the map every day and measured all the distances.) Wibicki, searching his memory, hesitated to give a reply. '250 leagues, isn't it?' 'Ah! Yes, Sire. 125 German miles.[1] That's right.'

'Then one can get there in six weeks covering six leagues a day. That's a trifle for my soldiers!' 'Oh, certainly! Your Majesty could easily be in Moscow in less time than that.'

On hearing this, the Emperor burst out laughing, a thing he seldom did, and said to the Polish conqueror: 'I much prefer to get there in two years' time. It is easy for you political gentlemen to cover distances like that. If Monsieur Barclay thinks that I want to run after him all the way to the Volga, he is very much mistaken. We shall follow him as far as Smolensk and the Dvina, where a good battle will enable us to go into cantonments. I shall return here, to Vilna, with my headquarters to spend the winter. I shall send for an opera company and actors from the Théâtre-Français. Then, next May, we shall finish the job, if we do not make peace during the winter. That is better, I think, than running to Moscow. What do you say, Mr. Tactician?' (addressing General Jomini, who was seated opposite him and next to Duroc,[2] the Grand Marshal). All flattery apart, the General's reply could only be in the affirmative. Was Napoleon sincere in making this declaration, or did he want to put us on the wrong scent about his real thought, as he had a habit of doing? That is something that nobody can affirm.

[1] A German mile is just under five English miles.

[2] Gérard-Christophe-Michel Duroc, Duke of Friuli (1772–1813), had been appointed Grand Marshal of the Palace in 1805. He was one of Napoleon's oldest friends, having met him at the siege of Toulon.

Captain Boniface de Castellane, who later became a Marshal of France but was at this time serving at Napoleon's headquarters, wrote in his diary for 7 July, in Vilna:

I am on duty. I follow the Emperor when he goes out riding. We go the whole way at a walk. His Majesty rides much less quickly these days; he has put on a good deal of weight, and rides a horse with more difficulty than before. The Grand Equerry[1] has to give him a hand in mounting. When the Emperor travels, he does most of the journey by carriage. It is very tiring for the officers who have to follow, because His Majesty is rested by the time he comes to mount, and therefore assumes that the same must apply to those who have covered the distance on horseback. He acts accordingly. Sometimes I could wish his confounded carriage to the devil. When His Majesty is on the move, one cannot expect a moment's rest in the twenty-four hours.

General Eblé[2] spoke to the Emperor about the lack of horses, and His Majesty replied: 'We shall find some fine carriage horses in Moscow.' So we shall probably head in that direction.

Sergeant Jean-Roch Coignet of the Imperial Guard, while on the march near Vilna, like everyone else could not fail to notice the serious effects of a sudden change in the weather.

On 29 June a violent storm broke before we came to a village which I had the utmost difficulty in reaching. Once in its shelter we could not unharness our horses. We had to unbridle them, cut some grass for them, and then light fires. The hailstorm was so bad that we had great trouble in controlling our horses, and it became necessary to tether them to the wheels. I was half dead with cold, and unable to stand it any longer I opened one of my waggons and took refuge inside. Next morning a heart-rending sight met our eyes. In the cavalry camp nearby the ground was covered with horses which had died of cold. More than ten thousand perished during this night of horror. When, numb with cold, I climbed out

[1] Armand de Caulaincourt, Duke of Vicenza (1773–1827), a former French Ambassador in St. Petersburg.

[2] Jean-Baptiste, Count Eblé (1758–1812), commanded the pontoon-bridging units, and was to perform outstanding service at the crossing of the Berezina at the end of November 1812. He died soon afterwards.

of the waggon, I saw that three of my horses were dead. I immediately divided the survivors among my four waggons. These poor animals were trembling so violently that as soon as they had been harnessed they broke everything, throwing themselves frantically into their halters. They were mad and pranced with rage. If I had delayed another hour I should have lost them all. I can say that we needed all our courage to bring them under control.

On reaching the road we found some dead soldiers who had not been able to withstand this appalling storm, and this demoralized a large number of our troops.

Albrecht Adam, born in 1786, began working as a confectioner, but soon made a reputation with his paintings of battle scenes, and in this capacity he accompanied Prince Eugène de Beauharnais on the Russian campaign. He describes the advance towards Smorgon in July.

The cavalry's march through a long thick wood was tragi-comic. Many riders who had fallen asleep on horseback out of sheer exhaustion banged their heads on trees. Helmets fell off, or held on lopsided solely by the chinstrap; a few horsemen slithered to the ground. The Italian *Guarda d'onore* fared particularly badly with their exceptionally tall helmets. Even the weary horses often stumbled and fell. In short, everything pointed to the declining strength of the troops. A further loss of horses resulted from such a march. Whole columns of hundreds of these poor beasts had to be led in the most pitiful conditions, with sores on their withers or backs stopped up with tow and discharging a stream of pus. They had lost weight till their ribs stood out, and looked a picture of abject misery. Already by the middle of July the army was in this state!

On 11 July I wrote to my wife from Olshany in Russian Poland: 'I am beginning to lose heart. Two whole months on the march and for what purpose? And through what country? It distresses me to be compelled to waste God-given time so wretchedly. War! That is a terrible word. It means no regard for the well-being or destruction of whole nations, and woe betide anyone who gets to know this termagant and still has a heart that beats for human beings. What I have witnessed in the way of distress this past fortnight is beyond description. Most houses stand empty and roofless. In the districts through which we have advanced, most people have thatched roofs, and this old straw has been used as fodder for the horses. The houses have been ruined or ransacked, the inhabitants have fled or else are so poor that they can scarcely avoid dying of hunger, because the soldiers don't leave them enough to do much else. The streets are strewn with dead horses which give off a dreadful smell now that the hot weather has come in, and more and more horses collapse. This is a horrible war. The campaign of 1809[1] seems a mere promenade by comparison. If things go on like this, I do not know how it will turn out.

'Despite our wretched existence and all the fatiguing moves, I have still managed to do a good many drawings, which are very valuable to me, but these drawings cost dear enough. And the outcome of this war will have to be extraordinarily advantageous if a painter is to be compensated for all the sacrifices he makes. This wandering about in miserable places and the consequent waste of golden time has already become intolerable. And I cannot hide the fact that I am looking forward to the first battle. I would rather hear the whistle of bullets than go on leading this cheerless existence.'

Lieutenant Paul de Bourgoing makes an interesting comment about singing on the march during the army's advance eastwards from Vilna.

It was the custom in French regiments to try to forget how long the march was by going through the whole repertoire of songs which the soldiers and officers could remember. Each nation made its contribution. Something that was sung once or twice was soon known by the whole group, and usually one or two verses were sung solo and then repeated in unison by the rest of the column. In our corps songs from Languedoc, Provence, or Picardy alternated with those from Paris, Piedmont, or other parts of the Empire.

The 5th *Tirailleurs* [of the Guard], like other corps in the Imperial Army, had in its ranks Frenchmen from Genoa, Amster-

[1] The victories over Austria at Eckmühl, Aspern-Essling, and Wagram led to the Peace of Schönbrunn.

dam, Mainz, and Erfurt, and so we sang in every language and dialect, though French songs naturally predominated. Here is one which was composed specially for our corps. I give only the chorus:

Les tirailleurs sans souci,
Où sont-ils . . . ? Les voici.
Où sont-ils . . . ? Les voici.

The verses were, as usual, sung in unison after being sung by the best tenor in the leading company. This question, posed by the strong voice of the first singer, and answered twice far down the long column of the battalion, had a gaiety all its own.

Lieutenant Karl von Suckow describes how, once across the Niemen, his troops could easily have believed they were in a cemetery.

Not a soul in sight, not an inhabitant in the villages we passed through. One would have said that even the animals wanted to escape notice. I remember that we were all struck by the absence of any birds flying up at our approach. However, a few officers who had very good eyesight did claim that they had spotted Cossacks in the distance.

These exceptional marches, added to the great shortages we had to put up with, thinned our ranks to an unexpected degree, and thousands of men disappeared within a very short time. Hundreds killed themselves, feeling no longer able to endure such hardship. Every day one heard isolated shots ring out in the woods near the road. Patrols were sent to investigate, and they always came back and reported: 'It's a cuirassier, a hussar, an infantryman, a Frenchman, or an ally, who has just committed suicide.'

Of all the unpleasant things we had to endure, one of the most unbearable was the thick dust which enveloped us on the march, much of the way in very dry weather. . . . I recall that at one stage, so as to prevent anyone taking a wrong turning, a drummer was stationed at the head of each battalion, and his job was to beat the drum all the time. This fact alone will indicate just how dense the clouds of dust were.

Captain Fritz ——, whose name it has not been possible to trace but who came from an ancient military and titled family in Pomeranian Mecklenburg, had campaigned in the Peninsula under Wellington's command before deciding to offer his services to Russia. He relates how the Russians continued their withdrawal towards the fortified camp of Drissa on the River Dvina, where Headquarters arrived on 11 July.

Having done two summer campaigns in Portugal and Spain, I was fairly well accustomed to heat and dust, but I must admit that I had never been so troubled by either in the Peninsula as was often the case on these marches during the summer of 1812 in Russia. The air along the wide sandy tracks running through endless dark pine-woods was really like an oven, so oppressively hot was it and so unrelieved by the slightest puff of wind. If one was unfortunate enough to be caught between the innumerable waggons, which ploughed along in deep sand ruts at the slowest pace of the draught animals, and to have to remain among them for hours on end without being able to escape, then one was enveloped in so much dust that one really thought one would suffocate. Eyes, nose, mouth, and ears were often so clogged with grains of sand that one seemed to have lost the use of all one's senses. The dust lay so thick on my dark-grey dolman, which was faced with red, that it was no longer possible to make out the slightest trace of this colour. Since there is very little darkness in a July night in Russia, we usually marched only by night, when it was cooler, and rested during the daytime.

An unnamed artillery lieutenant, serving with troops from Württemberg who were under the command of their own Crown Prince Wilhelm and formed one division of Marshal Ney's corps, stresses the disharmony between the French and their German allies.

Not only the 3rd Corps was on the march, but often the Imperial Guard as well and sometimes several other corps, all on the same road which, on top of all this, was frequently almost impassable for artillery. As a result serious disagreements were caused every day by the extreme difficulty in observing a regular order of march. The artillery was particularly bad in this respect, because if anything broke on a waggon or a gun, or if a horse had to be unharnessed on account of exhaustion, the vehicle in question would be cut off by the troops behind, and it was perhaps evening before it reached the bivouac and could rejoin its battery. Under these circumstances the French infantry were so unpleasant and brutal that their officers, so as to prevent an unfortunate, godforsaken gun from travelling near, let alone in front of them, would more often than not have bayonets levelled at the leading horses and strike the soldiers of the train. On our side this behaviour aroused intense hatred and the bitterest resentment. Such incidents were much more common and more unbearable with us than with the rest of the Württemberg artillery. Although General Beurmann's[1] brigade usually formed the advance-guard, it often had to flank the corps. It frequently happened that, after the battery had spent half a day following the brigade with the utmost difficulty and exertion along appalling tracks, we would be obliged to turn back because of some insuperable obstacle on the ground and to search for the road along which the infantry were marching. When we did reach this, nobody wanted to let us into the column, and we had to try and secure a tiny place on the road by dint of asking pleasantly, sometimes with insults and oaths, often at sword-point. I can honestly say that none of the hardships and dangers of this campaign irked me half as much as this daily bickering and squabbling on the march. As I was the only officer in the battery who spoke French, it always fell to me to conduct these wrangles.

In a report to the King of Bavaria, General von Scheler sought for reasons why the German troops suffered more than did the French from the lack of rations, despite the very real efforts of the corps commander to improve the situation. He himself commanded a Württemberg brigade in Ney's corps and later a division.

The principal cause by far lies in the different natures of the German and French soldier. Already when we crossed the Vistula all regular food supply and orderly distribution ceased, and from there as far as Moscow not a pound of meat or bread, not a glass of brandy was taken through legal distribution or regular requisition.

[1] Frédéric-Auguste de Beurmann was a native of Strasbourg.

Beyond the Vistula, as soon as the few stocks of food had been exhausted, the order of the day was at once issued: 'Let each man take wherever he can find it, and live as well or as badly as he can manage.'

Poland, and in particular that part of Poland through which the army corps marched, is poor and thinly populated, and the inhabitants, especially in the Russian part, had fled to the woods with their belongings. As a result, not a single place was under civil government, or else a shadowy administration was dealing with food supply, so the only means was to send detachments every day into the nearby villages and woods and let them take whatever they found.

At this point the difference between the German and French soldier became very apparent, and to the serious disadvantage of the former. In this respect the French soldier revealed an extraordinary knack and on these exhausting detachments lived only for the good of his comrades, almost ignoring his own welfare. He was satisfied to have found some provisions, packed up quickly, run after the regiment with whatever he had got, put up with very few hours' sleep, and was little worried by fatigue. If he could not arrive by daylight, he travelled through the night and felt himself rewarded by the thanks of his messmates.

The Germans were quite different, and unfortunately to the humiliation of the trained part. Too many detachments were required for each to be led by an officer, and even had there been enough, individual dispersion was inevitable. And so the soldier, left to his own devices, thought first of filling his own belly when he found anything to eat. In the actual hunt for food he was much too slow, because he was often busy with too many other things which could not be of use to him. Instead of being content with a quick refreshment, he wanted first to cook everything properly. After twelve hours on guard duty he wanted to sleep for another twelve. As a result he was late, could not overtake the regiment, which had received orders to march in the meantime; and he either turned marauder and stayed in the rear, or else threw his booty away to lighten his load, and rejoined the regiment with little or nothing.

Even the provision of more vehicles did nothing to remedy the situation, and strict discipline and punishments, which were very frequent, proved of no avail. It is true that after being punished, the soldiers straggled less, but they brought in no food and could always plead the excuse that they had found none. Unlike the French discipline, the German system lacked the many motives to awake the soldier's ambition, goodwill, and pride, and so the means of influencing the troops were exhausted once the strictness displayed at the top had shown itself to be powerless. Thus, continually on the march, there remained no other method, unfortunately, except to leave most of the supplies to chance or to the zeal of individuals, because the sending-out of detachments had to be abandoned, seeing that a number of men vanished to no purpose, whereas the French foraging parties returned well-laden to camp.

I did not fail to copy the example of several French regiments and organize mounted foragers, but even this, which served the French so well, was useless, because the temperament of the German soldier was not suited to conducting this foraging with the same cunning, speed, self-sacrifice, and camaraderie as were required when swift marches and few halts were customary.

If the Württembergers were in trouble, so too were the troops from Bavaria in Saint-Cyr's 6th Corps, as is shown by the gloomy report written for the King of Bavaria on 11 August by General Erasmus Deroy, commanding the 19th Division. Deroy, aged seventy-two, had nearly sixty years' service.

On the subject of marches, I have to inform Your Majesty that on two occasions my corps has encountered large swamps and areas covered with water, several of which lie on our route. We ought to have gone round them in single file along a path, but as this would have caused a serious hold-up, the men took off their shoes and gaiters and waded through the water. The first time a small section of the Imperial Guard was marching in front of us. They immediately removed shoes and gaiters and waded through, so I urged my troops to do the same. This they did, and went through with the water up to their chins. On the second occasion we were on a night march and had to cross even larger stretches of water.

. . . The number of my sick in the infantry and artillery is very considerable. Medicines have to be purchased, and they are almost unobtainable. In these circumstances we cannot, even by taking severe measures, prevent men from straggling every day and causing a great deal of disorder in the wake of the army. As the cavalry are all on detachment, it is difficult to collect them on the march, otherwise the best plan would be to leave some cavalry behind with the task of picking up the stragglers and forcing them to rejoin the ranks. . . .

The treasury is exhausted, and we cannot imagine how and when we shall get any more money. We are unable to pay for the slightest thing, nor pay the officers, most of whom are destitute, without a heller[1] in their pockets. We cannot pay the soldiers either. The food is bad, and the shoes, shirts, pants, and gaiters are now so torn that most of the men are marching in rags and barefoot. Consequently they are useless for service. Furthermore, I regret to have to tell Your Majesty that this state of affairs has produced a serious relaxation of discipline, and there is such a widespread spirit of depression, discouragement, discontent, disobedience, and insubordination that one cannot forecast what will happen.

Lieutenant Carl Anton Wilhelm, Count von Wedel (1790–1853), serving in the 9th Regiment of Polish Lancers, throws light on servants and foraging parties.

Since Vilna we had been on outpost duty. The horses were seldom unsaddled, and never at night, because we always had to be specially prepared for night attacks, since a hundred Cossacks, knowing the district and every track in it, could without danger to themselves put the wind up an entire army corps. If they found our outposts on the alert, they would retire into the darkness more quickly than they had come, secure in the knowledge that they would not be pursued; but if they caught their enemies off guard they would exploit their advantage to the full.

This constant outpost duty had exhausted men and horses alike, and the wet, cold weather since Vilna had produced widespread sickness. Yet we kept on advancing, unaware of what had happened to those left behind. And so, whereas the army lost men during its advance and outdistanced its supplies, the retreating enemy gained

[1] A copper coin of tiny value, say a farthing.

strength and drew closer and closer to his supplies. Much weaker to begin with than the French Army, the Russian Army grew stronger every day, while ours dwindled.

Every officer had a lancer, who was his attendant and had the task of grooming his horse and looking after the saddlery. He was exempt from service, and so had only to be in the ranks on the day of a battle, but even this regulation was not strictly enforced. I had picked my attendant from among the Westphalian cavalrymen entrusted to me in Hanover. His name was Rosemann and he came from Osnabrück. He was never eager to stand in the ranks when a fight was imminent, but he was a good fellow once he got there. In him I had a very loyal and honest servant.

In addition, each officer had one or more personal servants and the staff officers often had three or four. Some of them were pensioners who had been in their masters' service before the campaign opened, others were men who had been picked up on the march, in Prussia, Poland, and Lithuania: ragamuffins and tramps who had nothing to eat at home and went in search of adventure. My Joseph was one of these. For ten ducats I had bought him a Polish nag. Other officers had taken servants on condition that they brought a horse with them, and they did not bother where the horse came from. This was, in fact, nothing more nor less than a commission to steal a horse, which was an easy thing to do and one that earned great favour. If the thief was pursued by the horse's owner and a complaint lodged with the colonel, then the fellow either ran away or else got a thrashing and was sent packing, which meant that he stole a horse somewhere else and, several days' march later, returned to his master.

Besides these servants, each squadron had a sutler, usually accompanied by his wife, a coachman and a horse-thief as servants, and several washerwomen. This mob followed the regiment and came under the supervision of the farrier.

While the regiment marched along the high-road in good order, or wherever it was sent, this mounted rabble — or to give it its proper name, this robber band — swarmed round it to left and to right, in front and behind, and used the regiment as a base. They all carried large and small haversacks and bottles in which to hide their plunder, and they were armed with swords, pistols, even carbines if they could lay hands on such a weapon. These bands often roamed far and boldly on the flank, and if ever they got back again, brought supplies for the troops. The work was dangerous, and many lost their lives — in agony if they fell into the clutches of the infuriated peasants. . . . This swarm of plunderers also formed a sort of flank patrol for the army, because if ever they bumped into enemy detachments they came flying back with great haste and loud shouts.

Major Marie-Joseph Rossetti in the King of Naples's service and aide-de-camp to Murat, describes in his diary how he was sent to reconnoitre the Russian entrenched camp at Drissa and to go over under a flag of truce with money for a French general who had just been captured. On returning from this mission Rossetti reported to Murat on 19 July that the enemy had abandoned their camp. He was sent to tell Napoleon.

I reached Glubokoye at daybreak [20 July] and was at once received by the Emperor. He was quartered in a vast monastery which dominated the town where the houses looked like primitive huts. While I was giving him my report that the entrenched camp at Drissa had been abandoned, he seemed to disbelieve what I said, but having read the King of Naples's[1] dispatches and found there the sketches which had been made of this camp, he could not contain himself for joy and, striding quickly up and down, he said to the Prince of Neuchâtel [Berthier]:

'You see, the Russians don't know how to make either war or peace. They are a degenerate nation. They give up their "palladium" without firing a shot! Come along! One more real effort on our part and my brother [the Tsar] will repent of having taken the advice of my enemies.'

He then asked me several questions about the morale of the cavalry and the condition of their horses, and when I replied that the rest we had enjoyed over the past few days had benefited our horses considerably, and that the men were more devoted than ever, body and soul, to His Majesty, the Emperor remarked:

'Well, *Monsieur le Napolitain*, come back in two hours and I shall have dispatches for you to take to your King.'

[1] Joachim Murat (1767–1815) was given the throne of Naples in 1808 by Napoleon.

Several times already the Emperor had used this expression '*Monsieur le Napolitain*' when speaking to me, and I had never dared make any comment, but this time the circumstances appeared favourable, so I said:

'*Sire*, since I have been in the service I have always fought in the ranks of the French Army and for France,[1] and I shall never exchange my title of Frenchman for that of Neapolitan or of any other nation.'

The Emperor replied: 'This is good, and that is how I see the matter. What is your rank in the French Army?'

'I am a major.'

He turned and spoke to the Prince of Neuchâtel. 'I appoint him colonel.[2] Make a note of that.'

And the Emperor dismissed me, telling me to go to Desna[3] where the King of Naples was due to arrive during the day. Two hours later Prince Berthier gave me dispatches for the King, and I took my leave.

Major Heinrich von Roos was senior doctor with the 3rd Württemberg Regiment of Chasseurs à cheval *in Montbrun's cavalry corps.*

On 23 July we came in pouring rain to the River Dvina, which we had orders to cross. There was no bridge. For several days we had not been dry, and now such a cold bath was pleasant for nobody, all the more so because we were in a sickly condition. The Dvina was between eighty and ninety yards wide at this point, and the water rushed between great boulders. I accompanied the first squadron which moved down to the bank, and I followed the procedure I had recently grown used to: I ordered two well-mounted N.C.O.s to take me between them. They did so willingly, and — into the water and across we went. Swimming swiftly and easily, we soon reached the far bank, but were as soaked as the horses from our heels up to our thighs and even our ribs. Everyone who swam

[1] From 1796 Rossetti had for several years served in the Piedmontese forces against France.

[2] Rossetti became a colonel in the French Army on 4 August, and later a general.

[3] Twenty miles south of Drissa.

was drenched likewise. None of our men was drowned, but the next regiment did not get over without loss.

On the other side we at once built fires to warm ourselves, because the persistent rain did not allow us to dry our clothes. We exchanged greetings, filled our pipes, and everyone who had some schnaps in his bottle offered it round to his friends.

The people we pitied most were two wives of the regiment who rode little horses and had had their clothes and baggage immersed deeper than we had and now had just as little chance of drying themselves. I give their names because they belonged to the number of soldiers' wives: in fact, their husbands were sergeant-majors. The first, Frau Wörth, was able to fend for herself so well under all circumstances that she was highly esteemed by the officers and respected by the soldiers. The other woman, the careful Frau Weiler, had already proved extremely useful to us, and did so again when we advanced further into Russia, through her knowledge of the Polish language.

Albrecht Adam, the artist, relates that Prince Eugène de Beauharnais's corps was beside the River Dvina on 24 July and that Napoleon and the main body of the army joined them at Beshenkovichi, thirty miles west of Vitebsk.

The Dvina has a deep bed. On both sides of the river are high and fairly steep banks on the left of which stands Beshenkovichi. For a long time I stood on high ground and watched the great activity surrounding the Emperor who was on the bank with his marshals. Here I had an amusing adventure. I noticed a striking person wearing a light-blue coat trimmed all over in gold braid, red trousers edged with gold, a strange hat lavishly decked with plumes — in short, a person of whom I could make nothing. What struck me most forcibly was that he had so much to do near the Emperor who, like the whole of his suite, was on foot. In the end I asked an officer who was standing beside me: 'Perhaps you can solve a riddle. How is it that the Emperor has so many dealings with that drum-major?'

The officer looked at me in surprise and said: 'What do you mean?' I explained myself more clearly.

'My God!' he exclaimed. 'But that is Murat, the King of Naples.'

This was my first impression of that madcap. Soon I was to see him blackened with powder and driving the soldiers into action in all his wildness and in a cloud of the worst oaths.

Another, more favourable, portrait of Marshal Murat comes from Lieutenant von Suckow.

I can see that marvellous officer still, wearing an extraordinary costume: long black hair in curls; a Henri IV-style hat adorned with large white plumes waving in the wind and held in by a diamond clasp; his neck bare, with an ancient ruff in the Spanish style; a sort of light-blue velvet tunic, all bedecked with gold embroidery and held in tight to the waist by a silk sash of the same colour as the tunic and tipped at each end with gold fringes; white stockinet breeches; huge deerskin boots, like those which were fashionable during the Thirty Years War [1618–48], with massive gold spurs.

Such was the garb in which this hero showed himself daily to the gaze of the army, always as brave, always ready to fly to the place where his imperial brother-in-law's[1] plans had to be brought to success.

Albrecht Adam's wish to take part in a battle was fulfilled on 25 July at Ostrovna, west of Vitebsk, where a Russian rearguard fought stubbornly; and in describing it he points a contrast between Murat and Prince Eugène.

Here I saw Murat at close quarters, his wildness inflamed by fighting and opposition. He roared hither and thither, cursing and scolding, urging the troops into action. Dashing to and fro, he appeared to fly, and his noble horse was lathered. The noble Prince Eugène presented a very strange contrast. I saw him, both here and later, under fire, displaying complete calm and prudence.

[1] In 1800 Murat had married Napoleon's youngest sister, Caroline. He spoke in a hoarse voice and with a Gascon accent. Roos says that Murat wore a red or green Spanish cloak, and sometimes red, sometimes green or yellow Hungarian boots.

He always maintained his solemn, noble bearing, and only an injustice or something contrary to a soldier's honour could arouse his indignation. But it was precisely this quality which inspired love, trust, and attachment in all who served under his command. This was best seen in times of greatest need, because once Napoleon and Murat had left the army on the retreat, he alone was able to hold together the discouraged remnants. Napoleon said of him at that time: 'Eugène was the only one who did not lose his head.' He should have added: 'or the love of the soldiers'! . . .

My long-cherished desire to see a battle from close to and find myself involved in it at least once was now fulfilled. On those two days I saw enough to provide me with material for a lifetime of painting battles. Furthermore, on this occasion I really heard the bullets whistle, but I did not let this distract me from drawing. I still possess sketches done in the middle of the battle and autographed by Prince Eugène. I was the only German at his court, and although I was treated in a friendly way by the officers and aides-de-camp around the Prince, they still could not refrain from teasing me long before the action began. 'Just now our Adam is always around, but once the bullets start flying we shall have to hunt for him.'

'Just wait,' I thought. 'I will show you that a German heart is worth as much as a French one.'

When the first cannon-balls landed near us an aide-de-camp, who looked rather pale, remarked: 'Well, Monsieur Adam, how do you find this?' I replied quite curtly: 'I find that we are in a battle.'

Several hours later, when I was in a very unpleasant position, another well-intentioned officer came up to me and said I could go to the rear, as this was no place for me. I replied that I did not set greater value on my life than on the Prince's, and that if one wanted to paint battles one must have watched them. I proposed to follow my commander everywhere unless given a direct order to stay in the rear.

Because he spoke some Polish, Lieutenant Paul de Bourgoing found himself, at the end of July, attached to the staff of General Count Henry-François Delaborde, commanding a division of the Imperial Guard.

My new commander soon took a liking to me. When, along with the other divisional commanders, he was issued with the map of Russia which had been engraved specially for the campaign, these enormous and inconvenient rolls had to be cut up and stuck on to cloth. Two dozen red check handkerchiefs belonging to our General were used for this purpose. It was at Vitebsk, in White Russia, where the Emperor and his Guard made a fairly lengthy stay,[1] that I devoted myself to this manual labour as geographer, paster, and cardboard-maker, almost as well as the job could have been done in the workshops of our geographical bookshops in Paris.

The General was very grateful to me for this little piece of technical skill.

On 9 August Lieutenant Charles Faré of the Foot Grenadiers of the Old Guard wrote a letter from Vitebsk to his parents living near Tours.

We are all very keen that the Russians should stand and fight, because so far they have made war only on our legs and our stomachs. We are seven hundred leagues from Paris and we are not yet half-way on our career, *taking into account, of course, the distance we shall have to cover to return home.*

Up to now we have not exactly suffered from hunger, but we are far from being well off. I was quite wrong in relying on this campaign to restore my financial situation. We spend more here than in Paris, and even so do not live very splendidly. Everything is madly expensive because of the shortage of provisions and the immense crowd of consumers. The people who make up Imperial General Headquarters, with whom we are still stationed, are rich and pay for everything at its weight in gold; and in order to get anything we are obliged to buy at the same rate. The few local resources are in

[1] Napoleon was there from 28 July to 12 August.

the hands of the Jews, who profit marvellously from this circumstance: a pound of butter sells at forty sous, a white loaf at thirty, and vegetables in proportion. A bottle of vinegar costs four francs, and that for us is a prime necessity, because for two months now we consider ourselves extremely fortunate if we can obtain any for counteracting the bad water drunk in this country. So far we have been given no allowance, and there is no sign of our being granted one. We must hope that when the campaign ends, the Emperor will compensate us. He has already inspected us twice and has given the Legion of Honour to those Grenadier captains who had not got it; but nothing else. . . .

Les Amardières[1] must be looking charming! Has the harvest been good? Are the vines promising? The newspapers are full of reports of abundant harvests, but they often lie. Please let me know the news and happenings of your neighbourhood and of Tours itself.

Ten days later, Faré wrote again to explain why he, who had fought at Ulm, Wagram, and Fuentes de Oñoro, had lost much of his earlier enthusiasm for war.

First of all, for us officers of the Guard, the chances of promotion are less favourable in war than in peace. The Emperor can refuse nothing to regiments which have fought well, and a crowd of officers requesting to enter the Guard come and take our vacancies as captains. As a result there remains only the remote hope of some endowment, and I do not really know if this can compensate for the fatigue and privations of this war, the most dreary that I have ever been in, and *yet which so far is nothing compared with what it could become if prolonged through the winter*.

And then one's tastes alter with the years. I still like my state, but not with my earlier zest. The habit of seeing the court, great men treated brusquely by even greater, who in turn are handled in the same way by greater men still, and all feeling these annoyances all the more keenly because they are senior and yet, despite this, they envy men of still higher ranks and are as little content with the one they have as with those they will obtain later on; the little

[1] A property near Fondettes, on the north bank of the Loire some four miles west of Tours.

hope one has of rising except by favour, and my lack of aptitude for intrigue — all these things that I have read about a hundred times over, and far better described than I can do it, now have to be faced in the flesh, and their truth strikes me all the harder. It is not that I think myself mature enough to put into practice all the fine speculations of moderation in one's desires, of indifference to riches and honours, of love of agreeable mediocrity. I think I shall have to live some more years for that, but at last my thoughts turn of their own accord towards such things, and that does not displease me. This is, I believe, the true path towards the little happiness one can enjoy in this world. I do not know whether I ought to attribute my new tastes to the wearisome sight of the horrors of war, and also to the sort of book I read with most pleasure and always carry in my portmanteau. They are *Les Caractères* by La Bruyère,[1] *Télémaque*,[2] La Fontaine's *Fables*,[3] and above all Horace[4] — Horace for whom I want to relearn Latin when I have a chance. These tastes will not strike you as very novel. Have I not told you all along that I want to marry? That I do not believe that happiness exists without a wife and children? That, basically, is the summit of my desires, and you will perceive that for all my so-called philosophy, I am not such a moderate.

Major Raymond de Montesquiou, Duke de Fezensac, one of Berthier's aides-de-camp, found the Emperor's stay at Vitebsk disquieting.

Those of us who had nothing to do with administration or policing spent our time off duty discussing our first successes and promising ourselves fresh triumphs. Never had a campaign opened more brilliantly. The whole of Lithuania had been conquered in a month, and almost without a fight. The army, assembled on the banks of the Dnieper and the Dvina, only awaited its leader's command to penetrate into the heart of Russia. . . . Yet wiser men and officers of long experience were not without

[1] Published in 1688.
[2] By François Fénelon (1651–1715); *Les Aventures de Télémaque* first appeared in 1699.
[3] Published in 1668.
[4] Horace (Quintus Horatius Flaccus), author of *Satires*, *Epistles* and *Odes*.

misgivings. They saw how the army had lost a third of its strength since crossing the Niemen, and almost without having to do battle, thanks to the impossibility of supplying it regularly and the difficulty of extracting anything even by plunder from a country which was naturally poor and had already been ravaged by the Russian Army. They observed the frightening death-rate among the horses, the dismounting of part of the cavalry, the increasing difficulty of handling the artillery, and the convoys of ambulances and medical carts which were obliged to remain behind. In addition, when they went inside the hospitals they found sick men almost unattended. They asked not only what would become of this army if it should be beaten, but also how it would bear the losses which would result from further marches and more serious actions. While a prey to these worries they were struck by the admirable order in which the Russian Army had conducted its retreat, always covered by numerous Cossacks and without abandoning a single gun. They also knew that the Tsar Alexander was calling upon every Russian to defend the country, and that every step we took into the interior of the empire would weaken our forces and increase those of the enemy.

Heinrich von Roos relates that Montbrun's cavalry corps made rapid marches towards Smolensk.

We now saw crowds of infantry and huge artillery trains. But in a few days we were separated from the army, and wandered around the countryside meeting neither friend nor foe, except for occasional peasants busy with the harvest, who, the further away from our route they were working, the less they bothered about us and the harder they went on with their labours. Where exactly we went on this march I could not say. There was seldom an opportunity to ask the name of a little town or village, because the inhabitants fled or went into hiding. And if here and there we discovered information through our Poles, the foreign names were difficult to remember. We crossed the Dnieper several times and several smaller streams, and also main roads, from which we could ascertain whether Russians or our own troops had passed, because we recognized the horses' hoof-prints from the method of shoeing and from the wheel tracks. The troops always leave something behind by which one can ascertain their nationality. As soon as a column has gone past one notices a smell peculiar to each army, and veterans know it at once. We found arrows and a weapon, probably belonging to the Bashkirs,[1] which was neither knife nor sword, yet was shaped like a cross between the two, and was about four feet in length. I heard an officer complaining that one should have to defend oneself against such weapons, but Lieutenant Blattmacher, who owned the weapon, replied: 'Victory in war is the main thing, whether the weapon be a sickle, scythe, pole, or whatever else is in use.'

It is often more difficult to recognize the ownership of camp sites, but even here this campaign had the special feature that the excreta left by men and animals behind the Russian front indicated a good state of health, whereas one found behind ours the clearest possible signs that the entire army, men and horses alike, must have been suffering from diarrhoea.

[*One of the chief problems facing Roos was this diarrhoea, caused mainly by drinking bad water, which upset horses and men alike.*]

Hitherto I had had a few medicines and could give some help and healing to the sick, or else a measure of relief. It usually happened that as soon as we reached a new camp one or two field kettles would be hung over the fire and tea brewed from peppermint or camomile, and this would be served to all who needed it. If these items were not available, then people drank tea made from balm-mint and elder-blossom. To those who were particularly ill I allowed tincture of opium and Hoffmann's[2] drops with these drinks, and so long as my supply of these drugs lasted, we managed tolerably well. Men dragged themselves on without going sick completely, in spite of persistent symptoms. Many were given thick meal soup, or broth during severe attacks: this was particularly good, and I recommended it frequently. They met with approval, were more and more widely used, and eventually became

[1] A people living south of the Ural Mountains. Their soldiers often wore chain mail and were armed with a bow.

[2] Friedrich Hoffmann (1660–1742) was Professor of Medicine at Halle and personal physician to King Frederick I of Prussia. The drops were a mixture of alcohol and ether.

Russia Reacts

The French writer Madame de Staël, banished from France by Napoleon because of her book De l'Allemagne, *and hoping to reach England, entered Russia from Vienna in July with her children and her lover, and, after reaching Kiev, travelled to Moscow.*

I approached nearer and nearer to Moscow, yet nothing suggested a capital ahead. The wooden villages were no less spaced out. One saw no more movement on the vast plains, and heard no greater volume of noise. The country houses did not increase in number. There is so much space in Russia that everything becomes lost, even the *châteaux*, even the inhabitants. One would imagine one was crossing a country which had just been abandoned by its people. The lack of birds intensified the silence; herds of cattle are rare, or at least they graze a long way from the road. The spaces make everything disappear, except space itself, which haunts one's imagination like certain metaphysical ideas of which the mind cannot rid itself once it has been gripped.

When I reached Moscow people were talking of nothing except the sacrifices that were being made for the war. A young Count Momonov raised a regiment for the state, and would only serve in it as a second lieutenant. A Countess Orlov, a pleasant lady and rich in the oriental style, donated a quarter of her income. Whenever I passed these palaces set in their gardens where space was lavished in a town as is done elsewhere in the heart of the country, I was told that the owner of this superb dwelling had just given a thousand peasants to the state; another owner had given two thousand. I had difficulty in getting used to this expression, *to give men*; the peasants themselves volunteered with enthusiam, and their masters were only acting as their spokesmen in this war.

Ernst Moritz Arndt, the German poet and patriot whose violent attack on Napoleon in 1806 in his book Geist der Zeit *had obliged him to take refuge in Sweden, spent the summer of 1812 in St. Petersburg. He relates a telling incident in which Madame de Staël was involved.*

The French actors in St. Petersburg gave a performance of *Phèdre.*[1] Rocca,[2] Madame de Staël's friend, and her son went to the theatre, and the rest of us who had been invited to lunch at this famous woman's house were still at table, when lo and behold! the two of them came back quite soon and rather disconcerted. They explained that at the beginning of the play there had been so much noise and roaring in the theatre and such abuse of the French and the French play by the Russians that the performance had to be stopped. And that is what happened in fact; this was the last time the French actors played that summer in St. Petersburg, and public hatred and contempt was so bluntly, so roughly expressed that at the beginning of the next winter they had to leave the city. And Madame de Staël? She forgot time and space, and could only feel herself and her people. She got very worked up, burst into tears, and shouted: 'What barbarians, not to want to see Racine's *Phèdre*!'

On 8 July Prince Bagration, commanding the Second Russian Army, wrote to Count Alexis Arakcheev (1769–1834), a former Minister for War from 1808 to 1810, and an influential favourite of the Tsar.

I have no cause for self-reproach. I have been stretched like cat-gut along the whole front. The enemy attacks without firing a shot. We start withdrawing, I don't know why. Nobody in the Army or in the country will believe that we are not traitors. I cannot defend the whole of Russia on my own. The First Army must pull back at once and march straight for Vilna. What are we afraid of? I am completely surrounded. How am I going to extricate myself? I do not know. As best I can! I shall continue to bestir myself as long as

[1] Jean Racine's *Phèdre* was first performed in 1677.

[2] Albert-Jean (John) Rocca, born in 1788 at Geneva, became Germaine de Staël's lover in 1811, after service with a French Cavalry regiment in Spain.

my health lasts. For several days past I have been worried. I beg you to march at once against the enemy, otherwise he will be able to make us smart for it. And on our side it is not time to take matters lightly. The Russians must not retreat. We are worse than the Prussians! I shall extricate myself somehow or other and with losses. But it is you who have no shame: with your backs to an entrenched camp, your flanks open, faced by an insignificant force, you must attack. My tail is in action every day, at Minsk, on the River Vileika. My route is barred by forests, swamps, and bad roads. No rest, and not a moment for my own life! I have no objection, upon my word, to doing everything myself, but there must be a little conscience and justice. So you are going to do nothing but retreat while I try to break out. If I am here only to be destroyed, let me be relieved of *the burden weighing on my shoulders* and let me be replaced! What is the use of exhausting the troops for no object and without rations? I advise you to go ahead at once without listening to anyone. The cannon-ball is a foolish virgin and the bayonet a wise virgin: that, surely, is the parable of which Mr. Pfull[1] applies the first part to us.

Think of the Tsar and of Russia. Why do we offer no resistance to the enemy when we can so easily manage to do so? Let us advance all along the line, make a reconnaissance in strength with cavalry, and launch a general attack! There lies honour and glory! Otherwise I assure you that you will not even be able to hold on to your entrenched camp. You will not be attacked frontally, but outflanked. For God's sake attack! The troops will take courage again. On several occasions already we have received orders to fight, and then we do nothing but retreat. There is my frank opinion and my devotion to my Sovereign and my country! If you are not satisfied, replace me. I do not wish to witness evil consequences. A retreat — it's all right for a hundred versts,[2] but not five hundred! A man must really be a traitor to the Tsar and the country to lead us to destruction in this way. Now that we have told one another everything like good Russians, forgive me if I have judged wrongly.

[1] Colonel, later General, Ernst von Pfull (1779–1866), who with Clausewitz, Gneisenau and other Prussian officers — about three hundred — left their own Army when the King of Prussia signed a treaty with Napoleon in February 1812, and entered the Russian service.

[2] A verst = *c.* 1160 yards.

On 17 July Countess Maria Nesselrode, living at Kamennoe Ostrov (Stone Island) in St. Petersburg, addressed a letter to her husband Karl.

As I write, the local nobles are assembled at Count Bezborodko's house. We shall see what transpires, and I will let you know. They gathered first in the Kazan Cathedral[1] where a *Te Deum* was sung and prayers were offered for the success of our arms. Next the clergy read a moving address aimed at persuading the nobles to make sacrifices. You should also see the manifesto written for the occasion. Our clergy are setting a very fine example. Out of the money they have put by, they have offered a million and a half. The Metropolitan of the town is having all his silver melted down, and that is valued at fifty thousand roubles. All the bishops of the different provinces are contributing large sums. Furthermore, all the silver in the convents and religious houses which is not in use — in other words, everything held to be the treasure of these institutions — will be given up for the good of the state. The Russian and foreign merchants have already offered two millions.

. . . I was telling you that the nobles, when they assembled, displayed extraordinary enthusiasm. There were loud shouts calling for old General Kutuzov. He was instructed to organize the army which is being raised here for this Government and which comprises four men in every hundred. The financial contribution amounts to nearly a million in cash. There is a tax of five per cent on the houses of landowners, and God knows what else.

Four days later, giving his address as 'on the march, 24 versts from Dorogobuzh', Count Nesselrode, who was director of the Tsar's political correspondence, wrote to his wife.

Here we are quartered in a magnificent mansion belonging to a Monsieur Vaksel. It has fine rooms, beautiful orangeries, gardens laid out in the old style — in fact everything which contrasts with the image of war. It is so peaceful here that I should one day like to retire to a place of this sort. I have worked out a thousand novels on this theme in my head. God grant that the most modest of them

[1] Dedicated to Our Lady of Kazan, this building in the Nevsky Prospekt had been consecrated only a year before.

may become reality! I have almost forgotten about battles, operations on the left and on the right, flanking marches, movements to secure positions or to assure communications, to hold road junctions or to be astride a river; and I have also forgotten all ideas on tactics and strategy with which my mind has been stuffed these last four months. But tomorrow all this will reappear, because if I don't get news of the Commander-in-Chief at Dorogobuzh, I shall go to Smolensk to find out.

Major-General Sir Robert Wilson, who served as British Military Commissioner at Headquarters and reached Smolensk just in time for the battle, describes the Russian Army, which he knew well.

The infantry is generally composed of athletic men between the ages of 18 and 40, endowed with great bodily strength, but generally of short stature, with martial countenance and complexion; inured to the extremes of weather and hardship; to the worst and scantiest food; to marches for days and nights, of four hours repose and six hours progress; accustomed to laborious toils, and the carriage of heavy burthens; ferocious, but disciplined; obstinately brave, and susceptible of enthusiastic excitements; devoted to their sovereign, their chief, and their country. Religious without being weakened by superstition; patient, docile, and obedient; possessing all the energetic characteristics of a barbarian people, with the advantages engrafted by civilization.

The Russian soldier in general is extremely subordinate, and attached to his officer, who treats him with peculiar kindness, and not as a machine, but as a reasonable being whose attachment he ought to win, although he has authority to command his service. Punishment is not so frequent as in other armies, nor is it very severe.

The higher officers are particularly considerate of them [their men], and promote every occasion for their solace or encouragement. They share every hardship with a gallant spirit of example that cheers the soldier, and which would afford a valuable model to other armies. They enjoy pleasures within their reach, but they make no pre-arrangement to secure them, or murmur at a deprivation; and with astonishment foreigners must regard the abstinence, the endurance, the total indifference to accommodation, and even the common decencies of the better order of society, with which the high nobility, accustomed to every luxury, in Petersburg and Moscow, proprietors of palaces and royal revenues, encounter the rudeness of the most severe campaigns.

The Russian officer, although frequently making the greatest physical exertions, is, however, inclined to indolent habits when not on actual duty; loves his sleep after food, and dislikes to walk or ride far. This is one of the defects of education. At Petersburg or Moscow no person of rank moves on foot, and a journey of 50 miles on horseback would be an expedition for the city's talk. The Emperor met one morning at Petersburg an English officer [Wilson himself], and stopped his padroskin (or vehicle). 'Where is your carriage?' 'Sire, I am walking about to look at your capital.' 'Ah!' said his Majesty. 'I would give a great deal if my officers would imitate such an example, and appreciate justly the great value and utility of that custom which I hear so much prevails in your country.'

. . . No troops can and do defend ground in retreat better than the Russians. Their artillery is so well horsed, so nimbly and so handily worked, that it bowls over almost all irregularities of surface with an ease, lightness, and velocity that give it great superiority. The vivacity of their cavalry, and the unquailing steadiness of their infantry, make it a pleasure to command them in extremest difficulties; for, like the British soldier, the most unbounded confidence may be reposed, to use a sailor's expression, 'in their answer to the helm' in every stress of situation.

Robert Ker Porter (1777–1842), afterwards knighted, made a reputation in early life by his historical paintings on such subjects as the taking of Seringapatam and the death of Sir Ralph Abercromby in Egypt. As a result he was invited by the Tsar to visit Russia in 1805 and spent two years there until the Treaty of Tilsit. He accompanied Sir John Moore during the Corunna campaign, and in 1812 returned to Russia to marry the Princess Shcherbatov, with whom he had fallen in love at the time of his first visit. He also wrote a Narrative of the Campaign in Russia during 1812. *He gives this description of the Cossacks.*

Their persons, air, and appointments, and the animals on which they are mounted, seem so totally at variance, that you can hardly suppose a reason for so unequal a union. The men are robust and fit for service: their horses appear completely the reverse: mean in shape, and slouching in motion, every limb speaks of languor, and every moment you expect to see them drop down dead under their heavy burthen: but so false are these shows, that there is not a more hardy animal existing; it will travel incalculable journeys, and remain exposed to the heat or cold, day and night, without manifesting any sense of inconvenience. These little rugged beasts never, like our *war horses*, know the luxury of a snug stable and a well littered bed, nor ever enjoy the comfort of a currycomb or a wisp of straw. Their sustenance is of the most scanty sort. . . .

Their dress is military and useful; consisting of a close dark blue jacket, and very large full trowsers, under which they wear drawers and boots. Their head is covered with a high black cap of sheepskin: a red bag hangs from its top ornamented with a chain of white worsted lace and tassals [*sic*]: a red stripe, rather broad, runs along the outside of the trowsers, as well as a cord of the same colour around the cape and sleeves. A single row of buttons closes the jacket at the breast. A broad leather belt, containing cartridges, and to which is suspended a light sabre, confines their waists. Their principal weapons are a pike about eight feet long, and a pair of pistols. A black belt crosses their left shoulder, to which is attached a sort of tin cartouch box, holding ammunition, and surmounted with a ramrod. An uncouth saddle is bound on the horse, somewhat like a doubled pillow, under which is a square piece of oil cloth painted in various colours.

Sir Robert Wilson adds these details:

Mounted on a very little, ill-conditioned, but well-bred horse, which can walk at the rate of five miles an hour with ease, or, in his speed, dispute the race with the swiftest — with a short whip on his wrist (as he wears no spur) — armed with the lance, a pistol in his girdle, and a sword, he never fears a competitor in single combat; but [in 1807] he irresistibly attacked every opposing squadron in the field.

They act in dispersion, and when they do re-unite to charge, it is not with a systematic formation, but *en masse*, or what in Germany is called the swarm attack. Dexterous in the management of a horse that is guided only by the snaffle, they can twist and bend their course through the most intricate country at full speed.

At the end of July the people of Moscow enjoyed reading a prophetic pamphlet written by Count Fedor Vassilievich, from which the following extract is taken.

An inhabitant of Moscow, a retired soldier, recently heard in a cabaret that Bonaparte was coming to Moscow. Furious at this news, he addressed the enemy of Russia in the following terms:

'How can you take it into your head to come to our country? We beg you, come and celebrate the festival of Christmas with us. You will be properly received. If you do not give up your diabolical role, our prayers will be answered and you will perish. You would do far better to stay quietly at home and put a stop to your boasting. Your soldiers are dwarfs and little folk who will never be able to wear our heavy furs, our large gloves, our hats, and our fur boots. How do you expect them to exist in Russia? They will die of our cabbages and gruel. Those who survive and remain here for the winter will not be able to bear the cold weather in December and January. On every side they will be surrounded by want and disaster. Out of doors they will freeze. In our cabins they will suffocate with the heat. They will be roasted on our stoves. What more do you want? The pitcher keeps going to the well until it is broken.

Charles XII, of true royal blood, was more vigorous than you are, yet he met his end at Poltava[1] and never recovered from the blow he was dealt there. Not many of your men will survive. The Poles, Tartar, and Swedes were more skilful than you are, but our fathers beat them. The tombs one sees round Moscow bear witness to their deaths and our glory. Go! Your hour has come. You and those with you will perish. You do not seem to realize what our Moscow is — a veritable empire. You left behind you in France nobody but the blind and the lame, old men and brats. You cannot depend upon the Germans. At the first opportunity they will abandon you.

[1] Peter the Great defeated the Swedish King there in 1709.

Alexander Pushkin, the great Russian poet, was in 1812 a thirteen-year-old pupil at the newly founded school in Tsarskoe-Selo, a dozen miles south of St. Petersburg. A schoolfellow named Pushin describes how the war affected them.

To begin with we saluted all the regiments of the Guard which marched through Tsarskoe-Selo. We were always there as soon as they came in sight, and we even went out to meet them during lessons. We accompanied them with a fervent prayer, we kissed our relations and friends, and grenadiers wearing heavy moustaches blessed us with a sign of the cross without leaving the ranks. How many tears we shed! When military operations began, the parents of pupils brought us the latest news, and Kochansky[1] read them aloud in the classroom. The library was always full during recreation periods; we skimmed helter-skelter through Russian and foreign papers; we discussed and argued without let-up. The least event had exceptional repercussions with us. Fears changed to hopes at the slighest improvement in the military situation. The teachers taught us how to follow the operations and explained certain details which would otherwise have been incomprehensible to us.

Major Baron Woldemar von Löwenstern tells us that intrigues against Barclay de Tolly began to show themselves.

People resented General Barclay. Secret meetings were held and plots hatched. . . . The operations of the Commander-in-Chief were criticized openly; people wanted to make him disgusted with his command by a thousand vexations which were set in train at leisure. General Bennigsen,[2] Duke Alexander von Württemberg, and the Grand Duke of Oldenburg discussed freely, and with anyone who was prepared to listen, the errors that had been made and what they regarded as the incompetence of the man who had given the orders. They corrupted a group of officers who, as a crowning

[1] A teacher of Russian literature.

[2] General Count Levin August Theophil Bennigsen (1745–1826), a Hanoverian soldier of fortune who had commanded the Russian forces against Napoleon at Eylau in 1807.

misfortune, had the support of the Grand Duke Constantine;[1] and he — I do not know by what fatality — had been influenced by General Yermolov,[2] who deep down hated Barclay while pretending to be extremely attached to him.

The Tsar, who was aware of all these plots, decided in his wisdom to cut short all this intrigue and gossip by quitting the army and leaving Barclay in charge with full powers such as no Commander-in-Chief had ever enjoyed.

One now saw the ante-rooms, the vestibules, and even Barclay's court, which had been deserted for some time, suddenly filled by the very people who had so openly criticized him. He did not bat an eyelid on seeing this, and maintained his calm and courteous bearing with everybody.

The Tsar left us at Polotsk [18 July] to go to Moscow in order to encourage by his presence the arming of the Empire. He had resolved not to lay down arms until the enemy had been expelled from the holy soil of Russia.

Before leaving us he came to see the Commander-in-Chief. He found him at dinner in a stable, because such was Barclay's modesty or indifference to anything which concerned him personally that every lodging was a matter of unconcern to him provided it was near the army and the camp.

After spending an hour with him, the Tsar left Barclay, embracing him tenderly, and just when His Majesty was stepping into his carriage, he shook his hand warmly and said: 'Goodbye, General. Again goodbye and *au revoir*. I recommend my Army to you. Do not forget that it is the only one I have. Always bear this in mind.'

These very significant words from the master's lips may help to explain the cautious manner in which the Commander-in-Chief conducted operations and which was so criticized at the time.

[1] Grand Duke Constantine Pavlovich (1779–1831), brother of Alexander I, commanded the 5th Corps. At the time he was next in succession to the throne.

[2] Major-General Alexei Yermolov was Barclay's Chief of Staff.

Barclay de Tolly established his headquarters in Smolensk on 1 August and two days later the junction was made between his army and that commanded by Bagration. Major von Löwenstern relates their meeting, in which he had a pacifying hand.

When Prince Bagration, accompanied by all his staff, . . . came for the first time to see the Commander-in-Chief, I persuaded the latter to go out to the ante-room to meet the Prince, sword and hat in hand, and to say that he was on his way to pay him a visit. This step, which had not been anticipated by Bagration, had a tremendous effect on him and on all his suite, who had jealously noted that Bagration, though senior to General Barclay, had been placed under his orders by command of the Tsar. Barclay's modesty and his usual lack of pretensions, above all this considerate step, had all captivated them in his favour. . . .

The interview lasted only a quarter of an hour. Thereafter Barclay took over command of the two united armies, and although Prince Bagration was hurt to find himself placed under the orders of a junior, he mastered his keen disappointment and went openly to work.

In a confidential memoir addressed to the Tsar, General Barclay de Tolly explained some of the difficulties and opposition he had experienced.

Thanks to my junction with Bagration, Napoleon's manœuvres were thwarted as never before; but I must add that never did the commander-in-chief of any army find himself in so painful a situation as I did. The two commanders of the two united armies were equally answerable to the sole authority of Your Majesty and were equally entrusted with the full powers inherent in their office. Each had the right to address reports direct to Your Majesty and to make the arrangements he thought fit for the army entrusted to his charge. No doubt as Minister of War I had a particular right to speak in Your Majesty's name.

I was therefore obliged, in order to get a course of action common to the two armies and to make them aim at the same objective, to use every endeavour to restore the essential harmony between Prince Bagration and myself, because our earlier correspondence about the slowness of his movements had created considerable ill feeling between us. I was obliged to flatter his vanity and to give way to him in several matters against my better judgement, solely with a view to gaining agreement to the carrying out of more important enterprises. In short, I had to behave in a manner I find most repugnant, and one totally contrary to my character and feelings. However, I hoped thereby to gain my object, but the results convinced me of the reverse, because intrigues and party spirit soon reared their heads. Scarcely had the two armies linked up than offensive opinions and malevolent rumours began to circulate and were deliberately spread in St. Petersburg.

At the same time His Imperial Highness the Grand Duke Constantine came from Moscow and rejoined the army. I must also mention the attitude of several people who belonged to Your Majesty's military household and who followed the example of opposition set by your brother. This will give an idea, though a watered-down one, of what was going on at the time. I wish to mention the names of only a few important people who were at Headquarters in Smolensk and who each thought himself called upon to condemn everything that was done. Duke Alexander von Württemberg, Generals Bennigsen, Korsakov, and Armfeldt each had their supporters among Your Majesty's aides-de-camp and in the two armies, who reported everything that reached their ears.

Furthermore, my own Chief of Staff,[1] a man of talent, but false and an intriguer, acted towards me in an equally unpardonable fashion, with the sole object of flattering several of these notables, namely the Grand Duke and Prince Bagration.

These two official letters written by Count Rostopchin, the Governor of Moscow, throw light on the impact of war upon individual Russians. The first is dated 21 August.

The Commandant of Moscow, Lieutenant-General Hesse, informs me in a letter dated 7 August that, according to the report addressed to him by Kryazhev, the principal of a local com-

[1] Löwenstern wrote of General Yermolov: 'He is a man of merit, full of knowledge, energetic and strong-willed, but his nature is false, hard, and he uses every means to gain his ends. His heart is as black as his book, an expression the Tsar himself used to describe his character.'

mercial college, one of the regular pupils of that college, Gavrila Kruglikov by name, having been given leave in free time to go to the home of his grandmother, the merchant's wife, has without the knowledge of the college council and without proper discharge enlisted for service in the Cossack regiment which Your Excellency is raising. And since the said Kruglikov has to spend two more years in the college in order to complete his studies, . . . I advise Your Excellency to return the said Kruglikov to the college forthwith and to inform me when this has been done.

[*The second letter, dated 2 September, is addressed to the Chief of the Moscow City Police.*]

The Commandant of Moscow, Lieutenant-General Hesse, in a letter of 18 August, reports to me that the Moscow merchants' sons Platon Pavlov and Gerasim Simyonov, residing in the Pokrovsky district in the first block, have declared their desire to make rusks for the troops' rations and that other merchants intend to emulate them in this, provided they receive notice of permission from the district police authority. I have instructed the Commandant to inform the merchants' sons Pavlov and Simyonov that I accept with pleasure their zealous offering and I order Your Excellency to instruct all police authorities in the capital to publish an announcement that people of every class are permitted to make rusks out of their own bread for supplying to the troops and that they should report the quantity prepared to the police stations which will have had instructions from me as to where the rusks are to be sent.

Smolensk to Borodino

SMOLENSK was surrounded by an ancient brick wall, with loopholed battlements, about thirty feet high and fifteen thick at the base; thirty towers, some round, some square, butted out from the wall. A ditch, glacis, and covered way added strength to defences which, though in a poor state of repair, still presented a considerable obstacle to attackers, as the French soon discovered. Veterans in the Grand Army murmured that the thickness of the walls reminded them of the ramparts at St. Jean d'Acre thirteen years before.

On 16 August the town was in little danger, because the troops at Marshal Ney's disposal barely outnumbered the Russian garrison. If the French were to capture the place before the main Russian army came close, an immediate and powerful assault was imperative; but although Davout and Poniatowski arrived that evening, they were too late to do anything effective until next day, by which time Raevsky had been reinforced inside Smolensk, and Barclay and Bagration had hurriedly concentrated on the north bank of the Dnieper.

Early on the 17th Barclay, having decided that Napoleon might well continue his advance along the south bank and seize a river crossing further east, perhaps at Dorogobuzh, thereby blocking the road to Moscow, sent Bagration's army eastwards to Dorogobuzh as a precaution, to secure the line of eventual retreat. Meanwhile, inside Smolensk, Raevsky had been relieved by Dokhturov, who had 20,000 men under command.

That afternoon Napoleon launched Ney, Davout, and Poniatowski against the southern defences, out of range of Barclay's guns beyond the river. After four hours' fighting they had carried the suburbs, and Poniatowski's men were only just prevented from forcing one of the gates by the arrival of a Russian division under Eugen von Württemberg. However, the walls still defied assault, French 12-pounder guns having failed to make a breach, despite an intense bombardment. When Davout ordered his howitzers into action, the wooden houses of Smolensk quickly caught fire, and, as had already occurred in the suburbs, were reduced to smoking ruins, with blackened fruit hanging on garden trees.

At eleven o'clock that night, in the face of mutinous subordinates and a hum of bitter argument, Barclay de Tolly ordered the evacuation of Smolensk. He realized that Napoleon was beginning to outflank his own position, that Russian losses had been serious, and that Bagration on the march was unable to provide local aid. In any case, Barclay felt justified in ordering this withdrawal, now that the route to Moscow was secure. After the powder magazines had been blown up and the holy ikon of the Mother of God been carried away to safety, the army moved in two columns — the intention was to deceive Napoleon as to the direction of retreat — in darkness, and in a confusion exacerbated by lack of guides, bad reconnaissance, and much losing of the way in the woods, even to the extent of brigades turning in circles.

Many of the 15,000 inhabitants fled in the wake of their soldiers, who left behind hundreds of their wounded comrades without medical care and facing death from the encroaching flames.

On 19 August Ney and Murat were stopped by the Russian rearguard five miles east of Smolensk near Valutino Gora.[1] Fighting lasted throughout the day, with stubborn resistance and repeated counter-attacks until nightfall, when Ney, making a full-scale effort, eventually forced the Russians to abandon their positions. That afternoon Junot had come up from the south-west against the enemy's left flank, and although faced by no more than light cavalry, had refused Murat's entreaties to advance. Had he attacked vigorously, the Russians must have been cut off and severely mauled. Murat was so furious that he said to Junot: 'You are unworthy to be the last dragoon in Napoleon's army'; and the Emperor himself was no less indignant over the failings of an old comrade, for the day's struggle had cost his army another 7,000 casualties, rather more than on the Russian side, and once again he had failed to intercept Barclay's retreat.

After this battle the Russian general ordered his staff to find another favourable position on which to stand and fight. One, near Usvyatie, proved defective, so another was proposed five miles to the east, by Dorogobuzh on the Dnieper, but news of the French advance and a threat by cavalry to turn the Russian left wing induced even Bagration to advise retreat. To have fought there with barely 100,000 men would have been imprudent, especially as Russian morale was low, the men were hungry, the subordinate commanders protesting and unreliable.

The French had their troubles too. From Smolensk Napoleon redirected his main line of communication to pass through Orsha, Borisov, Minsk, and Vilna. In the town itself hospitals and magazines were established, but shortages were terrible — on the battlefield of Valutino, for instance, wounds had to be dressed

[1] This battle is known by the Russians as Lubino, a nearby village.

with hay and with paper from the archives of Smolensk; and too many of the Emperor's orders proved to be impracticable. Discipline declined still further, and even the generals and marshals were displaying gloom and discontent.

Much argument has centred round whether Napoleon should have remained in Smolensk for the rest of 1812, resuming his campaign the following spring, and devoting the interim months to reorganizing his patently failing supply and medical system, regrouping his various corps, perhaps establishing an independent Poland. But would he really have found it possible to support his immense army on a line near Smolensk? Would not a halt have appeared to the rest of Europe like an admission of failure? In any case, the urge to bring the enemy to battle and win a decisive victory was uppermost in his mind. In past years he had never failed to defeat his opponents in a single campaign, and he wanted to snatch from this side of Moscow the triumph which had eluded him at Vilna, Vitebsk, and Smolensk.

So he decided to continue the advance towards Moscow, another 310 miles by the post route. Led by Murat and the cavalry, with Davout's corps in support, the Grand Army moved forward again. Whereas Davout, rigid, unpopular martinet that he was, tried to conserve his men and horses, the dashing King of Naples fatigued and thinned his regiments, not only by losing no chance to attack Cossacks encountered along the way, but also, in the expectation of a decisive battle, by keeping most of his cavalry massed centrally, thus increasing the already unmanageable problem of feeding and watering the horses. His difficulties were not lessened by the Russian policy of burning villages, stores, stocks of hay and straw, leaving their pursuers to cut unripe corn as fodder or let their mounts munch thatch from local rooftops.

27 August saw the Russians evacuating Viazma, 112 miles from Smolensk, after setting fire to supply depots there. When, two days later, Barclay and Bagration reached Tsarevo-Zaimishche, just short of Gzatsk, they were joined by General Miloradovich with over 15,000 infantry and cavalry — a mixture of recruits, depot troops, and convalescents — and some 10,000 militia. Barclay was encouraged to offer battle. It now seemed reasonably safe to do so, and he was all too well aware of the feeling in the army and of his own position as focal point for abuse and resentment, even for such labels as 'foreigner' and 'traitor'. However, the decision was snatched from his hands by the appointment of Field-Marshal Prince Kutuzov to supersede him.

Ever since Smolensk, relations between Barclay and Bagration had been increasingly strained, with Bagration calling the other man cowardly, slow, and irresolute. It seemed obvious to many that once the two armies had united early in August, a single over-all commander should have been appointed, but the Tsar had been reluctant to hurt any feelings by taking such a step. However, pressure and voluble opinions from certain Army cliques indicated that unless changes were made, Moscow would be lost, since Barclay was said to be leading the country to ruin and betraying Holy Russia. Even his distant Scottish ancestry was a handicap, patriotic pride requiring that he should make way for a true Russian. As for the more obvious foreigners, Bagration was not alone when he remarked: 'The whole headquarters is so full of Germans that a Russian cannot breathe.'

Alexander called a council on 17 August, and even though they well knew the Tsar's dislike of Kutuzov since Austerlitz, the members unanimously proposed this one-eyed, shrewd, lazy, adroit, deeply patriotic veteran who at sixty-seven was corpulent, lecherous, and within nine months of his death. With neither inclination nor confidence, the Tsar accepted the decision of his council and Kutuzov became Commander-in-Chief.

On joining the army on 29 August he criticized the position selected by Barclay, and being still 130 miles from Moscow, in whose defence he was pledged to fight a battle, he risked his popularity by deciding to resume the retreat and look for a more advantageous field of battle. Covered by a strong rearguard marching a day behind, the Russians plodded as far as a village named Borodino.

Captain Eduard von Löwenstern, a brother of Woldemar and aide-de-camp to Count Peter Pahlen who commanded the Russian rearguard, recalls how they withdrew by forced marches to Smolensk, fighting continually.

Count Pahlen could no longer manage to travel on horseback, so we placed him in a drosky which we luckily still had with us, and we accompanied him to Smolensk, after picking up Dr. Macdonald.[1] In our last night camp outside the town our soldiers plundered several beehives. The angry bees immediately swarmed over the whole bivouac; our horses went almost mad, and I myself had seven stings on my head and face. You can imagine how swollen I was and what pain I had to bear. General Dorokov[2] took over command of the rearguard.

[1] Dr. Friedrich von Macdonald died in 1849 aged seventy-two.
[2] Major-General Ivan Dorokov, who was killed on 24 October.

At Smolensk we found General Raevsky, who was holding the storming French out of the town. As I now had no official duties, I rode out to a battery in order to watch the battle. Here I found General Schevich of the Bodyguard Hussars who was inspiring the gunners by his presence. Also standing there was a Russian priest from the town: he was personally laying several guns. The artillery officer, a young man of about my own age [twenty-two] distinguished himself, showed a bold front, allowed the French to come as close as possible and then, as soon as they came within case-shot range,[1] shattered great heaps of them to the ground. In the many battles and actions in 1806 and 1807, and also in this campaign, I had often seen soldiers fall, but never in my experience had I seen so many felled by a single salvo, weltering in their own blood and without arms or legs. A second earlier these poor victims of battle had advanced with fixed bayonets and pale faces. Now most of them lay dead or mutilated. Another column soon advanced and, with a hail of bullets, avenged the death of their comrades. Many of our artillerymen were shot.

I ducked behind a breastwork and the bullets whistled overhead. Being a mere spectator I had no job to do here, and did not wish to get myself killed to no purpose, so I made off and rode into Smolensk. The town seemed dead. A few wounded or drunken men staggered around in the deserted streets. The suburbs were on fire, the magazines and a few houses had been plundered, while outside the battle thundered. The blood-bath I had just witnessed had upset me dreadfully. I felt completely forsaken, and I was suddenly overcome by such fear that I would willingly have hidden in a mousehole. Every loud bang made me tremble.

I was never again to have such a moment of weakness. The wife of an apothecary was watching me tremble, and it can easily be imagined that I cut a pathetic figure, so much so that this woman could not stop laughing, despite the wretched circumstances. I was ashamed of myself, and did not breathe freely again till I had left Smolensk behind.

I found Pahlen in a little farmhouse less than a mile from the town.

[1] The most effective range was about two hundred yards.

Two rare examples of fraternization in this otherwise bitterly fought campaign occurred during the battle for Smolensk. The first is described by Carl Anton Wilhelm, Count von Wedel, a second lieutenant in the 9th Regiment of Polish Lancers.

At midday we witnessed a strange scene. Bruyère's division[1] was drawn up on the left wing in three lines, one behind the other, with Jacquinot's brigade in front. I found myself with my troop among the light infantry, and opposite us swarmed Russian dragoons and Cossacks. At one moment these men attacked our sharpshooters, at another they withdrew and tempted us towards the bushes in which infantry were hidden who opened fire and forced us to retreat hurriedly. This mutual banter lasted quite a while. Then the Russians stopped firing, positioned their own light infantrymen at distances of fifteen to twenty paces apart, and sheathed their swords as a sign that they did not wish to go on fighting. We followed their example and disposed our sharpshooters in the same way, at about a hundred yards' range, with orders not to shoot and to remain quiet.

Soon a Russian officer of dragoons rode forward a few paces, greeted us, and made signs with a bottle. I followed suit and placed myself in front of our line of *tirailleurs*. In this way we approached to within thirty yards of one another, whereupon the Russian shouted in French: '*Mon camarade!* It is useless to exhaust our horses and kill our men for nothing. Let us drink together instead. There will be plenty of time for fighting afterwards.'

We went nearer and enjoyed a friendly drink, while other troops continued fighting undisturbed in the distance. A few more Russian officers came up shortly. I wanted to withdraw, but the dragoon officer said: 'I promise you on my word of honour that they will do you no harm.'

So I stayed where I was and we talked amicably. I found his rum good, but could not give him any in return. It was not long before other officers arrived from both sides. Our sutler, Frau Ehmke, a pretty woman who always rode round among the light infantrymen and had two little casks of brandy on her horse, came past and poured the Russians a free drink, though she charged us a high

[1] Count Jean-Pierre-Joseph Bruyère (1772–1813) commanded the 1st Light Cavalry Division.

price for her liquor. A young lieutenant in our regiment named Piessac, who had an attractive, girlish face, was kissed by a bearded, elderly Russian. A Russian officer of uhlans, Polish by birth, who took us for Poles because we wore their uniform, wanted to make inquiries about his compatriots, and when he heard that a regiment of Polish lancers stood in the second line behind us, he rode confidently over to this regiment as fast as his horse would carry him. We thought he meant to desert, but this was not his intention at all. He merely wanted to see his fellow-countrymen and air his bitter views about the inglorious way in which Barclay de Tolly had chosen to wage war.

When he learnt that we wanted nothing better than a full-scale battle which would decide the outcome of the war, and that we were heartily tired of wandering around a country so devoid of resources, he replied that if we hoped for such a battle at Smolensk, then we hoped in vain. He would lay heavy odds that we should enter Smolensk next day, but that the Russians would, as before, slip away without fighting.

Meanwhile General Bruyère, who was some distance away, had noticed this scene and sent an aide-de-camp to recall the officers to their posts and to indicate to the Russians that they should retire behind their line of sharpshooters, otherwise they would be fired on. He gave orders for the Polish officer who had ridden through to our second line to be arrested, but the aide rode so slowly — no doubt on purpose — that the Pole was warned by another officer and hurried away.

We remained opposite each other for several hours longer, until the evening, but the friendship which had been struck up lasted, and not another shot was fired until both sides withdrew.

Lieutenant Hubert Lyautey, serving with the Artillery of the Guard, also describes a pause in the fighting, in the middle of the next day, 17 August.

We were separated from the Russians by a ravine with a stream of dark, muddy water. The need to water the horses was common to both sides, and each went down into the ravine. The horses were unharnessed from half our guns, which were left in battery formation, and I accompanied these horses and some of the gunners, leaving enough men up top to work the guns if need arose. The Russians drank on one side and we on the other. We conversed by means of gestures, without understanding each other very well. We offered drinks and tobacco, and in these we were the richer and more generous side. Soon afterwards these good friends fired cannon-shots. I found one officer who spoke French, and we exchanged a few words.

Lieutenant Christian von Martens, a Württemberg officer, relates how on 18 August the Russians, having destroyed the bridges, defended the Petersburg suburb on the right bank of the Dnieper in order to cover their withdrawal.

Quickly our 1st Infantry Brigade under General Ernst von Hügel pressed forward and crossed over to the suburb by a ford through which the troops waded up to their thighs in water. The Russian General Korff was still holding this suburb and defending it stubbornly so as to provide the army with a salient. A Portuguese battalion followed us and played a strong part in the bloody assault. After making some progress these troops were driven back to the bank by the enemy, who had meantime been reinforced, and they were able to hold out in houses and gardens only with great difficulty. At the same time we also lost our high ground, but linked up with the 2nd Brigade in the suburb of Stasnaya and with the light-infantry brigade occupied the left bank of the Dnieper, dispersed among the gardens.

With half the company I was assigned to a garden with fruit trees and a summer-house close to the river bank. Here I found a young French officer and about a dozen men already established. At once a fierce exchange of small-arms fire began, and was supported by our artillery, whose cannon-balls whizzed overhead and hit the enemy on the far bank. Delighted by the unexpected reinforcement, the fiery French officer grasped my hand and said: 'Come, my friend. Let us share our fate.' And he let me take a gulp of spirits from his water-bottle. I had scarcely thanked him for the refreshing drink and turned to my soldiers, who were spread out along the garden hedge with the Frenchmen, when an enemy case-shot smashed the head of this gallant young officer, whose acquaintance I had made only a few minutes before, so terribly that bits of his brain and blood were spattered over the summer-house wall. It was a horrible moment for me. For the first time in my life the enemy bullets fell about my head like a hail-storm which knocks the leaves off the trees. At midday we were fetched back from this unfriendly garden to the main street of the suburb, while the Russians also withdrew their troops from the far bank. . . .

Once this hot action ended, we camped in the streets. From the houses which had been so hurriedly abandoned by their occupants flour and lard were fetched, and with these precious ingredients I was just making what we called a 'sergeant', or meal mash, when an enemy ball landed in the fire and I dropped the pan full of mash. After all the grim events of the day this accident caused as much merriment as a very small officer of the 4th Regiment had done that morning when he found that he was unable to wade through the ford and so had himself carried across on rifles by four of his soldiers.

Captain Carl von Martens, serving in a hussar regiment in the 4th Russian Corps, wrote the following account of his experiences in the struggle for Smolensk.

I split up my detachment along a considerable stretch of our bank of the river, and sent my two trumpeters in opposite directions with orders to find a concealed place and there to blow lustily so as to mislead the enemy into believing that many troops were on the march and that my force comprised only the advance-guard. At the same time I sent a report to the general.

Here I saw very clearly how the result of battles and wars depends all too often on chance or on a higher Providence. The fate of the entire Russian Army, yes, the fate of the whole Empire, of Napoleon, and of the French Army, lay in the hands of an unimportant hussar officer. A word from me to the commander of the French corps would have sufficed to persuade him to cross the river and, led by me against the rear of the Russian Army, he would irrevocably have defeated the latter and forced it to surrender with bag and baggage. I understood my position and thought of the reverses I had suffered; but I also felt with pride what a man's honour means and I felt the infamy of treachery. For this adventure I received a letter of thanks from the Tsar, and this was printed in Army orders. But nobody thought to promote me.

The hussar came back with news that the army was in full retreat and he brought me an order from General Barclay to return to my regiment. But where was the regiment? I found General Korff's corps. This good man cut a sad figure as a cavalry general. He was so enormously stout that he could only be lifted on to a horse with the greatest difficulty. Furthermore, he had so little liking for musketry and the roar of the cannon that he always managed to organize a comfortable place of refuge. I found him sitting at ease on the grass and slicing off the head of a roast chicken.

He asked me where I came from, complained that he was afraid of being cut off, and asked me to send him a hussar in the event of my being fortunate enough to rejoin the army. However, he seemed quite unconcerned, as if the whole business was an everyday one, and he went on chewing his roast chicken contentedly. The aides-de-camp and other staff officers near him laughed and drank, and this whole section of the army was so calm that nobody would have imagined that the enemy were close. Even the most ordinary precautions had not been taken.

My horses and men were utterly exhausted. I selected ten of the best horses, and leaving the detachment behind with instructions to follow after the usual rest, set off to find the army. After two hours I met a colonel who was meant to lead a park of heavy artillery to the army. These guns belonged to General Baggovut's corps. The colonel had lost his way and taken a track which would have led him straight into the arms of the French. I had the utmost difficulty — indeed, I almost had to resort to threats — to convince him of his error and persuade him to turn about and follow me. I led the way at a trot and after an hour caught sight of our army on the heights by the Smolensk–Moscow road, a dozen miles from the former town. The French Army was drawn up in battle order on the opposite heights.

On one hill I spotted a group of generals who were studying the positions through their telescopes. I was told that Generals Tuchkov[1] and Yermolov were there: the former commanded the

[1] The Russian Army had three generals of this name. Tuchkov I is concerned here.

left wing of the army. I left my hussars at the foot of the hill, climbed up, and gave my report to the general.

'My God! That fellow Korff!' he exclaimed. 'Hurry back and tell him that he must arrive with his corps and that this is no time for dawdling.'

I pointed out that I had orders to find my own regiment. 'All right, then. Tell my aides-de-camp where Korff can be found. My God, if only Baggovut's artillery would turn up! We have no heavy guns and what are we going to do if we are attacked?' I told him that the guns should arrive within a quarter of an hour. 'That's impossible,' shouted General Yermolov, commanding the artillery. 'The guns are at least an hour's march away.'

After I had described my encounter with the artillery colonel, I heard a man wearing the scarlet uniform of an English general say in English to General Tuchkov: 'I am suspicious of this officer. He looks to me like a French officer.' I laughed, and said to him in English: 'No more than you do, General!'

Then General Tuchkov asked me: 'But you are not a Russian, are you?' 'No, a Livonian.' 'Which regiment?' 'The Y—— Hussars. Down there a sergeant-major and ten hussars of my detachment are waiting.'

The General summoned the sergeant-major and also asked him the name of his regiment. On hearing his reply, the General turned to me and said in French: 'Forgive my precautions, but I could tell from your accent that you were not Russian.'

The English general was the celebrated Sir Robert Wilson, who is now Governor of Gibraltar[1] and was at the time a volunteer with the Russian Army.

No sooner had General Tuchkov said these few words to me than the clatter of approaching artillery could be heard. 'Ah! There he is, thank God! Thank you. I will mention you to General Barclay.'

I often heard words like this, but they were never fulfilled. I moved away, found my detachment, which had followed me, and eventually two squadrons of the regiment, which had been utterly dispersed. Two days passed before complete squadrons had mustered again. The French did not attack us in this position,

[1] Wilson was in Gibraltar from 1842 to 1848, the year of his death. Martens's memoirs were published in 1848.

and our army retreated in excellent order along the Moscow road.

General Armand de Caulaincourt, Duke of Vicenza, recalled the night of 17 August outside Smolensk.

It was a cold night, so I went up to a fire which was burning in front of the Emperor's tents, and I was just dozing off there when His Majesty arrived with the Prince of Neuchâtel and the Duke of Istria. They watched the fire light up the entire horizon which was already aglow with our bivouac fires.

'It is an eruption of Vesuvius,' shouted the Emperor, tapping me on the shoulder and dragging me out of my drowsiness. Then he added: 'It's a fine sight, is it not, Grand Equerry?'

'It's horrible, Sir.'

'Bah!' retorted the Emperor. 'Gentlemen, remember the words of a Roman emperor: "The corpse of an enemy always smells sweet."'

We were all shocked at this remark.

At four in the morning a few watchful marauders penetrated into the town by means of old breaches which the enemy had not even repaired, and at five o'clock the Emperor learnt that Smolensk had been evacuated. He gave orders that the troops should not enter except as corps, but the soldiers had already got in through several ways which they had opened up and climbed. The Emperor mounted his horse and went to reconnoitre the eastern enceinte and then entered the town through an old breach. He rode through and spent the day at the bridge so as to hurry on the rebuilding of it.

All the public buildings in the main square and the finest houses in the town had been only slightly damaged. The arsenal, where very few things were left, was intact. All parts of Smolensk had suffered. The inhabitants had fled with the army, and only a few old women and some men from the lowest class had stayed, as well as a priest and an artisan. They told us all they knew of what had occurred in the town, but we could glean no information about the Russian Army, not even its losses. The Emperor appeared very satisfied, even exultant.

'Within a month,' he said, 'we shall be in Moscow. In six weeks we shall have peace.'

This prophetic tone did not convince everybody, at least on the subject of peace.

Colonel Rossetti accompanied the King of Naples when he, Napoleon, and Marshals Ney, Davout, and Berthier entered Smolensk.

Everywhere we stepped over rubble and corpses. Still burning palaces were nothing but shells, the walls cracked by the flames, and beneath their ruins lay the blackened skeletons of inhabitants who had been consumed by the fire. The few houses which survived were full of soldiers, and the owner stood at the door without shelter, with part of his family, weeping for the death of his children and the loss of his possessions. The cathedral,[1] celebrated in Europe and much revered by the Russians, became the refuge of the poor wretches who had escaped the fire; in this church, and very near to the altars, whole families were lying on rags. On one side an old man on his death-bed was turning to look for the last time at the image of the saint whom he had invoked all his life. On the other side, unhappy children in a cradle were being breast-fed by a terrified mother who shed tears over them.

After going through the town, the Emperor arrived at the gates of the citadel near the Dnieper, opposite the suburb on the right bank which the Russians still held. He went and stood on some mats in front of a hut and began a careful examination of the position just abandoned by the Russians. After a quarter of an hour he could no longer contain his joy, and exclaimed:

'The scoundrels! Fancy abandoning such a position! Come, we must march on Moscow.'

At this point a lively discussion began between Napoleon, the marshals, and the senior officers who surrounded him on whether the army should cross the Dnieper and pursue the enemy or whether it would be more prudent to halt at Smolensk. The Emperor took a few paces forward as if to separate himself from the

[1] The Cathedral of the Assumption, founded in 1676.

group. The King of Naples, Berthier, Davout and Ney, Caulaincourt, and Lobau[1] followed him, and we remained behind.

The Emperor's discussion with the army's commanders lasted for over an hour. We heard later that everyone except Marshal Davout had argued against the Emperor's plan for advancing, but that Davout, with his usual tenacity, had maintained that it was only at Moscow that we could sign a peace treaty, and the result of this conference, which was to have so important an effect on the destiny of France, was the order to depart the next day.

The Emperor mounted his horse, and we entered Smolensk. It was midday. The heat was prostrating. The King of Naples, who had been indisposed for several days, was taken ill, and we carried him to his headquarters where he was obliged to go to bed. At about three o'clock the Emperor sent for him. Murat sent a reply to the effect that he had nothing to add to what he had said in the morning, and that Napoleon could dispose of his life but not make him alter his opinion.

Baron Dominique-Jean Larrey,[2] Surgeon-in-Chief of the Grand Army, considered the assault on Smolensk one of the bloodiest he had ever witnessed.

The gateways, breaches, and main streets were filled with dead and dying, most of them Russian. Their losses were immense; it would have been difficult to count the huge number of dead we found in the town ditches, gulleys in the hills, on the river bank, and by the bridges. On our side we had about six thousand wounded and twelve hundred dead. Most had received first aid on the battlefield, while the fighting was in progress. I performed a large number of operations in the ambulances of the advance-guard, whence we removed the wounded with all possible speed, to collect them in fifteen big buildings which were converted into hospitals. Several were close to the principal points of the battlefield, others in the suburbs, and the largest in the town itself.

[1] Georges Mouton, Count Lobau (1770–1838), was one of Napoleon's aides-de-camp.

[2] On St. Helena Napoleon described Larrey as 'the most virtuous man I have ever met'. And to Larrey he once said: 'A sovereign is indeed fortunate to have dealings with a man like you.'

Here, as at Vitebsk, we were very short of all kinds of materials for dressing the wounded. As in many other circumstances I had to devise ways of supplying what we lacked. Thus, instead of the linen dressings which we had used up after the first few days, I made use of paper found in the Archives, whose building was set aside as a hospital. The parchments served as splints and bandages; tow and birch cotton (*Setula alba*) replaced lint, and the paper also served well for bedding-down the sick. But what difficulties had to be surmounted! What trouble we experienced in this predicament!

Prince Bagration wrote again to Count Arakcheev on 20 August when his disagreements with Barclay de Tolly were at their height.

I imagine that the Minister [Barclay] has already made his report on the abandoning of Smolensk. It is distressing, heart-breaking, and the whole army is in despair. To think that we abandoned the most important position unnecessarily; and I went to beg and impore him, I wrote to him, but all to no avail! I swear on my honour that Napoleon was in a trap as never before. He stood to lose half his army, without ever taking Smolensk. We have fought and we fight like nobody on earth. I held out for more than thirty-five hours with 15,000 men, and I was beating them, whereas he [Barclay] did not stay even fourteen hours. It is disgraceful. It is a blot on our army, and as for him, I consider he should not stay alive. If he talks of heavy losses, it is not true; 4,000 at the most, if as much. But even if the figure had been 10,000, that is war. And the enemy has lost masses. Napoleon was right up against it and compelled to make promises and give large sums of money to the commanders to capture the positions, yet they were repulsed everywhere. Our artillery and my cavalry did marvels. The enemy was hard pressed. What would it have cost us to hold on for two days longer? They would have left of their own accord, because there was no water for the horses or men. He gave me his word he would not retreat, and there he is, making arrangements for a retreat by night. That is no way to fight. We shall lead the enemy right up to the walls of Moscow.

. . . Barclay has no grounds for complaint against me: I am not only perfectly polite, but docile too, even though I am senior to him. It is sad, but I love my Sovereign and benefactor, and I obey. The misfortune is to see the Tsar trust a magnificent army to such people! Bear in mind that our retreat has cost us more than 15,000 men from exhaustion or sickness, and a battle would not have cost us as much. And what will Mother Russia say about our cowardice? And why has so good and dear a country been delivered to vandals? Why does she inspire in her children only disgust and contempt? Why on earth are we afraid, and of whom? It is not my fault if the Minister is a feeble, cowardly, muddle-headed dawdler — everything that is worst. The whole army weeps over it, and condemns him out of hand.

When, after the battle of Valutina (19 August), Napoleon visited the battlefield, Captain Heinrich von Brandt was in his suite.

The Emperor inspected Ney's troops and handed an eagle to the 127th Regiment which had just received its baptism of fire. This ceremony, impressive in itself, took on a truly epic character in this setting. The regiment formed square. In the ranks one could pick out many faces still black with powder, and much bloodstained leather equipment. The colonel and his officers were drawn up in a half-circle round the Emperor.

'Soldiers!' he said. 'Here is your eagle. It will serve as your rallying-point in moments of danger. Swear to me that you will never desert it, will always tread the path of honour, will defend our country and never allow France, our France, to be insulted.'

There was but a single reply: 'We swear it.' The Emperor next took the eagle from Marshal Berthier's hands and gave it to the colonel who in turn handed it to the colour-bearer. At the same moment the square opened, the soldiers formed line, and then the colour-bearer, preceded by the drums and band, moved to his battle station in the centre of the eagle guard.

A grenadier sergeant of the same regiment was promoted to second-lieutenant on the spot. 'Have this gallant fellow proclaimed at once,' said Napoleon. The colonel pronounced the sacramental words, but he abstained from embracing the new officer.

'Well, colonel? The accolade! The accolade!' said the Emperor sharply. This was not a case of forgetfulness by the colonel.

Decorations, promotions, and monetary awards rained down like hail. One could perceive that Napoleon felt an imperative need, within himself and within other people, to react against melancholy thoughts.

When he reached the 95th, he told the colonel to give him the names of those who had distinguished themselves the previous day, and this colonel naturally began with the officers, but when he reached the sixth or seventh name, he was interrupted by the Emperor.

'How is it, colonel? Are your soldiers all cowards?' And he personally summoned from the ranks the non-commissioned officers and men who were pointed out to him as meriting promotion or a decoration.

Watching this scene I understood and came under the irresistible fascination which Napoleon exercised whenever and wherever he wished. But he could not be everywhere!

On 20 August, after Smolensk and Valutina, Ney's 3rd Corps halted for three days, and according to one Württemberg officer of artillery, the time was spent in replenishing stocks and working out the expenditure of ammunition.

It was found that between 20 July and 20 August we had fired off 214 shells, 433 6-pounder cannon-balls, eleven howitzer shells, and thirty 6-pounder case-shots. The loss in horses was very serious, and the few replacements of small Russian farm-horses were of little help to us. The long-indulged hope of getting some captured remounts had already been disappointed often enough.

With 16 August began a new period in this campaign: what one might term the bloody period. Hitherto Russian opposition had not been very strong, but after Smolensk it became stiffer every day. This may well have been the reason why the war was henceforth waged with far greater devastation and horror. Not only villages but towns as well which happened to lie on our route were plundered and burnt. The first happened throughout and the second was mostly done by Russians themselves. Several Württemberg and even French officers began to shake their heads when it became increasingly clear that the Emperor intended to go to Moscow. I remember particularly the words of a French major who was aide-de-camp to General Montbrun[1] and whom I had got to know in Vienna in 1809. He said to me quite frankly: 'If we don't win a battle so decisively that we capture two hundred guns from the enemy, then our whole army is done for.'

Unfortunately these words were rendered only too significant by subsequent events. For my part, I must admit that my gift of prophecy was so poor that, quite apart from my natural thoughtlessness, I cherished so firm a trust in the political and military wisdom of the Emperor that all such fears seemed to me mere chimera.

Captain Victor Dupuy of the 7th Hussars, in describing the subsequent pursuit of the Russians, gives further sidelights on Marshal Murat.

Every day from five o'clock in the morning we skirmished with the Cossacks, and sometimes this lasted until ten or eleven at night. They carried away everything they could from the villages, and drove out the inhabitants who took refuge in the forests. Then they set fire to the villages. If, by a bold manœuvre or a sharp attack we did not allow them time for this, their artillery would fire incendiary shells, which produced the same result, setting alight the thatched roofs.

This method of waging war we found very prejudicial. After days spent entirely in fights and fatigues, we could scarcely find enough to eat and often had nothing to give the horses, whose number dwindled every day in alarming fashion.

The chief cause of the destruction of our cavalry was the little care taken. After fighting all day we were made to bivouac in windmills on parched heights denuded of all resources. Only with the utmost difficulty did we manage to procure a little bad forage; and often, in the middle of the day, the horses dropped with fatigue and hunger.

Though hard to credit, it is nevertheless true that at the battle of Borodino our division, which had numbered 7,500 horsemen at the crossing of the Niemen, had not even one thousand, and this immense gap was certainly not caused by the enemy's fire! But the King of Naples, who in face of the enemy knew so well how to

[1] Louis-Pierre, Count Montbrun, commanded the 2nd Cavalry Corps.

make use of the cavalry, did not know how to preserve it by ensuring supplies or at least by placing it within reach of subsistence.

This prince, herculean in strength, excessively gallant, admirably cool in the midst of danger, had inspired an extraordinary veneration among the Cossacks. His daring, his elegant costume, won their admiration. . . . If, as frequently occurred, he put himself in view of any Cossack skirmishers, these halted suddenly and ceased fire. One day I witnessed this almost magical respect. I received orders from my general to go and reconnoitre a path through a swamp which we had to cross, and I rode ahead with three men of the 7th Hussars. At the far end of a small wood which gave on to a narrow stretch of flat ground in front of the swamp I saw the King of Naples, all alone, while in front of him on the other side of the flat ground some forty mounted Cossacks were leaning on their lances and looking at him. Seeing us emerge from the wood they made a move. Thinking it was an attack, I shouted to the men with me: 'Hussars! cover the King!' We had no sooner taken up positions in front of him than the Cossacks fired several shots, one of which struck my horse in the leg. The King noticed this and said to me with a laugh: 'Just as well! What have you come for? They never say anything to *me*!'

A captain in the 16th Regiment of Chasseurs à cheval, *whose name is not known, also has some hard comments to make in his memoirs about Murat's handling of the cavalry.*

The King of Naples, who is personally very brave, has few military talents. It is mainly his fault that the cavalry was ruined, not only through being exposed frequently to no purpose, but also because it was posted far from water and forage.

Without being prejudiced, one can blame the marked wasting-away of the army and of the cavalry mainly on the way in which, during this campaign, the generals commanded the troops entrusted to them. The cavalry melted very quickly thanks to the engagements and excessive marches imposed upon it every day, above all to the neglect and selfishness of the senior officers charged with leading it and seeing to its needs. I will quote one example only from a host of similar instances. On the evening of the action at Viazma [29 August], I was in command of the outpost pickets with a hundred horsemen, and was left at my post until noon the next day without being relieved, and with definite orders not to unbridle. Yet the horses had been bridled since six o'clock the previous morning. Having nothing for my pickets, not even water in the vicinity, I sent an officer that night to state my position to the general,[1] requesting him to provide some bread and, above all, some oats. He replied that his task was to make us fight, not to feed us. As a result, our horses remained for thirty hours without food or water. When I returned with my guard, people were just leaving. I was given one hour to refresh my detachment, and then I had to catch up the column at a trot. I was obliged to leave behind a dozen men whose horses could not walk. The King of Naples, who was in command of all the cavalry, and the generals, copying him, were much more concerned with themselves than with their troops. We marched all day. We halted for an hour at a time, often for two hours, during which it would have been possible to cool off some of the horses; but we were absolutely forbidden to unbridle. Death resulted. We were made to bivouac in woods without anyone making sure that there was forage and water nearby. Next day we had to march and fight just as though we had been short of nothing. The method, which had become a mania, of forming large corps of cavalry, so as to give large commands to ambitious generals, is one of the causes of the cavalry's ruin.

Marshal Oudinot's wife Eugénie was living in Bar-le-Duc and, like many other wives, anxiously awaiting news from the armies.

The keen interest with which we watched the arrival of letters and newspapers had been fed with minor engagements only. Alas, at this period we had no more than four posts a week! Their arrival produced feverish moments, and in the intervals we vegetated painfully and counted the hours.

I was expecting a bust of my husband which a fairly talented artist in Berlin had modelled at the end of our stay in that city. One morning the arrival of an enormous case from Germany was announced. I dragged my mother with me and eagerly hurried on the opening. Trembling with excitement I saw the covering re-

[1] The 16th was in Piré's brigade of Count Nansouty's corps.

moved, then the first, the second, and finally the last wrapping-paper.

What was my shock on seeing that one of the shoulders of the cherished plaster was mutilated and about to break away from the body! Ominous thoughts seized my imagination. This foreboding was to be realized only too well, since, a few days later, the Marshal had his shoulder smashed by grapeshot.

Sergeant Joseph Schrafel took part in the August battle of Polotsk (see *page* 34), *but was not under fire on the first day.*

On the second day [18 August] we stood back on a hill while the 1st Battalion stood under fire further forward by a wood. On our right the division was drawn up, and the Russian artillery away to our left fired at this division, which was posted still higher than we were, and in particular at the cavalry. However, at such a range the Russian shells did not reach the division, and nearly all of them hit us and caused heavy casualties, perhaps without the Russians realizing it, because I do not believe the shots were aimed at us.

My wife came up during this affair and brought me some bread. We were surprised at her boldness, and the officers called out to her to inquire how she had escaped the hail of shot and shell in which she could so easily have been wounded or killed.

'If my husband is hit,' she said, 'I must look after him, on campaign just as much as at home. That is my duty.'

Eventually Colonel Baron von Habermann arrived and ordered Major Flad to lead the battalion out of range of the firing, as we could do no good there and were losing men to no purpose. We withdrew. . . .

On the third day we advanced towards a wood to attack the Russians. Here I caught sight of General Count Wrede who was walking near the front, because he was suffering from diarrhoea and could not go on horseback. We soldiers wondered how so distinguished a man, whose nourishment and care ought to have been a priority, could have been afflicted by this disease. But at that time nobody was spared, and the army suffered unspeakably from this epidemic.

We captured the wood in such a storming manner that we found the Russian fires with food cooking. Night fell, and we halted; on the fourth day we marched off across the battlefield which was strewn with corpses. . . . Several ammunition waggons, lying riddled by our bullets and French ones too, provided us with excellent cartridges. I threw all mine away and replaced them with double the number of Russian cartridges, which were all sized and therefore not subject to leakage. Besides, the powder, probably of English origin, was of outstanding quality, did not, as ours did, make a dirty crust on the vent, and had a strong propellant force. These cartridges were to serve me very well.

We moved forward through woods to a post-house where we halted. Here the regiment bivouacked among the trees. We were short of everything. There was no bread. We lived off wretched meat which was picked up here and there. Many soldiers went into the woods in search of roots and plants, but these were often harmful and caused illness and madness. . . .

In the end bread-waggons arrived, but with so little that sixteen men had to share one loaf. The most serious shortage was water. There was not a spring in the area. We had to fetch the water we needed from a large pool which had a brownish colour and teemed with thousands of tiny worms. This produced more illness, and the doctors gave orders for this water to be boiled and strained, so that we should not swallow any insects at least. We also dug holes in the hope of finding water, but we always came on the same brown liquid manure. Eventually a spring was discovered at the post-house and this produced good water, if a trifle sweet. A guard was placed over the spring so that we should not use up its water too quickly, but we soon drank it dry, and at the bottom — what a nauseating discovery! — we found a man's leg which had been amputated at the thigh and had probably been thrown into the spring deliberately by the Russians. This explained the sweetish taste of the water, and nobody drank any more from the spring.

It must have been at about midnight when I fell asleep on the ground, exhausted by hunger. Suddenly I was woken by someone. I started up. It was my wife. I stared at her.

'Where on earth have you come from?' I asked. 'From Polotsk,' she said. 'I found somebody to look after the horses, and have come to bring you some schnaps and bread.'

'But how did you get through all the troops who are behind us, and at night too?' 'Oh!' she said. 'They often challenged me, sometimes French soldiers, sometimes Swiss, or other Germans, but in reply to the "*Qui vive?*" I replied "*Bon ami*" with the best of them and in this way they all let me pass. I am a soldier's wife and have no need to be afraid of soldiers.'

And so my loyal wife brought me refreshment and allowed no obstacle to daunt her from seeking me out. When she had given me food and drink she set off back again, because she did not like to leave the waggon and horses for too long in strange hands.

Colonel Sebastien-Joseph de Comeau was chief of staff of the Bavarian corps under General Wrede. An artillery officer of long experience, he had entered the Elector of Bavaria's service in 1800 as an émigré *after eight years in the Army of Condé, and among the many battles in which he had taken part were Ulm, Jena, Eylau, Friedland, Eckmühl, Essling, and Wagram. At one stage of the battle of Polotsk Comeau was observing the Russian guns.*

I noticed a cannon-ball ricocheting towards me and spurred my horse to avoid it, but was too late! The ball removed a piece of boot from my left leg, tore right through my horse and struck my right leg, breaking it above the ankle. . . . Four grenadiers laid me on a door taken from one of the burnt houses and carried me out of the battle. They had no sooner got me out of sight than we were knocked down by blast without actually being hit. The grenadiers did not abandon me. Two case-shot bullets furrowed the door in two places, but they went on carrying me. Then another incident occurred: the Russians made a desperate effort, collected a large body of cavalry, and charged several battalions, only to be attacked in turn by our cuirassiers, who drove them back. I found myself lying on the door in all this mêlée, and I saw wounded men crushed by ammunition waggons. The four genadiers carried me down into a ditch and protected me from shock and blows. Then they took me on again and handed me over to an assistant surgeon who was moving about the battlefield with stretchers, which are provided for this purpose in Bavaria: a truly admirable service and one which I have seen used nowhere else but in Bavaria.

In this way, more dead than alive, I reached Polotsk and the square in front of the Jesuit monastery where crowds of wounded men were arriving from all directions. There, on the pavement,

Prince Eugène de Beauharnais, Viceroy of Italy, from the painting by Ary Scheffer

The Emperor's bivouac outside Vitebsk, 28 July, from the lithograph by Albrecht Adam

lying on my back with my head in the sun, I spent the rest of the day and then the night — something like thirty hours, without any attention, without a drop of water, and dying of thirst.

The fighting continued; and Wrede, still in command, went on advancing. That is why we, the first to be wounded, remained unattended. The battle had been won and the enemy was being pursued relentlessly. The number of wounded in the square grew all the time, and so did the tally of prisoners. Eventually some buckets of water arrived. Teams of surgeons, with their coats off and sleeves rolled up, laid out planks on upturned barrels. Prisoners brought them the wounded, and these gentlemen, their arms bare, proceeded to dress or to amputate.

I was one of the first to be laid on a stretcher made with two muskets, and a prisoner supported my leg hanging in a shako. I gritted my teeth with pain. A surgeon-major felt my pulse and found that I was too weak to stand amputation, so he signed for me to be carried to one side to join the hopeless cases, and gave instructions that another wounded man should be brought in. I was rolled on to the edge of the road leading to the bridge, and this circumstance saved my life.

Von Zoller[1] came along this road to fetch ammunition, recognized me, jumped down from his horse, and wrapped me in his coat. He had his gunners carry me to the beautiful Jesuit monastery which dominates the town. He knocked and rang, but nobody came. The monastery was shut and barricaded. He summoned his gunners, had them break down the door, and laid me in the first cell he could find in that part of the monastery which was built of wood and where classes were held. General Gouvion Saint-Cyr[2] occupied the stone-built part of the college. The gunners brought a truss of straw and laid me on it. Von Zoller embraced me and then departed. . . .

Several monks appeared and began to repair the broken door. In a dying voice I begged them for a little water to drink, and one of them brought me a jug. He was a Frenchman, Father Richardot by name. When I had drunk I felt such a tremendous sense of relief that I either fainted or fell asleep — I don't know which, for my thoughts seemed like dreams. When I opened my

[1] Lieutenant-Colonel Karl von Zoller commanded the Bavarian artillery.
[2] Laurent Gouvion Saint-Cyr (1764–1830) commanded the 6th Corps.

eyes a monk was kneeling at my feet, picking bits of boot-leather, clothing, and broken bone from my wound. Another monk, holding a book in one hand, held the other outstretched and was saying prayers over me. Father Richardot and his companion, Father Sedovitz, undoubtedly saved my life by their ministrations and prayers.

Father Richardot inquired my faith. I managed to tell him: Roman Catholic. He made signs of the Cross and said things which I failed to understand. He brought me some more water to drink, and then I fell asleep again. When I woke I saw General von Wrede with tears in his eyes, and General Saint-Cyr, who shook my hand. I was able to shake his and say: 'You have won a splendid battle!' A dozen fathers craned their necks to see what was happening, and General Saint-Cyr, shaking his fist at them, said: 'If you don't take good care of him until he breathes his last, I shall kill you all.'

[*Comeau's life was in danger for some days, but slowly and painfully he recovered, and he was still at Polotsk when the Russians under Wittgenstein reoccupied the town on 18 October. He was taken prisoner and received good treatment, thanks to Wittgenstein himself and to the fact that Comeau had fought in Russian service during Tsar Paul's reign. He spent a year in St. Petersburg and returned home to Bavaria at the very end of 1813.*]

Captain Heinrich von Brandt remembered how exhausting the march from Smolensk to Gzatsk proved to be.

The heat was extreme. Furious gusts of wind swirled up such dense clouds of dust that often we could no longer see the great trees which lined the road. The sacred soil of Russia which we were invading seemed, in obedience to the summons by the young fanatic of Smolensk, to rise against the invaders.

This constant burning dust was a real torment. So as to protect at least their eyes, many soldiers improvised dark spectacles out of bits of window glass. Others carried their shakos under their arms and wrapped a handkerchief round their heads, tearing only a hole large enough for seeing the way and breathing. Others made garlands of foliage. In this way the army presented a strange sight at times, but at the least shower of rain all this masquerade vanished.

Major Friedrich Wilhelm von Lossberg, a Westphalian serving with Junot's corps, wrote home to his wife in Detmold, describing the daily marches towards Viazma.

With regard to myself, I felt unwell this morning and was instructed by the regimental doctor to take some medicine. As a result I did not set off on horseback until several hours after the army corps had left, and this fact gave me an opportunity to observe at close quarters the disorder and misery left in its path. How many waggons, kibitkas [hooded sledges], herds of cattle, and drovers of all nationalities I met, either on their own or in large groups. In the latter many were dying, and most of them rode on miserable horses, called 'konias'! And even if I had not seen the high road to Moscow, I should only have needed to follow the smell, while every hundred yards at least I stumbled upon a fallen horse or a bullock which had been slaughtered and whose intestines lay on the road. At every village or isolated house I found dead, unburied soldiers, both friend and foe: nobody had taken the trouble to dig a grave for them.

So as to rest in the shade and drink some coffee — my servant had with him everything necessary for making it — I dismounted by a building which I then discovered was so damaged, so filthy, and so full of stragglers from every corps that I sat down some way off on a green beside a naked corpse, and was so insensible to every other emotion that I was able to give myself up to the single thought: how good it was that the dead men had not yet putrefied, because otherwise I should have been obliged to drink my coffee out in the burning sun.

Really! This day has convinced me that Napoleon is quite unconcerned over which of his soldiers collapse on the roadside and whether human strength is enough to pursue the Russian Army so as to attack and, if possible, destroy it.

Captain Girod de l'Ain writes vividly of the advance at the end of August through towns like Viazma, almost deserted by their inhabitants and half burnt or in ruins by the passage of troops, friendly and hostile alike.

The heat was excessive: I had never experienced worse in Spain; but there is this difference that in Russia it does not last long. The main Moscow road we were on is sandy, and the army, marching in several serried columns abreast, raised such clouds of dust that we could not see one another two yards away and our eyes, ears, and nostrils were full of it, and our faces encrusted. This heat and dust made us extremely thirsty, as can well be imagined, and water was scarce. Will you believe me when I say that I saw men lying on their bellies to drink horses' urine in the gutter!

. . . The road, very wide and lined with trees, was entirely taken up by the artillery trains and by horse-drawn vehicles moving two or three abreast. On each side of the road marched the infantry in close column by divisions — that is to say, on a front of about eighty men. . . . Outside these infantry columns and on either side moved the masses of cavalry by squadrons. From this you can judge the total effect of these corps all moving in the same direction. On this march, and in a rift in the dust-cloud, that is, after a sufficiently long halt to allow the dust time to settle, I at least had the pleasure of seeing together the heavy cavalry divisions composed of carabiniers and cuirassiers, forming in all fourteen regiments. Their cuirasses and helmets glinting in the sun made a splendid sight.

To begin with the Emperor had tolerated and even formally encouraged the luxury of carriages which the army dragged in its wake, in view of the considerable quantity of provisions with which they were laden. But estimating that these supplies must be exhausted, and that the vehicles which had carried them so far would henceforth be a useless liability, he suddenly gave orders that all those surplus to regulations were to be burnt. But this order was scarcely obeyed, as can be seen from the following incident which I witnessed in person. The Emperor had stopped beside a beautiful yellow carriage belonging to I don't know whom, and ordered it to be set on fire in his presence. In fact several blazing brands were brought over from the bivouac we had just left, and the Emperor waited until the carriage had caught fire before moving on. But he had barely gone a hundred yards before people hastened to put out the flames and the carriage joined the column, bowling along as before.

When Napoleon reached Viazma on 29 August, he was accompanied by General de Caulaincourt.

The enemy did not leave a man behind. They destroyed their magazines, and burnt their establishments, even large houses. Several people believed that this burning of the towns and villages we entered was due as much to the disorderly conduct of our advance-guard as to the rearguard of Cossacks, who did not spare Russia; and I am the first to admit that I shared this view, because I failed to understand what possible interest the Russians could have in destroying all their non-military establishments, including private houses, which could not be of much use to us. Several people spoke to the Emperor about these fires, and he ordered my brother[1] to take a strong detachment of the Guard next day and to press the enemy hard enough so as to enter Viazma with their rearguard and to ascertain for himself what was happening and whether the Russians really did start the fires. He instructed him to maintain order and not to let any soldier stay in the town.

All this was carried out punctiliously. The enemy's rearguard was in position, but withdrew after a fairly sharp engagement. My brother and the *tirailleurs* dashed into Viazma and found the place burning already at several points. He saw Cossacks lighting combustible materials, and found others in various places where fires broke out before the last Cossacks had evacuated the town. He used our troops to stop the fire from spreading. They all worked with a will and saved several houses, and stocks of grain, flour, and brandy. At the outset everything was saved from being pillaged, but this did not last. From details supplied by some of the inhabitants who had stayed in their homes, in particular by a very intelligent baker's boy, it became certain that, long before we arrived, everything had been made ready for lighting and spreading the fires by the Cossack rearguard detachment, and they had ignited the fires the moment we appeared. The fact is that in various houses, especially in those containing provisions, we found inflammable material methodically prepared and arranged for this purpose. In short, we had here, as we had already had and were to have later on, proof that the execution of these measures had been ordered and prepared in advance.

[1] General Auguste de Caulaincourt (1777–1812) was soon afterwards killed at Borodino.

These details, which had been supplied by a few inhabitants of other towns or villages, and which we had refused to credit, were subsequently confirmed at every step. Everybody was struck by the fact, the Emperor just as much as his army, though he affected to ridicule this new form of warfare. He often joked to us about 'these people who burn their houses in order to prevent us from sleeping a night there'. He tried to forestall solemn reflections which these terrible measures provoked about the results and the length of a war in which the enemy was making such sacrifices from the very start. The Emperor no doubt had serious thoughts just as we did, but he did not profit from them.

On 18 September the Tsar Alexander wrote to his sister, the Grand Duchess Catherine, who had married the King of Württemberg:

What more can a man do than follow his best conviction? That alone guided me. That decided me to appoint Barclay to command the First Army, on the reputation he had made during the wars against the French and the Swedes. That conviction also made me believe that his knowledge was superior to Bagration's. When this conviction was further strengthened by the latter's mistakes made during this campaign, mistakes which were partly responsible for our reverses, I thought him even less fitted to command the two armies which had united near Smolensk. Although I was not satisfied with what I had been able to see of Barclay, I thought him less bad than the other in matters of strategy, about which Bagration has no idea. Finally, I had no one better to put in his place. . . .

At St. Petersburg I found all opinions in favour of making old Kutuzov Commander-in-Chief[1]: that was the general cry. What I knew of this man made me turn down the idea to begin with, but when, in his letter of 5 August, Rostopchin informed me that all Moscow wanted Kutuzov to take command, finding both Barclay and Bagration incapable of doing so, and at this juncture, as if deliberately, Barclay having committed one stupidity after another at Smolensk, I had no other course than to yield to the unanimous clamour. I appointed Kutuzov.

[1] In July he had been elected to command the St. Petersburg militia.

Sir Robert Wilson knew the Russian Commander-in-Chief well, and has left us this brief pen portrait:

Marshal Prince Kutuzov was born noble and was still more nobly allied by marriage. In his youth he was regarded as a very gallant officer, and had served with distinction. Wounded several times, on one occasion he lost an eye,[1] but the expression of his countenance was still engagingly intellectual. . . .

A *bon vivant* — polished, courteous, shrewd as a Greek, naturally intelligent as an Asiatic and well instructed as an European — he was more disposed to trust to diplomacy for his success than to martial prowess, for which by his age and the state of his constitution he was no longer qualified.

When he rejoined the army he was seventy-four [actually sixty-seven] years old, and though hale, so very corpulent and unwieldy that he was obliged to move about, even when in the field, in a little four-wheeled carriage with a head, called a droshky.

General Bennigsen, Kutuzov's able though selfish and jealous chief of staff, was not the least vehement critic of the new Commander-in-Chief.

Prince Kutuzov is old, broken, ill, and has great difficulty in staying on horseback. Endowed by the Creator with very considerable natural intelligence, he is very amiable in society, in particular with the fair sex by whom he has always been very sought after and who, wherever he has found himself, have conducted affairs often to his great disadvantage, which on various occasions has made him pull back posts he was occupying. The disgust he has always felt for hard work and useful activities has, since he was a young man, got him out of the habit of application to study, so that he has no solid knowledge. Tactics is something he knows by name only. Moreover, wherever he has commanded, he has employed someone who guided him. Consequently, when he fell into good hands, things went well; but if, on the contrary, he fell into the hands of an ignoramus, things went badly. Having these principles and this manner of acting, he had no other desire or ambition than to evict from our country the enemy who could

[1] A Turkish bullet had done this at the battle of Alushta, when Kutuzov was twenty-nine.

not maintain himself there and asked for nothing better than to depart. The consequences of good opportunities let slip and of muffed strokes did not worry him, and in spite of the indignation of more than 100,000 men who had witnessed his timid conduct, his mind invented reports on bloody actions which had never existed. You will ask me how he came to fill so eminent and important a post. I must reply that there was a general desire, not without reason, that the honour of compelling Napoleon and his army to withdraw from Russia should fall on a Russian, because he certainly did not enjoy the confidence of the Court or the Army, nor of that part of the nation who knew him.

Like a number of other Prussian officers, Karl von Clausewitz had resigned his commission early in 1812 and entered the Russian service. The future director of the Berlin War School and author of Vom Kriege *was serving on the Russian staff, and reported that when Kutuzov arrived at the end of August to take command instead of Barclay, the Army was delighted. Clausewitz refers to himself in the third person.*

Hitherto, according to the Russians, everything had gone badly, so any change held out hopes of an improvement. Kutuzov's reputation was not, however, undisputed in the Army, and it can be said that one faction regarded him as a remarkable general whereas another did not share this view. But all were in agreement that at such a time it was essential to have a brave Russian at the top, a pupil of Suvorov,[1] rather than a foreigner.

Barclay was not a foreigner; he was the son of a Livonian pastor who had himself been born in Livonia.[2] Barclay had served in the Russian Army since youth, so there was nothing foreign about him except his name and also, maybe, his way of talking. He pronounced Russian badly and had adopted the habit of preferring to talk German than Russian.

In the circumstances this was enough for him to be considered a

[1] Alexander Suvorov (1729–1800), having won fame in the Seven Years War and in wars against the Poles and Turks, defeated the French in northern Italy in 1799.

[2] Livonia, with its capital at Riga, was later split between Latvia and Estonia.

foreigner. The fact that Colonel Wolzogen,[1] who had been in Russia for only five years, stayed beside General Barclay without being his orderly officer or serving on the staff, made the Colonel pass for the General's inspirer, and gave Barclay an even stronger foreign tint than before.

Wolzogen was persecuted with real hatred because his serious nature had none of the insinuating qualities which are needed when dealing with the Russians. Clausewitz heard one officer who had returned from Barclay's headquarters give free tongue to his spleen and remark that Wolzogen remained in a corner of the room like a large poisonous spider.

Since, according to the Russians, everything was going as badly as could be, this was attributed entirely to the perfidious advice of this foreigner. Nobody doubted that his secret counsels directed Barclay's every action.

. . . Barclay was rather a cold man, not readily accessible to other people's ideas, and it is difficult to win the confidence of men of this sort. Wolzogen was nothing less than satisfied with General Barclay and the role he played at his side. He tolerated it because he hoped to be able to do good sometimes or to prevent something bad happening.

At the very least his motives deserved not to be distorted. One would have needed the suspicious nature of a Tartar to consider as a traitor — and without the slightest proof — an officer who was aide-de-camp to the Tsar and enjoyed his confidence, merely because of the sound of his name. . . .

The arrival of Kutuzov revived confidence in the Army. The evil genius of the foreigners was exorcized by a true Russian, a slightly reduced Suvorov; and no one doubted that the battle would take place soon and would halt the French offensive.

[1] Ludwig von Wolzogen, a Prussian (1773–1845), had spent seven years with the Prussian army, and had fought the 1805 campaign with Württemberg troops before transferring to the Russian Army.

The Battle of Borodino

In the expectation that Kutuzov would accept battle, Napoleon gave his army two days' rest (2–3 September) at Gzatsk. The Russian Commander-in-Chief did resolve to stand and fight. His army, now totalling over 120,000 troops, had hurriedly built a line of fortifications. Of these, two stood out: one near the village of Shevardino in front of the Russian left; the other, the so-called 'Great Redoubt', just south of Borodino itself.

The Russian front formed a shallow convex curve. On the right sector, defended by Baggovut and Ostermann with cavalry support, the line followed the bank of the Kalocha, a tributary of the Moskva. In the centre, behind Borodino and its green-domed church on a wooded hillock, the front bent back a little before rounding the Great Redoubt to Semenovskoye village, then cut south for a mile and a half to Utitsa on the old Smolensk road. Generals Dokhturov and Raevsky held this part, backed by cavalry and the Grand Duke Constantine with the Guard. All the Russian reserves were too close to the front and from the outset suffered severely from French artillery fire. Whereas the right wing was virtually unassailable, the left was weak, being without the protection afforded by a stream, yet this weaker frontage was defended by Bagration's Second Army, distinctly inferior in numbers to Barclay de Tolly's command.

On 4 September, against mounting opposition and frequent rearguard skirmishes, the Grand Army's advance continued. Napoleon had with him about 130,000 men, 25,000 less than at Smolensk. He disposed of 587 guns against 640 on the Russian side. Next day Compans's division stormed the Shevardino Redoubt, with the help of Poniatowski's cavalry, who turned the flank, causing the Russian defenders to withdraw after nightfall to their main position.

6 September was spent in reconnaissance and preparation. The ikon of the Mother of God saved from burning Smolensk was carried through the Russian camps. To Napoleon's headquarters came two important visitors: first Monsieur de Bausset, Prefect of the Palace, bringing a new portrait of the young King of Rome which gratified the Emperor's paternal pride; then, to mar his pleasure, Colonel Charles Fabvier arrived from Spain with the

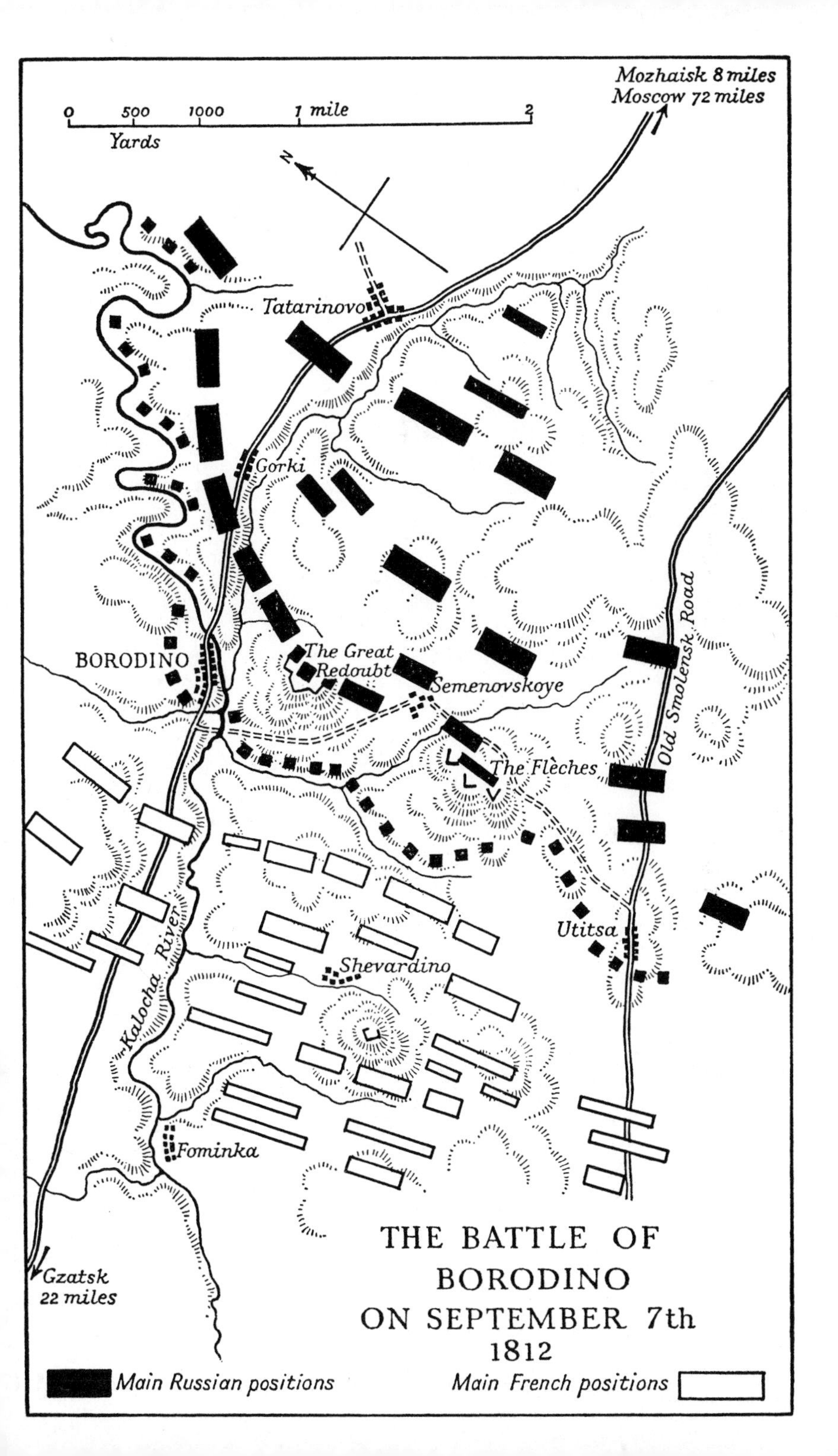

THE BATTLE OF BORODINO ON SEPTEMBER 7th 1812

serious news that Marshal Marmont's army there had been defeated at the battle of Salamanca six weeks earlier.

Napoleon rejected Davout's sound plan for turning the Russian left with the whole of his corps supported by Poniatowski, because he feared that such a manœuvre might hustle the enemy into a retreat. Anxious lest Kutuzov should take it into his head to escape, the Emperor decided on a frontal assault without awaiting the arrival of additional troops.

The battle which opened at 6 a.m. on 7 September was notable for savage fighting, costly attacks and counter-attacks, desperate struggles at close quarters, but not for manœuvre. Positions were taken, lost, and retaken. By midday the French and their allies had captured many of the Russian entrenchments and driven Bagration's men back over the Semenovskoye ravine, but only after prolonged and indecisive fighting in which Generals Compans and Dessaix were wounded. Davout was obliged personally to rally the attackers, and the Russian cavalry rushed upon his mauled divisions only to be flung back by French horsemen. Napoleon remarked: 'These Russians let themselves be killed like machines. . . . They are citadels that have to be demolished with cannon.'

At this juncture Murat, Davout, and Ney came to the conclusion that they could make no further advance without fresh reinforcements, and these the Emperor, who was unwell and not his dynamic, attentive self that day, refused to provide. The Imperial Guard was not committed in the hour of stalemate and crisis — for sound precautionary reasons, though it alone could have turned the scale and made Borodino — or the Moskowa as the French name it — a decisive victory for Napoleon. In the event, both sides claimed a victory.

Soon after four o'clock the battle died out from sheer exhaustion. Only on the French right did Poniatowski's troops, charged with turning their opponents' flank, fight on for another hour and more. The French losses of 28,000 included ten generals killed and thirty-nine wounded, ten colonels dead, and another twenty-seven out of action. Russian casualties were even heavier, but less serious than for the Grand Army far from base. Prince Bagration had been mortally wounded. Kutuzov, who had spent much of the day eating with his staff and leaving most of the work and responsibility to subordinate commanders, had intended to continue the battle next day, but was deterred from so doing by the extent of his losses.

An artillery officer from Württemberg who served with his battery on 5 September was sent back after the fighting with four waggons to obtain more ammunition, and had a difficult time.

Everywhere I met with refusal. The divisional reserve was unwilling to issue any ammunition because they said they needed it for the impending battle, and the large corps reserve was still far to the rear, some of it back in Smolensk. Eventually I came on a reserve park whose commander explained that he would give me as much ammunition as I required provided I brought him a note from the Intendant-General of Artillery, General Lariboisière,[1] who was usually in the Emperor's suite. I rode off hurriedly and found the Emperor in a monastery. I dismounted and went into the courtyard where the Emperor was with his staff, pacing up and down and indulging in the innocent pleasure of whacking his boot with a riding-switch.

Several officers from whom I inquired the whereabouts of General Lariboisière replied curtly: 'I have no idea.' But the Emperor, who must have noticed me stumbling about and asking repeated questions, called to me: 'What are you looking for?' 'Sire,' I replied, 'I am looking for General Lariboisière to get a voucher for ammunition from him.' 'Which corps are you from?' 'I belong to General Beurmann's light battery. Yesterday and this morning we fired all our powder and I do not think I can obtain the ammunition we are short of without a note written by General Lariboisière.'

The Emperor turned to his suite and shouted: 'General Lariboisière!' Everybody set about finding the General, and when he arrived the Emperor said to him: 'Give this officer what he needs.' I made the Emperor a deep and cheerful bow, and obtained all my requirements.

At six o'clock that evening, with two full ammunition waggons, I rejoined the battery which for lack of ammunition had remained close to where we had fought in the morning. At four o'clock on 6 September we broke camp and marched off to our brigade which had bivouacked only an hour away. At about ten General Beur-

[1] Jean-Ambroise Baston, Count de Lariboisière, born in 1759, commanded the artillery in the Grand Army. He was to die in Königsberg on 21 December 1812. In 1807 he had built the raft on which Napoleon and Alexander met at Tilsit.

mann summoned all the officers and made a speech in broken German, in which he informed us that the great battle would begin that very afternoon at two o'clock. He stressed that under no circumstances, even if enemy shells tore down whole rows of us, even if Cossacks attacked us in flank and from behind, were we to lose our 'presence of mind'. He expressly forbade the evacuation of the wounded during the battle, because otherwise too many men would be out of the fighting-line. The wounded would be taken care of after the battle. He closed by saying: 'I shall load you with decorations, because such brave men as you are can never be adequately rewarded.'

At one o'clock in the afternoon he returned and told us that on account of the thick mist which had only come up at noon, the Emperor had not completed his reconnaissance and therefore the battle would not begin until dawn next day. On receiving this news we spent the whole afternoon cooking and eating, so that whatever happened we should not have to make the journey into the next world on an empty stomach.

On the eve of the battle Hubert-Charles Biot, aide-de-camp to General Pajol, was sent to obtain orders from General Montbrun, commanding the 2nd Cavalry Corps.

I arrived. He was leaning over his map deep in thought. When I was introduced, he began by asking me if I had dined: I replied in the negative, whereupon he added: 'In that case you shall dine with us.' Soon afterwards his manservant came in and announced that a certain Verchère, orderly officer on the General's staff, had returned from accompanying Madame Montbrun as far as Warsaw.

'Bring him in,' said the General. The officer in question handed over a letter and a packet and on taking the latter Montbrun exclaimed: 'I know what this is. You did leave my wife in good health, did you not? As for her letter, we will read it after the battle.'

After dinner the General gave me his orders, adding: 'By the way, tell Pajol to be at the right-hand redoubt [Shevardino] at two o'clock tomorrow morning — the one that was captured yesterday and where the King of Naples gave me a rendezvous for last-minute instructions.'

Next day I accompanied my general to this redoubt. It was cluttered with dead and wounded. Our infantry were busy 'stripping' the Russian corpses of the bad brandy which they had in their water-bottles; short of everything, they did not despise this frightful drink. I too wanted to taste it, but the pepper and vitriol burnt one's mouth. After a good two hours of conference I was ordered to go and get the division mounted and on the move.

In the absence of General Saint-Geniès,[1] Colonel Désirad was commanding the 2nd Brigade. This senior officer, who had a liking for me, invited me to drink a cup of coffee. 'It will be ready by the time you return from the other brigades.' This was too good a windfall to be declined, so while the brigade was forming up we drank the coffee and what goes with it. This worthy man seemed to me sadder than usual. As he was leaving me he said: 'The battle will be a hard one, my dear Biot. We shall have to hold on tight to our hats.'

I learnt afterwards that on his way, Colonel Désirad met the dragoons of the Guard in which he had been a major, and he was heard to remark to several friends: 'I think this will be my last battle.'

The division debouched and entered the line, one brigade at a time. . . . We had hardly formed line when the cannonade began. At the second salvo I noticed a horse running across our front, his rider supine on his quarters. I recognized poor Colonel Désirad, whose skull had been removed by a Russian ball.

General Jean Rapp, aide-de-camp to the Emperor, was on duty that night and slept in Napoleon's tent.

The place where he rested was usually separated by a canvas partition from the room reserved for the duty aide-de-camp. The Emperor slept very little. I woke him several times to give him reports from the outposts which all proved that the Russians were expecting an attack. At three o'clock in the morning he summoned

[1] Jean-Marie-Noël Delisle de Falcon, Baron de Saint-Geniès (1776–1836), had been wounded and captured on 15 July.

his *valet de chambre* and had some punch brought in. I had the honour of drinking some with him. He asked if I had slept well. I replied that the nights were already cool and that I had frequently been woken.

He said to me: 'Today we shall have to deal with this celebrated Kutuzov. No doubt you remember that it was he who commanded at Braunau during the Austerlitz campaign. He stayed in that place for three weeks without leaving his room once. He did not even mount his horse to go and inspect the fortifications. General Bennigsen, although as old, is a much more energetic fellow. I cannot understand why Alexander did not send this Hanoverian to replace Barclay.' He took a glass of punch, read several reports, and then added:

'Well, Rapp! Do you think that we shall have a successful day?' 'There is no doubt about it, Sire. We have used up all our resources, and have simply got to win.' Napoleon went on reading and then said: 'Fortune is a shameless courtesan. I have often said it, and I am beginning to experience it.'

'Your Majesty will recall that you did me the honour of saying at Smolensk that the wine had been poured out and must be drunk. That is more than ever the case now. There is no time to withdraw. Besides, the army knows how it is placed. It knows that there are no provisions to be found save in Moscow and that it has only thirty leagues to go.'

'This poor army is sadly depleted, but what remains is good. And my Guard is intact.'

Napoleon sent for Prince Berthier, and worked until half past five. Then we mounted. The trumpets sounded, the drums beat, and as soon as the troops spotted us, there were acclamations all the way.

'It is the Austerlitz enthusiasm again.'[1]

[1] In the early hours of 2 December 1805, Napoleon, returning from a visit to the outposts, was greeted by his troops who held blazing torches of straw. Napoleon called this anniversary of his coronation 'the most glorious night of my life'.

Field-Marshal Prince Kutuzov, from the painting by George Dawe

The Battle of Smolensk, from a drawing by an unknown artist in the Musée de l'Armée, Paris

Colonel Louis-François Lejeune (1774–1848), one of Berthier's six aides-de-camp, had been busy throughout 6 September. He had already taken part in a dozen campaigns, been a prisoner in England, and had made a reputation as a painter of battle scenes.

At first light the Emperor, accompanied only by Prince Berthier, Prince Eugène, two officers, and myself, began to ride across the front of the Russian Army, which had taken up positions diagonally to the Moscow road, on heights separated from us by the very winding and marshy Kalocha stream, which at Borodino flows into the little Moskva River. All the way along, our outposts were barely a pistol-shot distant from the enemy's, but they did not fire at each other. It seemed as though the weariness of the previous evening had absorbed all irritation. The Emperor took advantage of this fact to reconnoitre in more detail and from closer quarters the ways of attacking the Russians. I was worried at the sight of him running the risk of being captured by a handful of men who might be hidden in the bend of a ravine, at the base of the fortified ridge, or in the centre of the enemy's line.

Napoleon, riding in front, came face to face with a patrol of twenty Cossacks, four yards away from us. These men, thinking themselves taken by surprise, were already turning about when they saw our little group set off at a gallop to make our escape, so they pursued us for several hundred yards. We eluded them thanks to the speed of our horses and to some fences surrounding private estates.

Before returning from this reconnaissance, which promised a great battle next day, the Emperor ordered me to ride carefully along the line again, to sketch the topography, and also to bring him some drawings of the ground. I spent the rest of the day in carrying out this honourable task, which obliged me to make a more exact study of the locality. When the Emperor received my drawings he thanked me and appeared satisfied. On his return he had instructed Bacler d'Albe, head of the topographical engineers, to have his men do the same work as I was doing, and the survey of the Russian positions was executed before evening came.

Baron Fain, who was First Secretary of the Emperor's Cabinet, had this to say about Bacler d'Albe and his work.

D'Albe was sent for when the Emperor wanted to read dispatches while referring to a map. D'Albe indicated, by means of red- or black-headed pins, the positions occupied by our troops and by the enemy. Then, with various colours, he marked the rivers, mountains, or frontiers which were most relevant. Finally, he calculated distances, presented a scale, and opened the compass alongside the map.

Thus the Emperor studied the dispatches as applied to the map. D'Albe gave him a summary, the Emperor following with his finger and moving the compass among the pins. Often the huge size of the maps obliged the Emperor to stretch at full length on the table and d'Albe to climb up as well in order to remain master of his preserves. I have more than once seen them both lying on this large table and interrupting each other with abrupt exclamations, right in the middle of work, whenever they bumped heads too hard. Their posture could only have been grotesque had one not simultaneously pictured to oneself the Emperor hovering like an eagle above distant plains on which his lieutenants were manœuvring, out of sight of everyone except himself.

Fain also remembered vividly the eve of Borodino.

The Emperor spent most of the night giving out final orders, and only took a few hours' sleep, and even these were interrupted. At first light he was up and about. He summoned the aide-de-camp on duty. Auguste Caulaincourt was not asleep, but half lying down on a camp mattress and wrapped in his coat, with his head propped up on his elbow: he was gazing sadly at a portrait of his young wife whom he had been forced to leave almost as soon as he had married her. One would have said he was bidding her eternal farewell. The Emperor's presence snatched him abruptly from his daydream, and he had time only to replace the portrait against his heart.

Napoleon drew back the curtains of his tent and appeared between the two sentries, who presented arms. He then moved forward to join a large group of officers who had already gathered.

'It is a trifle cold,' he said, 'but the sun is bright. It is the sun of Austerlitz.'[1]

Everyone emulated Napoleon with allusions to this good omen.

At five o'clock the Emperor mounted and set off at a gallop towards the right wing.

On the Russian side Captain Fritz ——, attached to Prince Karl von Mecklenburg's staff, spent most of that night by a great watch-fire with the grenadiers of the Fanagoria Regiment.

The soldiers were in fairly good order, and as they had had a rest during the last few days, they now sat, wrapped in their long grey coats, round the fires — and often joined in chorus to sing the monotonous, melancholy, dirge-like, yet not unpleasing national songs which the Russian people are so fond of. This singing before the battle had a strange effect on me, and I listened to it for several hours until eventually I fell asleep, exhausted, beside my horse, an ugly though sturdy little chestnut, which I wanted to ride during the battle.

7 September was just dawning when I was woken by the roar of cannon from our right flank by the village of Borodino, and the battle began.

Captain Girod de l'Ain provides a piquant vignette.

After a longish walk to reconnoitre the respective positions of the opposing armies, I returned to our bivouac and spent the time in having my first lesson in how to play chess from Major Fanfette,[2] who adored the game and always carried with him a little cardboard chess set which folded into eight pieces and which he had himself constructed with great ingenuity. I was obliged to mount my horse before the end of the lesson, and leave Fanfette there with his chessboard. But when I got back he showed me our game written down, as far as we had played it, and three or four months later we finished it in Berlin.

[1] The sun had come shining through the mist just as the battle began.
[2] One of Dessaix's aides-de-camp.

Lieutenant Roth von Schreckenstein was serving with the Saxon Regiment of Zastrow Cuirassiers which, with a division of Polish uhlans, a Westphalian brigade, and a Saxon and Polish regiment, formed Latour-Maubourg's 4th Cavalry Corps.

I had almost reached that part of the Saxon Life Guard Regiment which was gradually giving up its pursuit of the Russian cavalry when my horse fell back, pierced by several case-shot bullets which had been fired from somewhere away to the left. In this awkward predicament I had a moment for looking round. At the exits to the burning village [Semenovskoye] stood several Russian infantrymen who fired after the detachment of Life Guards dashing past the village. Colonel von Leyser was unable to halt this vigorous pursuit, and I believe I saw several detachments attacking infantry, while a small section of the Regiment pursued the enemy dragoons beyond Semenovskoye. . . .

To control and halt a regiment under such circumstances is a pious hope. Men who are imbued with true cavalry courage pursue and attack the enemy for as long as they can . . . and anybody who imagines that one can invariably control and direct a cavalry regiment just as one pleases by means of one's voice or a trumpet, as if on peacetime manœuvres, has never been in an action where all arms of the service co-operated. The Life Guards knew that four cuirassier regiments were following them and that they could count on their support, so they put their trust in their own courage and in God's help, while each man sought to distinguish himself and not to worry overmuch about the outcome of what he had undertaken. . . .

I looked about for another horse, but those nearest to me had been wounded. One Russian horse which I did mount refused to move, even when I clapped spurs to it, so I was on the point of moving off on foot, pistol in hand, without really knowing which way to flee, because, owing either to an illusion stemming from fear or else because they were really there, I could see enemies on all sides.

The thought of being captured and ill-treated overwhelmed me, and I gripped my pistol in much the same way as a person who is drowning clutches at the nearest straw. At very best this weapon would enable me to sell my liberty or my life more dearly. By some fortunate chance a riderless horse came past with a troop of Life Guards, so close that I was able to grab hold of it and escape with a swarm of horsemen who were withdrawing. Skill at vaulting stood me in very good stead, because I had no time left in which to mount in the normal way, and I was thankful when I eventually managed to reach the middle of the saddle. . . .

The Life Guard Regiment had no cuirasses, but in action they carried their cloaks rolled and slung across the chest, so that the men were reasonably well protected. The Zastrow Cuirassier Regiment wore very heavy, bullet-proof, black iron cuirasses, though only on the breast. Both regiments were equipped throughout with fairly long carbines, and every man had two pistols, though in battle the troops used only the sword. . . .

The horses of the Life Guards were on an average very large, and either black or very dark brown in colour, partly Saxon stud-horses but most of them so-called Holsteiners. The Cuirassiers of the Guard and the Zastrow Cuirassiers had much smaller though sturdy horses, which were purchased in the country or supplied by horse-dealers as Mecklenburgers. At that time it was still not considered fitting for a cuirassier to ride a chestnut, a grey, or a piebald, even though officers rode horses of all colours, spent a great deal of money on their horses, were very well mounted, and with few exceptions took a very active interest in breaking-in their horses. . . .

The regiments were very well clothed. The uniform, loose-fitting and comfortable, consisted of a white or straw-yellow jerkin and a similar doublet with sleeves, worn on routine duty in summer and in winter under the jerkin. Besides white leather breeches the men had grey cloth trousers, wore stiff boots, and their capacious riding-cloaks made of white cloth gave excellent protection against cold and rain.

At midday Louis-François-Joseph, Baron de Bausset, Prefect of the Imperial Palace, asked Napoleon if he wanted lunch.

The battle was not yet won, and he signed to me 'No'. I then was unwise enough to tell him that there was no reason in the world to prevent him from having lunch when he wanted. He dismissed me in a pretty brusque manner. Later he ate a slice of bread and drank a glass of Chambertin, without diluting it with water. He had taken a glass of punch at ten in the morning because he was suffering from a severe cold.

For his ambulance Dr. Heinrich von Roos had found a very suitable place close behind the front.

A gully, through which flowed a small, easily jumpable stream, was in places thick with bushes and served as a standpoint for myself, my assistants, and our horses. At the outset I had time to go nearer to the terrible game, but when a few balls of considerable calibre whistled close overhead I took this as a warning to curb my curiosity. Officers and other ranks, Saxons, Westphalians, French, Württembergers, and Russians too were brought in. Most of them were cavalrymen, with severe wounds and broken limbs.

. . . At noon the number of wounded men in the gully had increased so much that I could see myself being kept fully occupied until nightfall. There were several doctors whose assistance brought comfort and reassurance to many. A number of the wounded remained as corpses. Waggons arrived to take away the men who had been bandaged. Those from regiments were carried to our bivouac, while others went to the monastery [Kolotskoye] close behind the battlefield. Still others had orders to carry their wounded to nearby villages. This was unlike previous campaigns, when we doctors had been shown the collecting-points for the wounded well before a battle.

While we plied our bloody trade for some considerable time in this gully, our hands and instruments were busy and often had to be washed in the stream. Meantime a number of heavy cannonballs from the Russian redoubts flew over our heads. Some of them bored into the reverse slope of the gully, others rolled down the forward slope.

When Prince Eugène de Beauharnais made the mistake of sending Count Louis Morand's 1st Division on its own to attack Raevsky's corps, part of which was covered by the Great Redoubt, one of the officers who took part in this bloody and vain effort was Captain Charles François of the 30th of the Line, who had been campaigning on and off ever since Egypt and was wounded in the action.

Our regiment was ordered to advance. When we reached the crest of the ravine, we were riddled with grapeshot from this battery and several others flanking it, but nothing stopped us. Despite my wounded leg I did as well as my *voltigeurs* in jumping out of the way of roundshot which ricocheted into our ranks. Whole files, half-platoons even, went down under the enemy's fire, and left huge gaps. General Bonnamy,[1] at the head of the 30th, halted us in the midst of the grapeshot. He rallied us and we charged forward again. A Russian line tried to stop us, but at thirty yards range we fired a volley and passed through. Then we dashed towards the redoubt and clambered through the embrasures. I went in just after a piece had been discharged. The Russian gunners received us with handspikes and rammers, and we fought them hand to hand. They were redoubtable opponents. A great many Frenchmen fell into rifle-pits[2] jumbled up with Russians already occupying them.

Once inside the redoubt I defended myself with my sword against the gunners, and I cut down more than one. Our soldiers were so impetuous that we rushed fifty yards beyond the redoubt, but the other regiments of the division did not follow, because they were at grips with the Russians, all except a battalion of the 13th Light who supported us. We were obliged to retreat across the redoubt, the Russian line which had stood up again, and the rifle-pits. Our regiment was shattered. We rallied behind the redoubt, though still under enemy grapeshot fire, and attempted a second charge, but on our own we were too few in numbers to achieve success, and retired with only 11 officers and 257 soldiers. All the rest had been killed or wounded. The gallant General Bonnamy,

[1] Charles-Auguste Bonnamy (1764–1830) commanded a brigade comprising the 30th and the 2nd Baden Regiment.

[2] Literally *trous de loup*.

who never quitted the head of the regiment, was left in the redoubt after receiving fifteen wounds, and became a prisoner.[1]

I had been through more than one campaign, but I had never found myself in such a bloody mêlée and up against such tenacious soldiers as the Russians. I was in a deplorable state: my shako had been carried off by grapeshot; the tails of my coat had remained in Russian hands while I was engaged in hand-to-hand combat with them. I was bruised all over, the wound in my left leg hurt dreadfully, and after several minutes' rest on a plateau where we rallied again, I fainted from loss of blood. Some *voltigeurs* brought me round and then carried me to the field ambulance, just as they were attending to General Morand, who had been wounded by grapeshot in the chin. He recognized me, gave me his hand, and when he had been bandaged he signed to the surgeon to attend to me.

Lieutenant Louis Planat de la Faye, one of General Lariboisière's aides-de-camp, accompanied the Inspector of Artillery when he rode up to the battery supporting Ney's 3rd Corps early in the battle.

At Dorogobuzh I had again been smitten with the diarrhoea which had afflicted me so badly at Smolensk, and in the course of this day I went through the worst sort of agony one can imagine, because I did not want either to quit my post or dismount. I dare not describe just how I managed to dispose of what was tormenting me, but in the process I lost two handkerchiefs which I threw as discreetly as I could into the trench of the fortifications we passed. This was a serious loss in a country devoid of washerwomen, at least for us.

. . . The struggle which developed [the Russian attempts to recapture the Great Redoubt] was one of the most murderous I have ever seen. Leipzig [October 1813] is the only battle I can compare it to. The cannon-balls and shells rained down like hail, and the smoke was so thick that only at rare intervals could one make out the enemy masses. The Westphalian corps [the 8th, under Junot] was massed in close columns behind the redoubt, and now and

[1] See Meerheimb's account (pp. 135–9).

then was a target for shells which sent shakos and bayonets flying. Each time one of these shots landed, the poor soldiers fell flat on their faces. Not all of them stood up again.

Captain Jean Bréaut des Marlots, who later wrote an account for his sister Manette, has this to tell about his experiences at Borodino with a cuirassier regiment.

On every side one saw nothing but the dying and the dead. Twice during the battle I went to look at the faces of the cuirassiers in my squadron to see which of the men were brave. I was pleased and told them so on the spot. When I rode over to congratulate one young officer (Monsieur de Gramont) on his good bearing, I witnessed some terrible things. He told me that he had nothing to complain of and that all he wanted was a glass of water. He had barely finished speaking when a cannon-ball cut him in two. I turned to another officer and said how sorry I was about poor de Gramont. Before he could reply, his horse was struck dead by a cannon-ball. And a hundred other incidents of this kind. I gave my horse to a cuirassier to hold for half a minute, and the man was killed. I was covered with earth thrown up by shells, yet I escaped without the slightest scratch. This is what gave me the coolness under fire which is so essential. I said to myself: 'It is a lottery whether you survive or not. One has to die sometime. Would you rather live in dishonour or die with honour?' I had no difficulty in making my choice. When one is brandishing one's sword, when one is in action, the fire which tingles in one's veins wipes out all thought. Battle is often a game of prisoner's base. But to see death as almost a certainty, or rather to wait for it, is often more than the human frame can stand, and I believe that philosophy alone has the power to set us above these troubles by revealing to us the nothingness of our being.

General Jean Rapp, a brave man by any standards, found himself in the thick of the action.

The battle had been won, but the firing was still terrible. Cannon-balls and shells rained down all round me. Within the space of an hour I was hit four times, first quite slightly by two shots, then by a bullet in my left arm. It took away the sleeve of my coat and my shirt down to the skin. At the time I was at the head of the 61st Regiment, whom I had known in Upper Egypt [1798]. There were still a few of the officers from that period, and it was very strange to meet them again here.

Soon afterwards I received a fourth wound, when a grapeshot hit me on the left thigh and threw me off my horse. This was my twenty-second wound. I was obliged to quit the battlefield, but I warned Marshal Ney, whose troops were mixed up with my own.

General Dessaix, the only general in the division who had not been wounded, took my place, but a moment later he had an arm broken. Friant[1] was hit later.

My wounds were dressed by Napoleon's surgeon. The Emperor came in person to see me. 'So it's your turn again. How are things?'

'Sire, I think you will be forced to send in your Guard.'

'I shall take care not to. I do not want it destroyed. I am certain to win the battle without the Guard becoming involved.'

Lieutenant-General Count Mathieu Dumas, Intendant-General of the Army, was summoned to the Emperor's presence at about nine o'clock that night. Count Daru, the Secretary of State, went too.

His camp had been set up in the centre of the square formed by his Guard, a little behind the redoubt. Dinner had just been served to him. He was alone, and made us sit down on his right and left. After inquiring about the arrangements made for tending the wounded, and about the resources offered by the Kolotskoye Abbey, which was on the road two leagues away from the battlefield, and by a small number of dwellings near the village of Borodino, he talked about the outcome of the battle. A moment later he fell asleep — for twenty minutes or so. Then he suddenly woke up and continued talking: 'People will be surprised that I did not commit my reserves in order to obtain greater results, but I had to keep them for striking a decisive blow in the great battle which the enemy will fight in front of Moscow. The success of the day

[1] Louis, General Count Friant (1758–1829).

was assured, and I had to consider the success of the campaign as a whole. That is why I keep my reserves in hand.'

Count Roman Soltyk tells us that after visiting the battlefield, Napoleon returned to the bivouac where he had spent the previous night.

He was exhausted and had a bad cold, and needed rest and care. Yet he again slept in his tent, and this increased his indisposition to the point where he lost his voice completely. At daybreak I went to the Imperial camp to see if anything new had occurred, and to get orders from the Grand Equerry. In front of Napoleon's tent a large fire had been lit, and round this stood all the duty officers. Soon afterwards the King of Naples arrived and he stood with us to get warm, asked news of the Emperor's health, and inquired whether he was ready to receive visitors yet. A few minutes later Marshal Ney appeared. The two heroes of the battle greeted each other amicably, and the King said to the Marshal: 'Yesterday was a hot one. I have never seen a battle like it for artillery fire. At Eylau[1] the guns fired as many rounds, but it was cannon-balls. Yesterday the armies were so close that most of the firing was with grape-shot.'

'We didn't break any eggs,' said the Marshal. 'The enemy's losses must be huge and his morale has undoubtedly been seriously damaged. We must pursue him and exploit our victory.'

'However, the Russians retired in good order,' added the King.

'I find that hard to believe,' replied the Marshal. 'How could they, after such a pounding match?'

This interesting conversation went no further, because Ney, summoned by the Emperor, was at this point introduced into his presence.

After the fighting ended, Colonel Lejeune went back to Headquarters.

The Emperor's tents and those of Marshal Berthier were pitched at the foot of the battlefield, and this was no doubt a sign of

[1] Napoleon's army fought the Austrians and Prussians in a snowstorm on 8 February 1807 — a bloody victory for the French — at Preussisch-Eylau, just south of Königsberg.

victory; but the Russian Army was still within musket range of us. They too chanted 'Victory', and on our side all the commanders should have been preparing to renew the battle. The night soon got very dark, and little by little one saw the camp-fires gleaming on all sides — so many that one had serious thoughts for the morrow.

While waiting for the frugal meal which was to revive us, I cast my mind back over what I had seen during the day; and in comparing this battle with Wagram, Essling, Eylau, and Friedland, I was astonished to realize that I had not seen the Emperor, as in previous years, display that energy which compelled success. To-day he had not mounted his horse except to go to the battlefield; and there he had sat below his Guard, on a steep mound from which he could see everything. Several cannon-balls passed over his head. Every time I returned from one of my numerous missions, I found him sitting there, in the same position, following all the moves through his pocket telescope, and issuing his orders with imperturbable calm. But we had not been fortunate enough to see him going, as in the past, to galvanize by his presence any place where the enemy's stubborn resistance was prolonging the struggle and making success doubtful. We were all surprised not to find the energetic man of Marengo, Austerlitz, etc. We did not know that Napoleon was unwell, and this type of illness made it impossible for him, in the great events which were unfolding before his eyes, to act solely in the interests of his glory.

Colonel Ludwig von Wolzogen, one of the Prussian officers on Barclay's staff, in recording his memories of the aftermath of Borodino, throws light on the relations then existing between Barclay and Kutuzov.

At five o'clock that afternoon the cannonade stopped and suddenly complete silence reigned in both armies. Barclay could not understand why Napoleon did not exploit his victory; for he had in fact already gained possession of the principal points of the battlefield, namely the redoubt in the centre and the three bastions in front of Semenovskoye, as well as the village itself. Furthermore, a fairly general weariness had gripped the Russian Army. Many of the generals were dead or wounded, and almost all the regimental commanders too. As soon as I returned to the battlefield I had met a lieutenant with thirty to forty men behind the firing-line, and when I ordered him to rejoin his regiment immediately he replied: 'This is my regiment!' All the rest of the men were dead, wounded, or missing. Nearly all the Russian reserves had already been committed, whereas with the exception of several battalions of the Young Guard, Napoleon's Imperial Guard had not been seen in any attack. Therefore the Guard could in any case either continue the fight against the Russian centre or reinforce the Emperor's right wing and, by overthrowing Baggovut's corps, could attack the Russian Army in the rear. However, neither move occurred.

Barclay instructed me to find Prince Kutuzov, who had not appeared in the battle-line all day, and to report the situation of both armies to him and obtain further orders. But he added: 'Get his reply in writing, because one has to be careful with Kutuzov.'

I rode a long way before I found the Prince. I eventually met him — and his suite, who were so numerous that they looked to me like reinforcements — on the Moscow road about half an hour's ride behind the army. This suite consisted almost entirely of rich young Russian noblemen, who indulged in all kinds of pleasures and had taken no part whatever in the terrible and earnest events of the day. Colonel Toll was with them and busily eating a capon.

When I began my report with a description of the positions and state of the Russian Army and said that all important posts had been lost on the right wing and to the left of the high road and that the regiments were all extremely tired and shattered, Kutuzov shouted: 'With which low bitch of a sutler have you been getting drunk, that you come giving me such an absurd report? I am in the best position to know how the battle went! The French attacks have been successfully repulsed everywhere, and tomorrow I shall put myself at the head of the army to drive the enemy without more ado from the sacred soil of Russia!'

At this he looked challengingly at his *entourage*, and they applauded with enthusiasm.

This disgraceful reception made me all the angrier because I had only reported what I had seen with my own eyes during the turmoil of battle, whereas I knew that Kutuzov had spent the whole day in rear of the army among champagne bottles and delicatessen. However, I quickly regained my composure as I saw right through Kutuzov's sly, unfair motives in treating me as he had done. Certainly, I said to myself, his associates will not realize the true state of the army and, so as not to be able to condemn his prepared bulletin on the battle as lies, will leave him in the belief that the Russians have won a glorious victory. Besides, he assumed correctly that Napoleon, as he had been unable to gain a decisive victory between six o'clock that morning and five in the afternoon, and had, rather, broken off the action, would not renew the battle; consequently the Russians would remain in control of the battle-field overnight. As I was convinced that I had correctly guessed at the motive for his fierce diatribe against me, I replied quite calmly that I must leave him to take my report how he chose. Meanwhile General Barclay wanted to know, by written orders, whether he was to continue the fight or what was to happen instead.

At this Kutuzov took Colonel Toll on one side and talked to him. After a time Toll wrote out an order for Barclay which Kutuzov signed and handed to me. I rode back to Barclay at once and found him by Gorki Hill. The order contained an instruction that, as long as Napoleon did not reopen the battle, nothing should happen on the Russian side. Meanwhile Barclay should try to bring the army into line so that its right flank rested on Gorki Hill, with its left extending towards a strip of woodland beyond the old Smolensk road; this wood was to be held by Baggovut's corps. . . . In addition, however, everything had to be prepared for the next morning, so that Kutuzov could attack the enemy.

Barclay shook his head and said to me that he did not know where he was going to find enough force for this. If we could attack the French on the spot and straight away, this might perhaps be feasible; but next day the troops, who had exerted themselves for twelve hours without any food and could still not get anything to eat during the night, would be so exhausted that a further attack would be out of the question.

However, Barclay carried out Kutuzov's orders as best he could, and when darkness fell he and his staff went to the village of Gorki, which had been almost destroyed, and where we soon fell into a much-needed sleep, only to be woken again at three o'clock by one of Kutuzov's adjutants, who brought Barclay an order to send the reserve artillery and baggage back through Mozhaisk immediately and, as soon as all these had got far enough ahead, to follow with the army.

Once he had replaced all the ammunition expended and had promoted various men to be non-commissioned officers in place of casualties, Colonel Lubin Griois visited the battlefield.

There was the most appalling confusion. Several cavalry charges had taken place and the ground was strewn with weapons and guns as well as with dead horses and men, above all Russian cuirassiers. Among the last-named were many wounded who had not yet been removed, and no doubt many of them died on the very spot where they had been knocked down. The resources of our ambulances, considerable as these were, did not suffice, and the French wounded had to take precedence.

Such wounded Russians as I saw, overcome by their sufferings and by the cold of the night, made no complaint. Indifferently they watched the passing troops, and tried as far as possible to avoid being kicked by the horses. This insensibility, which I believe stems from a stronger and less sensitive make-up than our own, was increased still further by their fervent devotion to their great St. Nicholas. Nearly every wounded soldier clasped a medallion or image of the Saint which they kissed eagerly and which helped them to forget their pain.

One senior officer who was wounded and captured during this battle was Colonel Franz Ludwig August von Meerheimb, who commanded the Cuirassiers of the Saxon Guard, which formed part of Latour-Maubourg's cavalry corps. At one stage he became surrounded, and in desperate hand-to-hand fighting was knocked unconscious after his horse had been wounded. When he came to he was being plundered by several Russian cuirassiers, and had it not been for the intervention of a French-speaking officer and above all of an elderly grey-haired cuirassier who ordered off the thieves, he would probably have perished.

The old man bound up my head with a cloth, lifted me on to a second horse, took its bridle, and led me with care and patience through a birch copse. Whenever he met any armed peasants, who formed a reserve militia to transport, escort, and guard prisoners he always made a detour and gave me to understand that it was dangerous to fall into their hands.

I became very weak and could barely keep myself up in the saddle. But he kept on telling me not to lose heart and he frequently called out: '*Hauptquartieru nie daleko!*', which meant, as I later discovered, that the Headquarters was not very far.

My helmet, which he had taken as booty, seemed to give him especial pleasure. The good man probably believed it was made of gold and would ensure him a carefree existence in old age.

After we had ridden for about half an hour, we came to some houses which lay on the main road but belonged to another village. Several rows of guns and a great many powder waggons stood here in reserve, and several militia battalions, which must have totalled some four thousand men, guarded them. These were the only available troops I could see. The appearance of these Russian militiamen was dreadful, and if they had worn long cowls of hide instead of dark brown and grey clothing, one would justifiably not have been able to tell them apart from deer. Many had so much hair on their faces that nothing was visible except the nose and eyes.

[*Meerheimb was taken into a field ambulance, where a young Swiss named Bernhardt took pity on him.*]

Meanwhile more and more wounded Russian officers were brought in. They all assured me that the battle was going to turn out well for their side, that several of our batteries had already been captured, and that my King — they mistook me, Heaven knows why, for one of Murat's aides-de-camp — had been taken prisoner.

The Swiss eventually managed to find a senior divisional surgeon, and not before time, because I was near the end of my tether, having lost a great deal of blood from a thrust wound in the left jawbone, where a blood vessel had been pierced. This surgeon, a native of Württemberg, was an agreeable and helpful man, although he expressed sharp anger over our politics and our march to the north. 'I should like to see you all, yes, every one of you, thrashed and shot, so that I could have you here under my dressings!' And yet, despite these hard words, he treated me with admirable care, washed away the blood, stitched and fastened me up, and assured me that none of my wounds — I had four in the head and three on the body — was mortal, provided nothing untoward occurred.

I had scarcely been bandaged when I lost consciousness. The sympathetic young Swiss had had me carried on a truss of hay behind a railing in one corner of the room, and there I slumbered. . . . How long I lay on the hay I cannot say exactly, but to judge from the late hour at which I reached Mozhaisk, it must have been at least an hour. I was woken by a violent shaking. It was the young Swiss, my guardian angel, shouting at me to get up at once. 'I cannot,' I replied. 'I am very weak and lame. Leave me to my fate.' 'Certainly not,' he said. 'You must get up. Do your utmost. Every delay is dangerous. In a few minutes it will be too late to save you. One side of the house is on fire already, and the whole village will soon be in ashes.'

This excellent young man and the cuirassier grabbed me under the armpits and pushed and carried me outside. He remained with me and sent the other man to fetch a waggon which would transport me to Moscow.

[*Meerheimb travelled on a two-wheeled cart and reached the city that evening.*]

We found ourselves in the field ambulance. However exhausted I may have felt, this new scene of extreme human suffering was very upsetting. I was shown a corner and told to wait there until my turn came for surgery. Probably I was taken for a *grand mutilé*, and indeed what remained of my clothes gave no indication that I was an aide-de-camp to the King of Saxony and commanded his Horse Guards. The torn and blood-spattered collar which had been returned to me I wore on my arm, because I could not have it put on again. The rest of my costume comprised a flannel waistcoat and an old cloak of the Bodyguard which had been thrown round my shoulders in the first village. I had no headgear at all, and my face and forehead were swathed in bandages. Only with difficulty and effort could I speak even a few words, because every utterance caused me severe pains in the chest and ribs, and my throat was so swollen on account of the hoof-marks that a fortnight went by before I could wear a collar with my shirt.

Eventually we came to a wretched little house, half fallen down and with only the ground floor standing, yet it seemed like a palace to me, since I should at least be able to get some rest there. I found a French general named Bonnamy lying on some hay in one corner of the room and groaning. He had been taken prisoner in one of the Russian redoubts which had been captured and then lost.[1] He had thirteen bayonet wounds, of which one in the left breast caused him a great deal of pain and, since it was deep, endangered his life. When the Russian surgeons arrived to treat his wounds, he begged them to bleed him to afford some relief. 'For God's sake bleed me, or I shall die,' he repeated at least a hundred times; but just as often came what seemed to me the very reasonable answer that he was too weak to allow this.

Not until seven o'clock next morning did the militia officer who was to accompany us turn up. He told the General that the special ambulance waggon was ready. This sort of waggon for the conveyance of wounded officers is very comfortably fitted. It is shaped roughly like a large four-seater travelling waggon, but holds six people and has spring suspension. The floor is double, so that in order to lie more comfortably one can stretch out one's legs when necessary. Instead of a window there are shutters with small round apertures. The sides are padded with leather cushions.

At last, on 10 September, we approached Moscow. Through chinks in the shutters I saw mounds on the right-hand side of the main road. Whether the view of the capital from this side was impressive I could not judge because of the helplessness of my condition.

The waggons waited for a long time at the door. A crowd of curious people, mostly from the lower classes, surrounded it, and the various grimaces and gestures they made with tongue and mouth indicated in which category of guests they placed us. When General Bonnamy, who was always full of the most sinister ideas and, as a former revolutionary and upstart, was familiar with the activities of the mob, saw these figures of terror, he called out in tones of high tragedy: 'Ah, we are done for. This rabble is going to massacre us!'

[1] See Captain François's account (pp. 127–8).

[In fact the wounded were very well received in Moscow, were placed in a house and properly looked after, the Russian Government making some payment in roubles to Bonnamy, Meerheimb, and others. Bonnamy returned to France from captivity in August 1814.]

Colonel Raymond de Montesquiou, Duke de Fezensac, who had been one of Marshal Berthier's aides-de-camp at Headquarters, arrived on 12 September at a village east of Mozhaisk to take command of the 4th Regiment of the Line. The previous colonel, Massy, had been killed at Borodino.

From the very first day I was struck by the exhaustion of the troops and their numerical weakness. At G.H.Q. only results were judged, without thought for the cost, and people had no idea of the army's situation. But when I assumed command of a regiment I had to go into all the details which I knew nothing about and to learn how deep the trouble went. The 4th Regiment was reduced to 900 men out of the 2,800 who had crossed the Rhine; furthermore, the four battalions only formed two on the ground, and each company had a double-cadre of officers and N.C.O.s. Every article of clothing, and in particular the shoes, was in a bad state. We still had enough flour and a few herds of bullocks and flocks of sheep; but these resources would soon be exhausted. To replenish them we had constantly to change from place to place, since in twenty-four hours we ravaged the country we went through.

What I have said about my regiment applied to all in the 3rd Corps, and especially to the Württemberg division, which was almost destroyed. . . . We had never suffered such heavy losses; never had the Army's morale been so damaged. I no longer found the soldiers' old gaiety: a gloomy silence had replaced the songs and amusing stories which previously had helped them to forget the fatigue of long marches. Even the officers appeared anxious, and they continued serving only from a sense of duty and honour. This depression, natural in a defeated army, was remarkable after a decisive action, after a victory which opened to us the gates of Moscow.

Baron Fain states that when night fell Napoleon's headquarters moved into a ruined village on the Moscow road, where the plain begins.

We were not more than half a league from Mozhaisk; on the morning of 9 September our advance-guard entered this little town after quite a sharp action.

We found the principal houses full of wounded Russian soldiers who had been abandoned by their comrades without any form of relief. The corpses of these wretches lay among the living.

On reaching the square the palace quartermasters noticed on the left-hand side a new house which had not quite been completed. It had no doors, but had closed windows and several stoves. The Emperor came and occupied the first floor. He had hardly settled into this lodging when he wanted to start up the office work which had been suspended for the past five days. But he lost his voice so completely that he was not able to dictate or even to talk. This was the result of a heavy cold aggravated by spending the last few cold nights in a tent. In this embarrassing situation he had recourse to his pen, and this was a sharp break with Napoleon's routine. However, he resigned himself to it, sat down, and began to cover sheets of paper with all the orders teeming in his head. His secretaries, Méneval and Fain, the Cabinet vassals, d'Albe, Mounier, and Deponthon, copy at great speed; Count Daru and the Prince of Neuchâtel also take a hand in the work. But at every line we are held up by difficulties in deciphering the handwriting, and yet the Emperor, who keeps on finishing another order, bangs constantly on his table to have someone remove the drafts which accumulate. The day goes by in this dumb work in which Napoleon's hurrying pen and his mallet are the only sounds!

A vivid description of conditions in Mozhaisk comes to us from the recollections of Alexandre Bellot de Kergorre, a young commissary born in Nantes. He reached the town after nightfall on 10 September and rejoined Headquarters, bivouacking in the middle of the square by a fire belonging to the Guard.

Next morning we found the Intendant-General and a stable in which we installed both men and horses. I was on duty with

Monsieur Trousset, the director,[1] and we had a temporary assistant named Ligerot who had arrived that very day from Milan. . . .

After two days the Headquarters left, and Ligerot and I found quarters in a little house near Monsieur Trousset's. The evenings were beginning to turn chilly, and we used to light fires to keep warm. I slept on a truss of straw and was never able to change it during the three weeks I spent in Mozhaisk. We lived with Trousset and every day his cook prepared liver, kidneys, brain, and beef tongue. We had spirits distilled from grain and potatoes which we mixed with water from the Moskva. We had no candles, but we eventually made some out of butcher's grease. We ate off tin plates belonging to the director. As for linen, we had long since given up using it.

Every day we had visits from a number of friends who were on their way to Moscow and came asking for bread. It was heart-breaking when they did so, and the circumstances were so dreadful that we decided to have a few loaves in the house, and these we cut into hunks to give to those who were worst off. . . .

When I took up my duties I had to look after the needs of the hospitals. These contained three thousand patients lying in two stone-built houses, the only ones in the town. The Intendant-General departed, leaving me nothing but one barrel of flour which we distributed to the generals, four or five pounds apiece. There were twelve divisional commanders and fourteen brigadiers. As for the other wounded, they were excluded from this issue. So as to be able to feed the wounded we had collected from the battlefield, Ligerot was sent with a detachment of troops and some waggons to scour the countryside and try to collect some grain. He was fortunate enough to find a quantity, but we still had to grind it. I found a soldier who was a carpenter by trade, and I had him repair a mill which was situated on the Moskva half a league away. While waiting for corn to be found, brought in, ground, and converted into bread, I had to prevent our wounded men from starving to death. So with the town major I stationed myself sword in hand at the entrance to Mozhaisk and there we stopped the first stragglers who came by, and also a few little local carts on which

[1] Trousset was a *commissaire ordonnateur*; Bellot was a *commissaire des guerres* (*2e classe*).

they had some provisions. Partly by force and partly by persuasion we collected some of these men who then helped us with our arrests. In this way we obtained some flour, but inevitably this supply, being so small, quickly ran out. Word soon got about that we were stopping passers-by on the main road, so they no longer entered the town, but went round.

Our poor unfortunate wounded were dying of hunger and thirst. They were bandaged with hay for lack of lint and linen, and they groaned dreadfully. For the first few days they lived on the few grains they could find in the straw they lay on, and on the little flour I was able to give them. When soup had been made, it had to be taken to the wounded, and we had no receptacles! Providentially I came upon a fairly large number of small bowls intended to be used for lamps, so we were able to give the patients water. The absence of candles was a terrible privation. In the early days I had the painful misfortune to lose some men who, hidden in the straw, were not spotted in the evening when the food was distributed by the light of a flaming pine torch. A shocking thing was the impossibility of removing the dead from among the living. I had neither medical orderlies nor stretchers. Not only was the hospital full of corpses, but so were the streets and a number of houses. After attending to the most pressing needs of the living, I used some little carts I had found to remove corpses from the hospital. On my own I took away 128, which had been serving as pillows to the sick and were several days old. I then had all corpses removed from the streets and houses. As far as possible I joined the wounded together by putting them under a leader whom I selected from the healthiest of the non-commissioned officers, and these reported to me every morning on their condition. Many officers were on their own, so I urged them in their own interests to get together.

. . . Six hundred wounded Russians had fallen in the gardens, and here they lived on cauliflower stalks and human flesh. Of this there was no shortage! In the first week I could give each man no more than half a pound of meat. Many of these wretches died. The others, as they recovered through Nature's care, went away, because they were not under guard. In fact, we could not guard them, because then we should have had to feed them.

To begin with I had strong arguments with the director. We had been expressly forbidden to touch the convoys destined for Headquarters, and had orders to live off the country. The director was not prepared to take anything bound for Moscow, but I decided to stop whatever seemed to me essential for maintaining the hospital. As I could not induce him to follow my advice, I told him I would take all responsibility for levying a tithe on the convoys, since I preferred to be court-martialled for feeding the wounded entrusted to my care than to leave them to die of hunger. I even ventured to seize a convoy of flour, which was a proceeding not without danger. However, I was fortunate to have my conduct approved subsequently. . . .

The Abbey of Kolotskoye, full of wounded, asked us for help every day. The unfortunate sick who had been crowded in there dragged themselves on to the main road to implore a little food from the few passers-by. We had no means of dressing their wounds and no medicines. Amid so many horrors, Nature furthered the cause of medicine. I had very few fever cases and, apart from two or three hundred deaths in the first days, I saved all my patients.

Moscow

WHILE Napoleon remained temporarily at Mozhaisk, the Russians continued their retreat to a village on the outskirts of Moscow named Fili, where, on 13 September, Kutuzov, who had vowed to defend the ancient capital, summoned a council of war. Various proposals were debated for fighting *in situ*, but no really good defensive position was available, and the troops numbered little over 70,000. Other generals proposed a retreat either north-east or southwards. Eventually Kutuzov, arguing that so long as the Russian Army continued to exist, hope of ultimately winning the war would be preserved, whereas to risk destruction of the Army was to risk all, decided to resume the retreat — south towards Kolomna, thus guarding the more fertile southern provinces and the arsenal at Tula, known to contemporaries as 'the Sheffield of Russia'. He likened Moscow to a sponge which would suck up Napoleon's hitherto irresistible flood.

General Miloradovich covered this move with his rearguard, and enabled not only the Army but something like a quarter of a million inhabitants to leave the city. Of the 15,000 who remained, many were French or other foreigners, and several thousand wounded soldiers had also to be left behind. Taking advantage of the keen French desire to capture Moscow intact, Miloradovich obtained an armistice which ensured his unmolested departure on 14 September. That afternoon a chagrined Napoleon, having waited vainly for a deputation of officials to surrender the city, entered the almost deserted streets, and as soon as a few fanatical defenders had been disposed of, took up residence in the Kremlin.

Two days later the fires which had broken out, being fanned by gale-force winds, had enveloped large areas of the most inflammable city in Europe and became so threatening that the Emperor was obliged to escape through the conflagration and lodge for two days in the Petrovsky Castle just outside Moscow. The flames cast a glow upon the countryside for thirty leagues around, and even four miles from the outskirts a letter could easily be read at night. A subject of prolonged argument, this great fire was in part deliberate — the work of incendiaries posted on orders of the Governor, Count Rostopchin, to destroy magazines and markets —

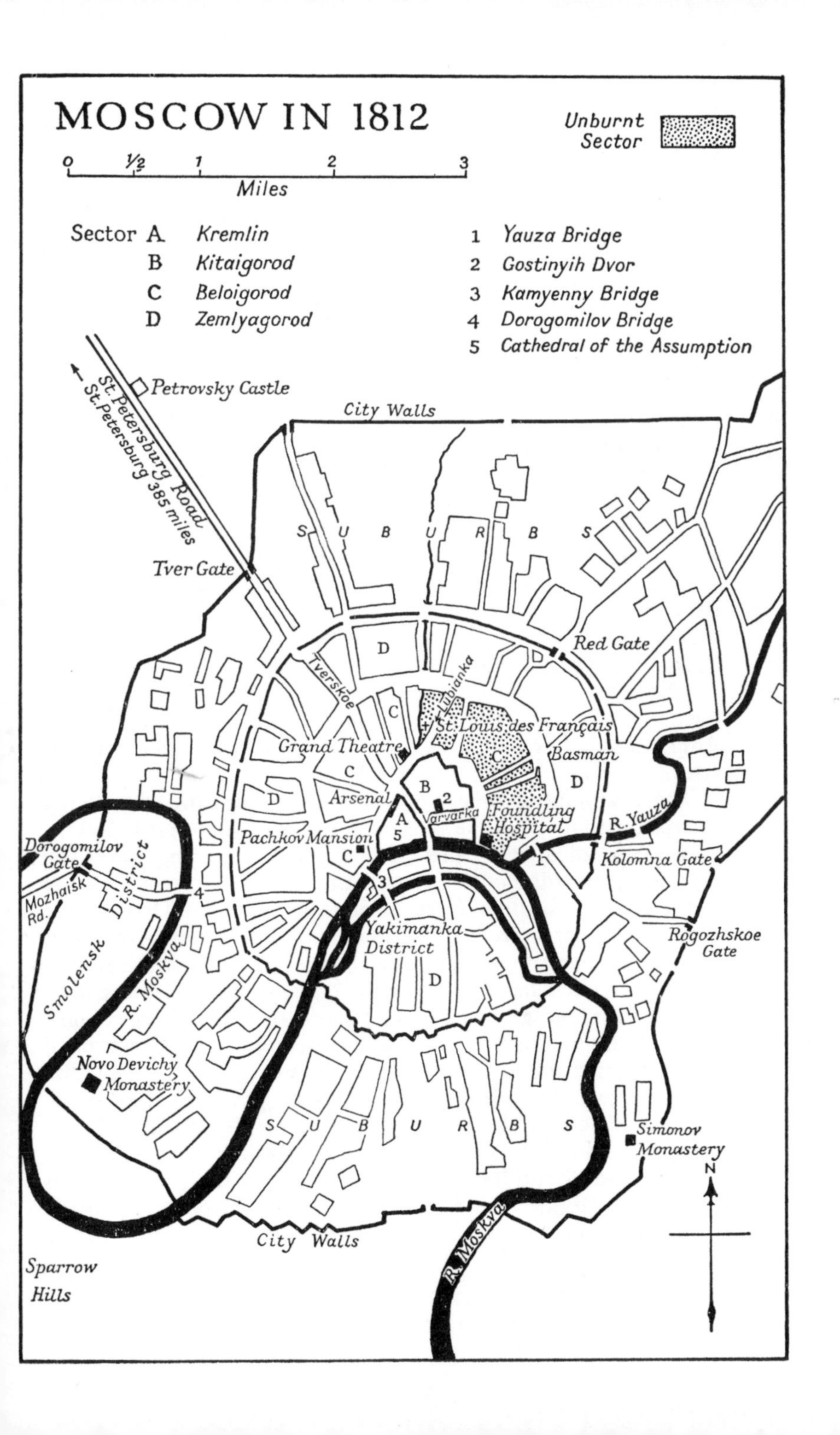

MOSCOW IN 1812
Unburnt Sector
0 1/2 1 2 3
Miles
Sector A Kremlin
B Kitaigorod
C Beloigorod
D Zemlyagorod
1 Yauza Bridge
2 Gostinyih Dvor
3 Kamyenny Bridge
4 Dorogomilov Bridge
5 Cathedral of the Assumption
St. Petersburg Road
St. Petersburg 385 miles
Petrovsky Castle
City Walls
SUBURBS
Tver Gate
Red Gate
Tverskoe
Lubianka
St. Louis des Français
Grand Theatre
Basman
Arsenal
Varvarka
Foundling Hospital
R. Yauza
Pachkov Mansion
Kolomna Gate
Dorogomilov Gate
District
Mozhaisk Rd.
Yakimanka District
Rogozhskoe Gate
Smolensk
R. Moskva
Novo Devichy Monastery
SUBURBS
Simonov Monastery
N
City Walls
R. Moskva
Sparrow Hills

and partly unintentional. Of Moscow's nine thousand houses,[1] two-thirds of them stone-built, only 525 in stone and 1,797 in wood survived intact; while half the churches were burnt to the ground and nearly all the others damaged. The furnace afforded full opportunity for plundering, both systematic and haphazard, for licence, and for disgraceful sacrilege.

When he returned to the Kremlin Napoleon had three main tasks: to obtain peace; to restore discipline in his cosmopolitan army, which was fast deteriorating into a rabble bent on plunder; and to collect centrally such resources as the city still contained. All three proved beyond him, and beyond Marshal Mortier, whom he appointed Governor of Moscow. Neither disorder nor destruction affected Russian determination not to make peace. Messages and letters sent by intermediaries drew no reply. Nor did the Emperor's bitter criticisms of the wrecking of so beautiful a city as 'atrocious and useless conduct'. Napoleon apparently failed to grasp that Alexander could not negotiate without risking assassination or dethronement. As for provisions, an even greater problem than shelter, despite the fire, the Russian peasants could not be tempted to bring in corn and hay for sale to the Army, and foraging parties outside often incurred serious casualties. Troops found sugar, preserves, and spirits, but went short of bread and meat. They had furs to wear, but often lacked uniform and shoes. Ammunition, however, was found in abundance, and saltpetre also.

The Tsar's intransigence was backed by Kutuzov, who altered the retreat route from the Kolomna–Ryazan road towards Kaluga — a westward swing. Then the dispatch of strong forces by Napoleon towards Podolsk caused the Russians to move further south as far as Tarutino. Here, during the first half of October, the Army was reorganized and reinforced to a strength of about 100,000 infantry, 20,000 Cossacks, and over 600 guns. Already in September guerrillas had started to harass Napoleon's convoys, detachments, and garrisons along the over-extended lines of communication. Baggage-trains and convoys of sick and wounded were captured; stragglers, marauders, and couriers were hunted down by merciless peasants; and Russian prisoners were freed. Partisan leaders like Denis Davidov, formerly Bagration's aide-de-camp, Chetvertakov, an illiterate but skilful dragoon, and Figner, the epitome of ruthlessness, achieved a good deal, yet they received very cautious help from Kutuzov, and were often obstructed by a Government which feared that the peasants would turn their weapons against the landlords.

[1] Authorities differed on this figure: police registers gave 6,532, Rostopchin 7,632, Lecointe de Laveau and the official returns 9,158.

Napoleon, oppressed by these and other problems, still waited for the Tsar to come to terms as he had done after Austerlitz and Friedland. But as Alexander made no move to open peace talks, Napoleon, reluctant to admit defeat yet feeling his position to be deteriorating fast, took the initiative on 5 October by sending General Lauriston to the Russian Headquarters to request a pass to the Tsar in St. Petersburg. This *démarche* produced no tangible result, yet Napoleon still hung on. 'Moscow,' he stated, 'is not a military position; it is a political position.' And he needed to show Europe that he had compelled the Tsar to sign a peace *in* Moscow. What would be the effect of a retreat on the rest of Europe, where his hold was precarious? He could not safely winter in Moscow, and realized the danger of waiting there *if* he had to continue the war. France would not get used to his absence, he declared, whereas Prussia and Austria would take advantage of it.

Early in October his plan to march on St. Petersburg had been turned down by the marshals, who protested against advancing towards the wintry north while Kutuzov remained to threaten their rear. Napoleon had not insisted. Then warnings about the impending winter were ignored or treated with contempt. It is true that October was exceptionally mild for Russia, and the really severe weather did not come until early December, but Napoleon could not forecast this. Russian prisoners gave warning: 'in a fortnight your nails will drop off and your weapons will drop from your benumbed and half-dead fingers.' When General Rapp told him: 'The natives say we shall have a severe winter,' Napoleon retorted scornfully: 'Bah! You and your natives! See how fine it is.'

Usually a master of his decisions, he was still hesitating, still debating, when, on 18 October, a shock decided matters for him. The Russians had suddenly left Tarutino and, at Vinkovo, attacked Murat, who, slackly relying upon a truce which had no official status, was taken by surprise and lost 2,500 men in hitting back and then retiring. But for Kutuzov's refusal of reinforcements to Bennigsen, who was directing the action, Murat would have had great difficulty in extricating himself. Bennigsen could not resist sending the Tsar a most violently worded report on the battle, and was dismissed by Kutuzov.

Napoleon realized that he must march south before Kutuzov could bar his route. One might have expected the Grand Army to have retreated along the northern route through Zubtsov and Bielyi to Vitebsk, but to have done so was not in Napoleon's character. A bolder move was required: along the southern flank to Smolensk, not by the old and devastated route through Mozhaisk, but further south through Kaluga, where he reckoned to find at least some of the villages intact. Critics have argued that from Kaluga he should have gone into the rich, untapped southern provinces; but had the Army time to do so? Could it risk scattering in order to derive full benefit from these riches? Had he not set up supply depots along the road from Smolensk to Minsk and onward to Vilna? The depots in these towns, and at Orsha and Kovno, were full, despite the incompetence of several garrison commanders.

Partly to save face and show that he might still return to the capital, but still more in retaliation for the Tsar's silence, he left a temporary garrison of 8,000 men under Mortier with orders to blow up the Kremlin and Arsenal and many other public buildings. This was done on 21 October, but damp fuses and half-heartedness reduced the damage far below Napoleon's expectations. On 19 October the evacuation began — 107,000 troops, thousands of civilians, and a clutter of waggons and carriages, too often laden not with provisions or winter clothing, but rather with booty taken as presents for wives or fiancées who would soon become widows or girls mourning lovers. When success depended upon swift, sudden manœuvre, the Grand Army was a slow-moving, clumsy monster, not a mobile force designed for flexibility and speed.

Count Rostopchin's fourteen-year-old daughter Natalya described in her memoirs, which were partly devoted to defending her father from various charges, what happened to her on 21 August and how people began to leave Moscow.

My mother had sent me to father with a letter which she had just received and which required an immediate reply. I found him sitting at his table, head in hand. He appeared to be plunged in grief and I hesitated to approach, but the rustle of my dress roused him from his stupor. He stared sadly at me for a moment and then, picking up a dispatch, said: 'Take your mother this letter from Barclay. Smolensk has fallen, and we shall soon have the enemy at the gates of Moscow.'

The news of this frightful disaster spread instantly all over the town and produced general consternation. However, my father soon recovered his good spirits and, as always, tried to soften the unduly sombre colours in which the public saw this important event. In his public bulletins and in conversation with the people he stressed the prodigies of valour displayed by our generals and by our poor dear soldiers.

. . . My father began to busy himself with putting the treasures of Moscow in a safe place. An enormous number of carts and horses were used to transport into the interior of the country the riches which were scattered in churches, convents, public libraries, and museums. If we had to deplore the loss of several *objets d'art* or precious manuscripts, the fault lies with those who arranged the means of transport and who safeguarded their own belongings instead of attending to those which had been entrusted to their charge by the Government.

Moscow soon began to empty. Every day one saw hundreds of equipages going through the streets, mostly full of women and children. However, the refugees occasionally included some young or old noblemen who followed the example set by the weaker sex. The crowds who collected at the barriers expressed their contempt of these *émigrés* in vehement terms, accusing them of cowardice and treachery. It was often difficult to repress these outbursts of patriotic indignation. And so, to escape the gibes and insults of the populace, men of all ages were seen to adopt the costume of their wives and mothers, hoping by means of this disguise to avoid any disagreeable comments.

Madame Louise Fusil (1774–1848) was a French actress and singer who had been living in Russia since 1806. Her memoirs provide one of the most illuminating civilian accounts of life in St. Petersburg, then in Moscow before and during Napoleon's occupation, and of the retreat, which she survived.

The fall of Smolensk did nothing to allay anxiety. The French Army was approaching rapidly. All the nobles departed, and the treasure in the Kremlin and the riches deposited in the Foundling Hospital were taken away. There was a continuous procession of vehicles, carts, furniture, pictures, belongings of all sorts. The city was already deserted, and as our soldiers advanced, the emigration gathered pace.

As I had been born in the Duchy of Württemberg, at Stuttgart, I hoped to obtain, through the protection of the Empress-Mother, who was also from the Duchy, a passport for St. Petersburg.

Despite a recommendation from Count Markov,[1] the former Russian Ambassador in France, I was refused one.

. . . As we feared a food shortage, everybody was making provision. Soon the alarm became widespread, because there was talk of people burying themselves under the ruins of the city. People moved into the outer districts, and as Moscow is very large, it was reckoned that the part through which the army would pass would be the first, and perhaps the only, part to be burnt. We could not imagine that the whole of this immense city could be sacrificed, but people fled from districts which had wooden houses. All those palaces built of stone and covered with sheet-iron seemed as if they could never burn, and people took refuge in them for preference.

I had left the house I was living in and joined a family of artists who occupied a large palace belonging to Prince Galitsin, situated on the Basman, a very isolated district and at the opposite end of the city from where the French Army would enter. My friend's husband, Monsieur Vandraminy, had been commissioned by the Prince to make an engraving of his superb picture gallery. He and his family lived in a small wing of this palace, looking on to a vast garden which would serve as a hiding-place if the mob went to extremes, and would preserve us in case of fire.

. . . We were fairly quiet for a week or ten days — this was the first half of September — but after that people came to say that the army was close.

We kept on climbing to the top of the house, where we could get a long view, and one evening we spotted the bivouac fires. Our servants came into our rooms in great alarm to announce that the police had been knocking at every door to urge the occupants to leave, as the city was going to be set on fire, and the fire-pumps had been taken away. 'We do not want to remain here,' they added. And in fact we learnt that the police had left, which was scarcely reassuring.

[1] Ackady Markov, Minister of Foreign Affairs and twice Russian envoy in Paris.

The following account comes from a Russian woman who worked as a servant in the house of Prince Lobanov. She was married to a serf named Soimonov, and her story was written down by her daughter.

We were living at that time in our house on the Vshivaya Gorka, and our store-room was large, standing as a separate building. We had the idea of dividing the store-room with a stone wall, seeing that we had our own stove-makers and that bricks for the alteration were lying in the yard. The wall was begun, and all the family's trunks, boxes of crockery, linen, and different things — everything imaginable! — were dragged there. All our belongings were put on top, and the wall rose higher and higher. From above they had already started to throw feather beds and pillows from the whole house. When the wall was finished, all but the last two feet, a man we knew suddenly looked into our store-room from the neighbouring yard and began to entreat us to let him hide his property there as well. All kinds of trash was brought. It wouldn't have been worth hiding, but you know nobody wants to part with his own, and you have to help people in trouble. After all, kind folk were helping us. We trusted in his gratitude.

The wall was built up to its full height and partly plastered, otherwise it would have been as clear as daylight to anybody that it was new. They dragged all the shabbier stuff to the front of the store-room and crammed it full. 'Smash it, carry it off, if you like,' they said. 'You won't get very rich on it, you cursed Frenchmen.'

. . . Well now, to avoid any unpleasant happenings the master's family went off to Vladimir.[1] They had some relations there and they were waiting there for the master. But he could not leave. Whether he stayed on business or on duty, I cannot say. I only recall that every morning he put on his uniform and drove to where all the gentry gathered to put their heads together as to how best to make things hot for the Frenchman and how not to let him get into Moscow. But it's clear they did not think of anything.

St. Alexander's Day[2] passed. Suddenly the master arrived home and gave orders to harness the droshky to one horse; he saw that one horse would not carry him, so quickly another jade was

[1] A hundred miles east of Moscow.

[2] 12 September, on which day the revered saint and national hero Alexander Nevsky was celebrated.

bought — they found it somewhere or other and harnessed it with ropes. The master, accompanied only by a coachman, mounted the droshky in his uniform which he had been wearing in the morning. I can remember how he said good-bye to us, how he took out his last money and ordered us to buy a horse and ride out by the Tver Gate to our country house near Moscow, and if anybody was not afraid of staying at our Moscow house, then he was to stay. We said good-bye to him and he set off.

We servants began to consider where we should all go. Six or so remained at the house, the others left for the country house eighty versts away. My mother-in-law would not let me go with them so far away, nor would she leave me in Moscow. Her own sister lived on the other side of the Moskva River with the Arsenyev family, and they were intending to go to a village in Orel province; and the Frenchmen, it was said, would not get as far as that. Mother-in-law was afraid for me — I was very young and pretty. She hurriedly got me ready, tied up my bundles, and blessed me. 'Dunyasha, go to your aunt and beg her on your knees to take you with her. Misfortunes can happen so easily.'

. . . Shcherbinki, their country house near Moscow, was twenty-five versts from the gate. Somehow we dragged ourselves there safely. Had there not been such distress on the way, it would have been a pleasure and real fun. Some people were riding in carriages, some on horseback, some pulling their children in little carts. Here a cow was being led, there a goat was trying to escape. Hen-coops were attached to carts. A big tub was being carried on a *troika*.[1] People were sitting in the tub and looking out. Some were making their way alone, others with their whole family, children clinging to their mothers, howling because they could not keep up or had grown hungry and were looking for something to eat.

Löwenstern's recollections provide a glimpse of Kutuzov and Barclay de Tolly just west of Moscow on 13 September.

Prince Kutuzov instructed General Barclay to reconnoitre the position outside the Dorogomilov Gate,[2] the right of the line to be

[1] A vehicle with a team of three horses abreast.

[2] The Smolensk road led to this gate on the west side of the city. The Sparrow Hills rise a little to the south-west.

in front of the village of Fili, the left on the heights of Vorobievo [the Sparrow Hills]. This position was entrenched, because at one time there was talk of giving battle to the enemy before abandoning Moscow to him.

The Prince installed himself in the open on a camp chair which was always carried by an aide-de-camp. General Dokhturov had lunch served and wanted to do the honours, but General Barclay de Tolly, who never paid any attention either to the little comforts of life or to the pirouettes people danced round the Prince, mounted his horse and rode off. Then, noticing that General Dokhturov had not followed, he sent me back to Kutuzov to claim him, adding: 'Bring him to me, even with a cutlet in his mouth.'

'That's what they are all like,' he went on. 'Always seeking happiness and favour in the Prince's every glance, and not realizing that these blessings must come from over there' — he pointed to the enemy.

When I went up to the Prince, he asked me what I wanted. I told him that I had come to fetch General Dokhturov.

'Go,' said Kutuzov to the General. 'You must not keep General Barclay waiting. I shall lunch all right without you.'

And poor General Dokhturov, who was an excellent man but something of a courtier, was obliged to mount his ambling horse and follow me. General Barclay de Tolly said nothing unpleasant to him, rode rapidly along the position, found it a bad one, and an hour later rejoined the Prince.

It was at this point that Count Rostopchin arrived from Moscow.

At ten o'clock in the morning Rostopchin went to Kutuzov's headquarters to concert plans for the security of Moscow.

I found Prince Kutuzov sitting by the fire, warming himself. He was surrounded by generals and aides-de-camp who asked for orders. One by one he sent them off, now to Barclay, now to Bennigsen, sometimes to Count Toll, the Quartermaster-General, his great favourite and deserving in every way of the protection Kutuzov gave him. The Prince received me with great courtesy and took me on one side. We stayed alone together for half an hour, and our conversation showed me the baseness, timidity, and indecision of this Commander-in-Chief, who was named the Saviour of Russia, even though he did nothing to deserve it.

He told me that it had been decided to give battle to Napoleon at the very spot where we now stood. I pointed out that the ground behind this position sloped fairly sharply to the town, and that if our front line were forced to withdraw, it would enter Moscow helter-skelter with the enemy, that there would be no means of extricating our troops, and that he risked losing the entire army in this way. However, Kutuzov continued to assure me that he would not be forced out of this position, but that if, as the result of some unexpected development, he felt himself obliged to retreat, he would move back on Tver.[1] I observed that he would be short of provisions there. At this point Kutuzov let slip these words: '*But we must concern ourselves with the north and cover it.*' The Commander-in-Chief had in mind solely the Tsar's residence, and he overlooked two things: first, that if Wittgenstein's[2] corps were destroyed, then Saint-Cyr would be in St. Petersburg before Kutuzov; secondly, that Napoleon could not be intending to march on St. Petersburg after occupying Moscow in September — a march that would take at least six weeks. Besides, by taking the road to Tver, Kutuzov would be leaving behind all the reinforcements, and the enemy would become masters of the country as far as the Black Sea. I asked him if he did not think he would do better to put himself on the Kaluga road along which all supplies from the interior were routed to Headquarters. He replied evasively. As the King of Naples had gone in this direction after the battle of Borodino, Kutuzov probably wanted to avoid an encounter with him.

The Commander-in-Chief started talking again about the battle he was going to fight, and asked me to come next day with the Archbishop and the two miraculous images of the Virgin which should be carried right along the line of the army. The clergy would lead the procession, holding sprinklers of holy water, and be accompanied by cantors and monks carrying banners. Kutuzov ended by asking me for a dozen bottles of wine, and warned me that nothing would happen in the camp next day. 'I know Napoleon's method,' he added. 'He will halt this evening, will allow

[1] A hundred miles north-west of Moscow on the St. Petersburg road.

[2] Ludwig Adolf Peter von Sayn-Wittgenstein-Ludwigsburg (1769–1843).

his troops to rest for a day, will make a reconnaissance on the day after tomorrow, and will then come and attack me.'

At the end of this conversation we went back to the fire, where we found all the generals arguing. Dokhturov, who was to command the left wing, came to report that there was no means of bringing up the artillery on account of the escarpment on the banks of the river and a steep hill. I spoke to Barclay de Tolly, who said to me: 'You see what they want to do. The only thing I desire is to be killed if we are mad enough to fight here where we are.'

Duke Eugen von Württemberg (1788–1857), in the Russian service and commanding the 4th Infantry Division, was also there, and wrote in his diary:

Gradually more and more troops filled the valley between the Moskva and the heights of Vorobievo, and very soon they were jammed in confusion within this constricted area. General Barclay was not satisfied with the disposition of the troops, and staff officers were sent to reconnoitre the heights and to find better positions. General Konovnitsin and I accompanied them. All were of one opinion, namely that it was impossible to select a position there.

I took this news back to General Barclay. Kutuzov was sitting in an armchair, set on a small hillock beside the road and surrounded by innumerable generals. As far as I could gather, opinions were sharply divided. Barclay, who said little, held the correct view that where we stood was not the place to accept a battle, and that we must either go forward or withdraw. Kutuzov, whose inward disquiet was apparent, listened in silence to many of the opinions expressed. In truth no less a decision was at stake than to rise boldly above all responsibility and, in spite of the views held by the Army and the nation, to yield the old imperial capital to the enemy after a battle which had been announced as won — after a retreat which had been voluntarily undertaken, and with an army which, it was claimed, again totalled 90,000 combatants, including the militia and the Cossacks.

This already tense moment was suddenly interrupted by thunderous firing by the rearguard, indicating the enemy's approach. To most people the possibility of further withdrawal seemed to be ruled out by the demands of honour. In their view Moscow was the goal and the grave of the Russian warrior, as are the depths of the tomb to the wanderer on earth. The beyond lay in another world. In the local situation in which the Army found itself, a defeat was naturally to be assumed.

When I had served in the Vilna garrison in 1810, Kutuzov had been Military Governor and he had shown himself well-disposed towards me. I remember very clearly what he said to me when he left the assembly and referred to the decision he had already made for retreating. '*Ici ma tête, fût-elle bonne ou mauvaise, ne doit s'aider que d'elle même*,' Kutuzov said, getting up out of his chair and whispering in my ear, as I, well aware of the many different opinions which had been expressed, looked at him.

Count Rostopchin, Military Governor of Moscow, came up to me soon afterwards and said with great fervour: 'If I were asked my opinion, I would say "Destroy the capital rather than surrender it to the enemy!" That is Count Rostopchin's view. As for the governor of the city who is called upon to look to its preservation, he cannot give such an opinion.'

I was so struck by this thought that on my return to the divisional camp I passed it on to everybody round me. 'It is scarcely credible,' I exclaimed. 'It would be a gigantic task, but in this terrible crisis the proper expedient.' My companions at the time will confirm this incident. But I must admit that I soon changed my mind about believing the Russians had any share in the burning of Moscow, and, like General von Clausewitz, only reverted to that belief in more recent times.

A council of war was held towards evening. Those present included Generals Bennigsen, Barclay, Dokhturov, Count Ostermann, Konovnitsin, Yermolov, and Colonel Toll. . . . Konovnitsin wanted to attack the enemy, Toll was for sending the army on a flanking march sideways from Moscow, in the direction of Kaluga. Yermolov vacillated between these two proposals, while Barclay advised unquestioning retreat along the road to Nizhni-Novgorod. Kutuzov decided on the wisest course by declaring that the army should move south-east towards Kolomna, where we should, while remaining in touch with the southern provinces, gain the advantage of deceiving the enemy about what we intended next.

During the night of 13–14 September the whole army received

orders to march through the city in good order and in silence, and to take up positions fourteen versts further on, near Panki.

A young Russian officer named Nikolai Muravyev (1794–1866), who later became a general and during the Crimean War captured the fortress of Kars in Armenia after the Turks had withstood siege for six months, went to Moscow on 10 September.

I found the capital in a woeful state, with weeping and clamour everywhere. Along the streets lay dead and wounded soldiers. The inhabitants had got away from the city, in which disorders had already broken out. Crowds of people stood everywhere.

I galloped to the house of Prince Urusov, expecting to find my father and brothers there. . . . The house was nearly empty. Prince Urusov had already left with his father for Nizhni-Novgorod, where all the Moscow nobility had taken refuge. In the house there remained only a few of our servants and those possessions which in their haste they had been unable to take away.

. . . During our stay in Moscow Vasili Novikov, the manager of Prince Urusov's cloth factory, arrived in haste. He lived in a village forty versts from Moscow, and was not expecting the French, when suddenly an enemy detachment arrived at his house and sacked the village. Novikov himself was beaten and robbed. . . . We judged it possible that the Commander-in-Chief might be unaware of the appearance of the enemy in that quarter, so I hurried to Vistitsky with this information and found Headquarters at Fili, which is six versts from Moscow.

My commander, General Vistitsky, ordered me to report this matter personally to the Commander-in-Chief. I went to Kutuzov, who was sitting in an armchair in the centre of the room, surrounded by the corps commanders. I suppose they were holding the council of war at which the surrender of Moscow was under consideration. They were all talking; Kutuzov alone was silent. When I reported to him, he only replied 'Very good', and I returned. Clearly he already knew the direction in which the French detachment had advanced. Back in Moscow it was being rumoured that the city would be defended, and the digging of trenches for a fortified camp had begun.

. . . Save for an inconsiderable part of the common people,

nobody remained in the city. Almost all the nobility had left. Carriages appearing on the streets now were stoned by the populace. Rostopchin's aim was to burn the capital, in order to deny to the enemy the stocks of food which were to be found in the houses. As the surest way of attaining this end, the fire-hoses had been removed from Moscow.

On 14 September our troops made a detour round the city across the Sparrow Hills. Miloradovich[1] had remained in the rearguard with orders to conclude a twenty-four-hour truce with the enemy, so as to have time to evacuate the wounded. The truce was arranged, but the hospitals contained some twenty-five thousand sick and wounded, some of whom were burnt to death in the general conflagration. In Moscow there also remained many officers who had called in at their homes. Some of them, not anticipating so swift an appearance of the enemy, were taken prisoner. One such officer was Second-Lieutenant Vasili Perovsky of the Quartermaster's corps. At the moment of capture he was removing muskets from Count Razumovsky's family arsenal and throwing them down a well. The French suddenly caught him while he was thus engaged, and sent him off to France with the other prisoners.

I would also have been taken prisoner, had it not been for our comrade Lukash galloping up to our house with the news that the enemy was already at the Dorogomilov Gate. I hurried with him to the gate to assure myself of the fact, and hearing French drums I galloped home, gave orders for a cart to be got ready, and then set out to leave the city. I drove towards the gate through which our rearguard had passed and caught up with the army. I believe the gate in question was the Vladimir. . . .

We were quite unable to get used to the idea that we were abandoning Moscow to the enemy, who would be master and give orders in our ancient sanctuary.

[1] Mikhail Miloradovich (*c.* 1770–1825) had fought against the Turks and Poles, then served under Suvorov's command in Italy in 1799, and later in the Austerlitz campaign.

General Bennigsen, who had strongly opposed the Fili decision to evacuate Moscow, describes what ensued.

At eleven o'clock that evening [13 September] our artillery began to move through the town, and at three in the morning the infantry columns set off. Outside the town there was still a crowd of vehicles of all kinds, and first the guns and then the troops prevented these from passing. Imagine the difficulties attending this march across a town about six miles wide, with many narrow streets — a town which nearly all the inhabitants had left or were in the process of abandoning, where the doors of the cellars, especially those of taverns, had been left open or were broken into by soldiers, servants, carters, hauliers, and by the lowest classes of the population, and where the least damage to a team of horses stopped the entire column in the street! The best and strictest precautions would certainly not have been enough to prevent disorders of all sorts in such a retreat. And what might it not have cost us but for the presence of mind of General Miloradovich, who commanded the rearguard and who, under enemy pressure, soon saw himself obliged to enter Moscow, where the streets were blocked by artillery, troops, waggons and horses, carts laden with provisions, hauliers and drunkards stretched out in front of the cellars, while enemy soldiers under the King of Naples's command on the one hand and, on the other, the Viceroy of Italy's advance-guard on the road from Ruza,[1] were entering the town almost at the same time as the last troops of our rearguard.

In these critical and difficult circumstances, which could have cost our army very dear, General Miloradovich thought up an expedient which saved us in large measure from the losses threatening us. He sent a flag of truce to the King of Naples and proposed an armistice lasting several hours, so that he would have time to evacuate and surrender the town, adding that if the King of Naples did not agree, then he would make him pay dearly for the possession of Moscow and would not let him enter except over corpses and ashes. The enemy, who was anxious to preserve this great town and who was unaware that he would find there nothing but empty houses, except for the huts of the poorest inhabitants, consented without making difficulties. Both sides agreed not to

[1] A town about fifty miles west of Moscow.

engage in hostilities for several hours, to give us time to evacuate the town.

A. A. Shcherbinin (1791–1876), a young officer in the Quartermaster's department, throws more light upon Miloradovich and his rearguard.

Miloradovich reached the head of the column when it was approaching the Kremlin. At that moment Nashchokin returned with the news that the King of Naples had accepted the proposal and halted the advance. Miloradovich then went ahead of the infantry and rode with his suite to the Dorogomilov Gate, at a distance of seven versts from which he ordered the rearguard to halt for the night. Riding through the Kremlin we saw two battalions of the Moscow garrison leaving with band playing. Miloradovich addressed the garrison commander, Lieutenant-General Brozin, as follows: 'What blackguard gave you orders that the band should play?' Brozin replied that when a garrison left a fortress on capitulation the band should play. 'It is thus laid down in the regulations of Peter the Great.'

'But where in the regulations of Peter the Great,' retorted Miloradovich, 'does it say anything about the surrender of Moscow?'

Eugen von Württemberg affords us a brief portrait of General Mikhail Miloradovich.

He was a rare military phenomenon. He was a knight in the strictest sense of the word, unsurpassed in bravery. His calm indifference to danger was immense and so astounding that one hesitated to believe one's eyes and ears. His wit remained unquenchable under the heaviest fire and even in the face of imminent death he could draw an involuntary smile from his audience. He never got angry or punished except with biting satire, he never lost his self-control in the worst tumult and in moments of general confusion, and laughed heartily on such occasions at his own misfortune. His orders of the day in 1812 were sometimes incomprehensible in their originality. One seldom knew where he had established his headquarters, but one was certain to see him gallop up at the first cannon-shot. Even then his usual friendly greeting would be followed by an assurance to the commander on the spot: 'Act as you think best, and look on me solely as your guest.'

Prince Nicholas Boris-Galitsin had been hit on the head during the battle of Borodino and, feeling in need of a rest, had set off for Moscow, where he arrived on 12 September.

How different this great and imposing capital already was from what it had been earlier! The streets, formerly so busy, were now all but deserted. The traffic had almost entirely stopped, the nobles and a majority of the inhabitants having moved out to the provinces. The few people one met in the streets looked more like souls in torment who appeared to have a presentiment of some great catastrophe. One had only to appear in military uniform to be accosted on all sides, questioned about events, the battle of Borodino, or the likelihood of a battle at the gates of Moscow. To all these questions I was hard put to find answers; nevertheless I took it upon myself to calm those who asked me whether they should hurry up and flee from the city, by assuring them that as it seemed impossible that Moscow could be given up without the armies coming to grips again, there would be time to decide about leaving when the guns began rumbling. I admit that on this point I was under a complete delusion, fortified as I was by my knowledge of the order which had been issued to take the offensive on the morrow of Borodino. I could not conceive for a moment that Moscow would be sacrificed without firing a shot in its defence. This feeling I shared with all the members of the Army who, like me, did not know the outcome of the council of war held near Moscow, at Fili.

Next day, 13 September, was a Sunday, and I went to the Kremlin, to the Cathedral of the Assumption. This was to be the last time Archbishop Augustin would celebrate the holy office there. But who could have foreseen that? The church was full. I can truthfully say that I have never attended a divine service at which every heart seemed to be so universally disposed to pray or where a more religious spirit prevailed. The truth is that misfortune teaches us to pray. The memory of this service, all sincerity and genuine fervour, will never leave me. The pontiff himself officiated with the most touching sincerity, and at the moment when, raising his eyes to Heaven, he pronounced in a voice filled with emotion the words: 'Lift up our hearts and give thanks unto the Lord,' the eyes of all present filled with tears and turned spontaneously towards the only consolation of the afflicted. . . .

On 14 September, a day to be remembered by Moscow for ever, I rose early, mounted a horse, and rode quickly towards the Smolensk barrier to try to discover what had been decided. I was burning to take part in the battle which I assumed to be imminent. I had still not gone through the barrier when I caught sight of General Kutuzov from a distance; he was preparing to enter Moscow, escorted by his numerous staff. Here was a most favourable opportunity for me to set at rest all my uncertainties, so I attached myself to his suite.

We rode across Moscow in a melancholy silence, nobody expressing what was in his thoughts, and each apparently absorbed in sombre reflections. The solemnity of this silent march, of which no one except the Commander-in-Chief knew either the destination or the duration, had something sinister about it as we passed through these streets, usually so thronged, now all but empty. Here and there we encountered a few groups of inhabitants whose faces bore signs of anxiety and apprehension, and who received no replies to the urgent questions some of them addressed to us. Eventually, after riding for more than three hours through Moscow's tortuous streets, we spotted in the distance the posts of a barrier. 'But whichever barrier is that?' we asked in an undertone. 'It must be the Kolomna barrier.' 'Where are they leading us to?' 'God knows!' Such were the questions and exclamations which broke the gloomy silence which had presided over this march, so impressive in its mystery amid the dangers threatening the capital. Here we found the Governor, Count Rostopchin, whose impassive face gave nothing away. He seemed to be expecting the Commander-in-Chief, and after exchanging a few words with him in undertones, he returned into the city, and we . . . we abandoned it. And from this moment we realized the sad truth: Moscow was going to be surrendered to the enemy without a defence.

Baron Woldemar von Löwenstern adds further first-hand impressions of how Moscow was abandoned.

General Barclay remained in the saddle for eighteen hours and had all the parks and waggon-trains file past him in the street. The columns of infantry and cavalry went by one by one without a break.

General Barclay stationed his aides-de-camp in the various districts of Moscow to see that order was maintained. I was posted by the Pachkov mansion. We each had a Cossack escort to turn soldiers out of the cabarets and prevent them entering houses. Any who in contravention of these orders were found with bottles of brandy or liqueurs were arrested on the spot and the bottles broken. In this way the fruits of their disobedience were destroyed. They were punished on the spot.

It was by such exhausting yet vital measures that General Barclay managed to save the Army from inevitable destruction and got it out of Moscow in the best possible order.

General Miloradovich fought while awaiting the French advance-guard. By his presence of mind and personal bravery he covered himself with glory, and he saved part of the Army by arranging an armistice with General Sébastiani and the King of Naples, who, delighted at being able to occupy Moscow without bloodshed, granted General Miloradovich more than he had asked for. And so one had the curious spectacle of friends and enemies mingling higgledy-piggledy in this huge town. This agreement, for which all the credit goes to General Miloradovich, made possible the evacuation of Moscow without loss, except for dangerously wounded men who had to be left behind in the hospitals. . . .

As soon as he was outside Moscow, General Barclay and his suite halted for an hour to allow us and our horses to rest and also to be more on hand to find out what our rearguard was doing.[1] Once this force had finally evacuated the town, we continued on

[1] Wolzogen, on Barclay's staff, writes: 'Some distance from the Kolomna road we spotted a crowd of vehicles escorted by soldiers, and as the convoy approached I noticed that it comprised the fire-engines from Moscow. I thought this most extraordinary, and asked Rostopchin, who had joined us, why he had brought them. He replied that he had good reasons. "However," he went on, "I have brought for myself only the horse I am riding and the clothes I stand up in!"'

our way and that night reached Prince Kutuzov's headquarters. We found him fast asleep at Panki on the Ryazan road.

It would be difficult, indeed wellnigh impossible, to describe our feelings after Moscow was abandoned, because interests and points of view differed so sharply.

Whereas one man grieved over the loss of his house, another regretted the loss of homes belonging to his parents or friends, while others — and they were the majority — were preoccupied with the humiliation at seeing this ancient capital occupied by foreigners. But quite spontaneously everyone forgot his personal concerns and thought only of the affront the enemy had just inflicted on us, and, far from being disheartened, we felt more passionately determined than ever to continue the war and to make every conceivable sacrifice. One felt as if a burden had been lifted. After the capture of Moscow we had the Empire to save, not just a town; and from this moment everybody said: '*The war is only just beginning!*'

Early on 14 September Count Rostopchin and his son Sergei rode out of Moscow, and that evening reached Headquarters. Rostopchin wrote to his wife Catherine:

Kutuzov deceived me when he said he would fight.[1] I have done a day's march with what we are pleased to call an army. To give you some idea of the disorder that prevails: for thirty-six hours nothing but equipages filed by three abreast. The Tsar, who does not allow officers to have horses, is unaware that there are sixty thousand in the Army. The troops are worn out, even ill with exhaustion. They say: 'We shall end up by retreating as far as Siberia, and our Tsar wants us to leave the country to the enemy so that he can proclaim liberty there — something he himself wants to do but does not dare.' Kutuzov's aides-de-camp declare that it is shameful to wear uniform after abandoning Moscow in such a cowardly fashion. Our soldiers go pillaging under the very noses of the generals. Indeed, yesterday I saw them break down

[1] That morning Kutuzov had told Rostopchin: 'I can assure you that I shall not leave Moscow without giving battle.' Rostopchin said to his sixteen-year-old son, who had fought at Borodino: 'Salute Moscow for the last time. Within an hour it will be in flames.'

the door of a house and remove all the contents. In this neighbourhood every village is devastated by night, and I believe the inhabitants are less afraid of the enemy than of their own protectors. In fact, in my view everything is done for. Kutuzov is an obstinate old woman. Tomorrow he is going to move along the Vladimir road without knowing why.

Sergei Glinka (1776–1847), serving in a militia regiment, watched the Army leave Moscow.

Outside the gate Kutuzov was sitting in a droshky, buried in deep thought. Colonel Toll drove up to the Russian general and reported that the French had entered Moscow. 'God be praised,' answered Kutuzov. 'That is their last triumph.'

Slowly the regiments marched past their commander. How the faces of the Russian soldiers had changed between morning and evening! In the evening anger and grief burned in their eyes, their mouths uttered loud cries of 'Where are we being led?' 'Where has he brought us?' His right hand resting on his knee, Kutuzov sat motionless, as though seeing nothing, hearing nothing, and pondering the announcement: 'The loss of Moscow is not the loss of the motherland.'

Meanwhile the evening twilight thickened, gloomy over orphaned Moscow; and beyond the city the passage of the soldiers, the crowded masses of the populace, and the serried carriages and carts had caused the dust to rise in pillars and hide the dying rays of the setting sun over Moscow. Suddenly there was a crash like thunder and a flame shot up. This was the explosion, near the Simonov Monastery, of a boat carrying Army stores; the flames were carried from a wine shop which had caught fire on the other side of the Moskva River. Quickly our soldiers turned to look at Moscow and exclaimed sadly: 'Mother Moscow is burning.' Overcome by a heavy and deathly grief I threw myself to the ground and my hot tears mingled with dust.

General Yermolov held strong views about these events.

I observed very carefully the effect which the abandonment of Moscow had produced on the troops, and contrary to expectation I noticed that the private soldier had not lost heart and was by no means disposed to grumble, whereas chagrin was evident in the commanders and the loss of the ancient capital had dumbfounded them. Already there were very few inhabitants left in Moscow, and those who remained were the poorest, who had nowhere to seek refuge. The houses were empty and shut up; the vast squares resembled steppes, and in some streets one did not meet a single soul.

In accordance with previous orders, all sick and wounded had been sent beyond Moscow, and before danger threatened the city the unpleasing spectacle of some thousands of suffering men had been diverted from it. In the town of Gzatsk Kutuzov changed my orders concerning the sick and wounded and dispatched officers in all directions with orders to bring them into Moscow; there were some twenty-six thousand of them. On the last night I sent word to the commandant to announce that we were abandoning Moscow and that all able-bodied men should leave. There were no vehicles in which to evacuate them. The Government, which had not been warned, had no means of transport whatever for the purpose, and the consequence of this ill-advised order by Kutuzov was that no less than ten thousand remained in Moscow.

The impression this produced on the Army had to be seen to be believed.

Lieutenant von Wedel describes his first sight of the Russian city spread out below him.

'*Moscou! Moscou!*' was shouted in the ranks. Is that really Moscow? Yes, it is: the longed-for Moscow. A thousand voices rejoiced in the ranks. We have reached our goal. The war is coming to an end. The promised winter quarters lie before us.

All difficulties, shortages, pains were forgotten. We, who had fought bravely day after day under Murat's eyes, we, whose numbers had dwindled to half, we would stay in Moscow under Murat's care. The troops behind us who had suffered little from the war (or so we believed) would be cantoned in the neighbouring country. Rewards now awaited us from the Emperor, in accordance with our efforts and the dangers we had been through. Promotions awaited us, and many of them surely, because there were so many vacancies. Happiness and plenty would now accrue from trials and shortages.

That was how our thoughts ran, how we talked among ourselves as we gazed at the huge town with its golden towers, its roofs painted in red and black, with its palaces and more modest houses and the large green parks inside the town, which bears no resemblance to our towns and has a wholly oriental character.

Suddenly an orderly officer of the Emperor galloped past, and immediately afterwards the order rang out: 'Column, halt!' Then the Imperial Guard *en grande tenue* went by as if to a parade. 'There is the Guard who have not fought once throughout the campaign! They are going to show off in Moscow. As for us riff-raff, we shall not even be allowed to stick our nose inside! It's a disgrace, a scandal!' shouted the officers one to another. With suppressed rage we watched this splendid, envied, favoured Guard go past, and already our fine fantasies began to melt away.

From the top of the Sparrow Hills, on which we had halted, we could see on the plain beyond Moscow a long black column, and with telescopes we made out masses of people on foot, on horseback, or in vehicles who were leaving the town. No chimney smoked. Could the inhabitants have fled? Is it possible for 400,000 inhabitants[1] to leave their homes just as a few hundreds quit their village?

While we were looking at Moscow like this, stirred by a variety of emotions, a strong force of Cossacks appeared away to our left. '*Tête de colonne à gauche! Marche! Adieu Moscou!*' The Cossacks rode through the Moskva, we followed them over the river, and soon they had gone out of sight.

We established a bivouac close to one of the suburbs, on a hill by the main St. Petersburg road. This time the camp had a particular animation; everyone was excited by the nearness of the town, by hopes of peace, by annoyance over the supposed slight by the Guard, who were regarded as mere parade-ground troops.

[1] The population of Moscow was around 250,000.

One of those most reluctant to believe that the French had arrived in Moscow was the husband of Elena Pokhorsky. He was deacon of a small church, and though taciturn by nature, enjoyed composing sermons. He had complete faith in his God, his Tsar, and in the Governor of Moscow. His wife Elena relates:

One day I was sitting at my window and knitting a stocking. Suddenly the sacristan's wife ran up. 'Mother,' she said, 'the street boys are saying that Bonaparte has reached the Dorogomilov and Kaluga barriers.' I dropped my knitting and started shouting: 'Dmitri Vlasich, do you hear?' My husband was seated in the next room, writing. Hearing my shouts, he asked: 'Whatever is going on?' 'Bonaparte has arrived,' I replied. 'The sacristan's wife says so.' He burst out laughing. 'What a fool of a woman you are! You believe the sacristan's wife and you will not believe the Governor. Here is the Count's poster.[1] I have read it to you, haven't I? Well then. You would do better to prepare the samovar. Meanwhile, leave me in peace. I am writing my sermon.'

I served dinner. Suddenly we heard shouts in the street. The deacon went to the window and looked out. Then he put his cup of tea down on the table, and I noticed that his hands were shaking. He was as pale as if his face had been coated with flour. I said: 'My good man, what is the matter?' His tongue seemed to be stuck to his palate. He could only mutter: 'The French!' and then sat down. I gave him some water to drink and began telling him that one must never despair, that God is merciful. He said nothing. Bit by bit he regained his composure, and colour returned to his face. Then he stood up, seized Rostopchin's poster, tore it to shreds, went back to the window, and stayed there without moving, just as if he were dead. As for me, I was so frightened that I did not dare speak to him.

[1] Rostopchin had, in good faith, issued a proclamation that Moscow would be defended.

A middle-aged French resident in Moscow, François-Joseph d'Ysarn de Villefort, was one of many who expected the Russian Army to offer battle again close to the city, but when it became clear that this was not to be the case, he decided to await 'the catastrophe'.

Above all I owed it to my creditors to protect to the last moment the house I had given over to them as security on the loan. Painful experience had taught me too often that the man who abandons the game loses it. This was not the moment to listen to one's fears or to consult one's own convenience. My job was to stay — and stay I did.

I spent 13 September doing various errands on foot in the German quarter, and I came home in the evening absolutely exhausted, but determined to go out early next morning to get news of the approach of the French. I left my house at eight o'clock in the morning and soon saw the crowd of people making their departure. Carriages, droshkys, carts, horse-drawn vehicles of all kinds, and people on foot carrying their loads went by in a constant procession. I saw poor women of the people crushed with the weight of burdens far beyond their strength, carrying off even the smallest pieces of furniture in their homes, and followed by their crying children who wailed in despair. In fact, it was a wholesale emigration. This concourse of departures lasted from eight in the morning until about midday, and as for various reasons the streets were becoming rather unsafe, everyone kept indoors and awaited the future with apprehension.

We knew that Prince Kutuzov had gone through the town at nine o'clock that morning, followed by some troops, but this was not the army. The silence which succeeded the morning's turmoil gave us leisure in which to estimate our probable chances. We awaited the passage of troops or the beginning of hostilities. From my windows I could see a few Cossacks moving along the ramparts, and after them other troops who rode quietly by at a walk.

Eventually our heightened attention was arrested by a fanfare of trumpets and we looked more closely at these troops. They were French! What a moment of consternation!

A postal official named Andrei Karfachevsky wrote in a letter:

A few days before the enemy entered Moscow the people were confident that this capital would never be taken. However, having a presentiment of something, they lost heart and left it; but in spite of this, more than twenty thousand inhabitants were to be found who, either for want of the means to leave the city or out of love for their country, remained to defend the capital city and their families. On 13 September there were already less people on the streets than previously: only wounded soldiers who had been in the fighting at Borodino were walking about, smashing up taverns and shops in the markets.

At the news that the enemy was to be fought in front of the walls of Moscow, those inhabitants who had remained behind were preparing for the battle; but on Monday the 14th, in the morning, the city police moves out, together with the officials and the fire-hoses; guns were being transported through the city and numerous Russian troops were moving at a rapid pace, coming from the Tver Gate and making for the Rogozhskoe Gate. In the afternoon the wounded soldiers were given orders to take the Kolomna road; and in the meantime muskets and swords had been distributed to the people from the Arsenal.

At that time shots were audible close to Moscow. All believed the battle had begun and, praying God to grant victory, hastened with their arms to the aid of their countrymen. Suddenly, however, there appeared in the Kremlin itself troops who ordered the running populace to throw away their weapons and say *pardon.* Anyone who resisted or who did not understand their language was stabbed and cut down mercilessly. It was then they guessed that this was our enemy, and all in fear and trembling ran for their lives, crying: 'The French are in Moscow.'

One of the first officers into Moscow was Count Roman Soltyk, who went on ahead as soon as Marshal Murat had passed the barrier in order to obtain important information for Napoleon.

I first went along a fairly wide street which extends across the Smolensk district and has houses built of wood yet plastered over and then painted yellow. This gives the wood the appearance of stone. I found all the doors and even the window shutters closed. Nobody was out in the streets. Everything was deserted and silent and I came to believe that all the inhabitants had taken refuge in the side streets, so I went off to the left in search of them. I had hardly gone a few hundred yards when I heard someone call to me in Polish from a first-floor window. I stopped, and soon discovered that this house contained several hostages (rich landowners in White Russia) whom the Russians had taken and now led behind their army. They were guarded by a detachment of enemy foot-soldiers who had stayed behind and who just then were busy plundering nearby shops and breaking-in casks of brandy.

Such was our confidence then that although alone, I did not hesitate to dismount, and after entrusting my horse to one of the Poles who ran up, I entered the house and soon found myself surrounded by about thirty Russian soldiers who were completely drunk. They did not think of grabbing their muskets which were propped against the walls of ground-floor rooms. True to the respect the Russian troops have for rank, they took off their police helmets on seeing my epaulettes and stood up as best they could, as do soldiers under arms. Their own officer could not have been better received.

The owners of the house, finding themselves delivered from the rapacity of these marauders, hastened to offer me some much-needed food, and the Poles embraced me effusively, thankful to have their freedom restored in so unexpected a manner. However, not wishing to waste any time, I quickly remounted, followed by the hostages who carried the muskets of the soldiers, and by about fifteen Russians whom we had thus disarmed. The remainder had already fled.

This singular anecdote reflects accurately the state of the Russian Army at the time. . . .

We did not delay in rejoining the Emperor, whom we found at the entrance to the Smolensk district. He was standing on the left of the road. A very large-scale map of Moscow was laid out before him on the grass. He studied it closely and then questioned the people who were brought to him from the centre of the city. I had to wait for a favourable moment to speak to him; consequently I was present at everything that took place. All the reports agreed in assuring Napoleon that the majority of the inhabitants had fled from Moscow and that the authorities had also left. Several reports even went so far as to state that the place was deserted. Later I had occasion to convince myself that they were exaggerated, and that when we made our entry more than half the population was still there; but they had shut themselves indoors or taken refuge in the most remote districts.

Be that as it may, no deputation waited on Napoleon, nobody of note came forward, and most of the people brought to the Emperor were foreigners.

That morning of 14 September Napoleon rode up on to the Sparrow Hills and dismounted to gaze down on Moscow. Captain Brandt was among the Emperor's entourage.

We saw him standing on a hillock, scanning the horizon through glasses. Seen from the top of this last hill, Moscow had an oriental or, rather, an enchanted appearance, with its five hundred domes either gilded or painted in the gaudiest colours and standing out here and there above a veritable sea of houses. It was a magnificent sight. Nevertheless, I noticed many anxious expressions among the French officers. There was surprise at seeing no deputation come out. 'They will wait a long time,' said a veteran of our regiment. 'All those Russians will emigrate to Siberia rather than surrender.'

Alexander Ivanovich Herzen was six months old when Napoleon's army occupied Moscow. In after years he wrote novels and political works, was imprisoned and exiled for his revolutionary opinions, and later took refuge in England, where he published a Russian newspaper and various political writings. His memories of 1812 stem from the experiences of his nurse.

'Dear Vera Artamonovna, tell me the story of how the French entered Moscow.' In the evenings I often used to say this as I lay in my little bed, which was screened with linen to prevent me falling out, and snuggled cosily under my quilt.

'What's that? You've heard the story so often already. It's time to go to sleep now. You had better get up rather earlier in the morning instead.' That was the old woman's usual reply, though she enjoyed telling the story quite as much as I enjoyed hearing it.

'Only a very little bit of it, then! Now, what was the first news you had? How did it all begin?'

'Quite simple. You know that your father[1] would always put off doing everything. He dragged out the preparations till it was too late. Everybody advised us to leave as quickly as possible. What was there to wait for? Nobody was left in town. But no! First he had to discuss all the preparations with Pavel Ivanovich.[2] And one of them was invariably late. Still, we eventually had everything packed, and the carriage stood at the door. The men were having breakfast when suddenly our chef ran white-faced into the dining-room and announced that the enemy had already entered by the Dorogomilov Gate. Our hearts missed a beat from sheer fright. All we could say was 'Holy God! Be with us.' We all lost our heads, and while we were still dashing about and wailing, we spotted dragoons wearing strange helmets with long flowing horse-hair plumes galloping through the streets. All the gates were closed, and so it came about that your father had to remain in the town and you with him. Your nurse was breast-feeding you. You were tiny and very weak at the time.'

I laughed proudly and happily, none the less, because I too had taken part in the war.

'At first things were bearable. In the early days only a few soldiers came and went, and indicated by signs that they were thirsty and wanted a drink. If we gave one of them a little glass of schnaps, he would go away and say "Thank you", raising his hand to his shako. But when the fires broke out, there was terrible confusion. Men began to steal and rob, and one horror followed another. At the time we were living in one wing of the Princess's house. It caught fire and so Pavel Petrovich invited us into his stone-built house which stood deep in a courtyard and was surrounded by thick walls. So we moved, masters and servants all together without any distinction.

'When we came to the Tver Boulevard we saw that even the trees were on fire. At last we reached Pavel Petrovich's house, but when we approached we saw that flames were licking out of every window. Pavel Petrovich was horror-struck and unwilling to

[1] Herzen was the natural son of Ivan Yakovlev, a Knight of Malta, a courtier of Catherine the Great, and a close friend of the Grand Duke Constantine.

[2] Pavel Ivanovich Golochvastov was the husband of Herzen's aunt.

believe his eyes. Now you know that behind the house there is a large garden: well, we wanted to take refuge there, but we had scarcely sat down on a seat, feeling very depressed, when a party of drunken soldiers came up. One of them accosted Pavel Petrovich and tried to take his travelling-fur, but the old man resisted, so the soldier drew his bayonet and caught him a blow right across the face: he carried the scar for the rest of his days. Another soldier snatched you from your nurse's arms and unfastened your napkins to see whether any banknotes or jewels had been hidden there, but on finding none he deliberately tore the napkins and threw them away. . . .

'Dead tired and having had nothing to eat, we sheltered in a house which had been spared by the flames and lay down to rest a little. But within half an hour people ran in shouting "Get out! Get out! Fire! Fire!" I was so frightened I tore the covering off the billiard-table and wrapped you in that as protection against the cold night wind. We arrived in the Tver Square, and here the French were busy putting out fires because their commander had taken up his abode in the Governor's house. We sat in the middle of the street which was full of mounted *gendarmes* and policemen. It was dreadful. Your nurse's milk had stopped, and you were extremely fidgety and crying as hard as you could.

'None of us had even a piece of bread. We had with us at the time a maid named Natalya Konstantinovna who was mad. When she noticed a few soldiers eating in one corner, she took you in her arms and went across to them and said, pointing at you, "Give the little one something to eat". At first the men gave her hostile looks and shouted "*Allez! Allez!*" But she was not to be intimidated and kept on at them, loading them with curses and reproaches. The soldiers did not understand a word and roared with laughter, but eventually they produced some soaked bread for you and a crust for herself.'

Captain Fritz ——, a German in the Elisabethgrad Hussars who had been wounded at Borodino, left Moscow on 14 September.

It was not until late in the evening that we arrived with our two heavily laden carts in Ryazan, where we bivouacked in open fields. I had already spent many hundreds of nights bivouacked among soldiers, but never among fleeing townspeople, crying children, and complaining women, and so I witnessed and heard many things that night which were rather strange to me. I infinitely prefer a bivouac with hussars to one full of refugees from a large town, although we were not short of food and I found a comfortable billet for the night in my cart.

On the 15th we continued on our way, because my hospitable host had decided to flee to Tula,[1] where his wife's father owned a large business. He and his good wife very kindly offered to take me with them and assured me that I should receive a very warm welcome from their relatives. As my wound was such that I could not possibly think of rejoining the army for a month to six weeks, and having nowhere else to turn, because to travel to my relations in the Ukraine would be too far, I gratefully accepted this unusually friendly offer.

It was during the night of 15–16 September that we first saw an immense glow on the horizon, indicating that a great fire had broken out in Moscow. Although the swarm of refugees had gradually scattered along various roads and into different neighbourhoods, we were still surrounded by many hundreds of people of every age, sex, and rank. When these poor wretches, who had often been able to save only a tiny part of their belongings, saw the fiery glow of their blazing home town in the night sky, they began wailing and complaining. The women in particular showed this by violent outbursts of grief, whereas the men often did no more than clench their fists and swear bitter revenge on these insolent enemies of their motherland on whom they now laid the blame for the downfall of their proud city. The glow was so bright that it almost lit up the road, and we were able to travel almost the whole night through, since sleep was out of the question and we could maintain our horses on full rations of fodder.

On 14 September Baron de Bausset and General Count Philippe de Ségur, with a detachment of gendarmerie d'élite, *were sent to inspect the Kremlin with a view to Napoleon's occupying it.*

We returned there at ten o'clock at night with employees of all the services so as to settle them in and prepare everything for

[1] A hundred miles south of Moscow.

Napoleon's reception. As on all these missions we had been unable to fetch our servants and carriages, Ségur and I were obliged to spend the night fully clothed and stretched out on chairs or armchairs. We selected the room which had been reserved for the Emperor: here the windows had no shutters and no curtains. I emphasize these details because they are connected with what followed. With such uncomfortable beds, I slept fitfully despite the exhausting day. Between midnight and one o'clock I noticed fairly bright glows, though they were some distance away. I went to the windows and saw flames leaping up in whichever direction I looked from the eminence of the Kremlin.

The Kremlin was not a palace. In fact it was merely a citadel on a very high point on the bank of the Moskva. It contains fine buildings, large barracks, a superb arsenal, magnificent churches, and a miserable dwelling for so powerful a sovereign as the autocrat of All the Russias. A light crenellated wall serves as a military defence. A stone bridge built across the river leads to a fortified doorway placed in the corner of a large piece of ground used as a public square and not as the courtyard of a palace. On the left, at the far end of this square, is a great outdoor staircase, devoid of ornament or decoration, very long, very straight. It is called the 'red staircase' and leads to a very ordinary terrace on a level with the apartments reserved for the Tsar's use. These consist of three large drawing-rooms, a state bedroom, and on one side a large hall known as the 'Hall of the Tsars'. The factories, kitchens, and stables are situated below the terrace and the palace. The outside of this palace looks extremely mean and irregular. There is not a nobleman in Moscow who is not better housed than the Tsar.

Captain Louis-Joseph Vionnet,[1] who had campaigned in Italy, Prussia, Poland, and Spain, and was now serving with the Fusilier Grenadiers of the Old Guard, describes Moscow in his memoirs, and after referring to the Kremlin gives an account of the next of the city's four districts — this was Kitaigorod.

The word Kitaigorod means 'Chinese town', because it is in this part of the city that the caravans coming from China unload

[1] He later became Lieutenant-General Vionnet de Maringoné (1769–1834).

their merchandise. China, although very far from Russia, nevertheless borders on this empire. This part of Moscow contains many shops and goods used by Orientals, and it is also where the merchants of all nationalities live.

The third district surrounds the first two and is called Beloigorod, or 'white town'. It owes its name to the fact that most of the houses in the area are built of stone and have been whitewashed.

Lastly, the fourth and outermost district. It forms a huge circle and encloses the other three. It is called Zemlyagorod, or 'earth town', and it is thought that this name was given because, during the wars fought by the Russians in the reign of the Tsar Fedor Ivanovitch,[1] it was surrounded by earth bastions.

The suburbs number thirty. Everywhere one finds immense palaces which could be mistaken for churches. Most of them are decorated with balconies, pillars, balustrades, and other ornaments.

. . . Green is the national colour and the Russians' favourite. The soldiers' uniforms are made of green cloth. The domes of towers and church belfries are usually painted green when they are not gilded. The shutters and doors of fashionable houses are of the same colour. Finally, the figures of saints and the illuminated points which one sees in private houses always have some green ornaments. It appeared to me that the colours used in Russia in the arts and painting are much brighter than ours, and they resemble Chinese colours very closely.

Colonel Jean-François, Baron Boulart, who had fought with the Artillery of the Guard at Jena, Friedland, Madrid, Essling, and Wagram — he was wounded in the last two battles — was sent into Moscow on 15 September.

The fire had not yet reached the great loop formed by the Moskva, between the Kremlin and the entrance by the Mozhaisk road. It was in this district that I placed my guns, on a very large square to the right of the gate and not far away. I billeted my men in nearby houses and I also installed myself in one of them. The

[1] Fedor I (1557–98) was ill, and allowed his brother-in-law, Boris Godunov, to rule in his stead.

house was a fine one, but it had no occupant to do the honours. All was quiet around us, and even this silence had something frightening about it.

. . . The fire was still gaining, and as a strong north wind had got up, its progress became faster, so that during the night it approached the district I was in. Indeed, sparks carried on the wind were dropping near my park. I was extremely worried and never remember spending a more harassing night. No orders reached me, yet it seemed clear that I should eventually be engulfed in the flames, so I decided to go myself to the Kremlin to report matters to General Curial[1] and to ask permission to quit this inferno. While waiting for daybreak, I had hay and straw carried well away from my ammunition waggons. I posted gunners to watch for the fall of sparks, although there was little to fear with waggons as well enclosed as ours were and covered with sheet-metal. I also gave orders that if, while I was away, the fire should threaten our only escape route, the men were to move out of the city.

François-Joseph d'Ysarn de Villefort was posted at a window to watch the progress and route of the conflagration.

At about five o'clock on the Wednesday evening I saw flames cross the town wall from the direction of the Varvarka, one of the largest business streets in the Kitaigorod, and within half an hour the fire had reached the surrounding wall of my house, on the side of the church.

A few neighbours who had been driven from their houses by the fire had taken refuge in my courtyard, and they joined me in knocking down the fence of planks facing the church. The wooden house over the ice cellars caught fire, but I did not care very much, because in my defence plan I had prepared to sacrifice all the outbuildings made of wood in order to save the main part of the building.

Unfortunately the crowd of refugees in my house took fright at seeing the coach-houses on fire, and everybody fled, even the

[1] Philibert-Jean-Baptiste-François, Count Curial (1774–1829), commanded the 3rd Division of the Imperial Guards (*Chasseurs à pied*). Boulart was in charge of his artillery.

occupants, my tenants or actors from the French theatre. From the room I occupied in one of the wings I was busy carrying out whatever I most needed when this defection took place. I was so little aware of it that for a long time I remained in the courtyard lending a hand wherever it was most urgently required. Eventually I went indoors, quite worn out, to see what my tenants were doing. I visited the ground-floor rooms — nobody. I climbed to the first floor — nobody. I felt very upset by this desertion and lost all heart for defending the house against the fire, especially when I noticed that in the attic staircase the rafters were on fire. In a state of distress, I returned to the ground-floor rooms and saw that the flames were attacking a window. There was a remedy in the vaulted rooms, but the furniture would have to be moved, and I was on my own.

I resigned myself to surrendering the house to the flames, but sheer curiosity led me to look into a room beside the front door, and there I found an old man named Monsieur de Trassène, who was infirm and deaf. He said to me: 'Everyone has gone. I stayed here so as to live or die with you.'

This was certainly a fine example of devotion, but how helpful! To get him to safety I hurriedly led him through smoke-filled rooms towards a little staircase near the well. I reckoned on being able to shelter in the cellars on that side. I led the way down, at the risk of being crushed by sheet-iron which was falling from the roofs on all sides. What was my horror when I found the door to the cellar burning! I only had time to climb quickly up again and to take my companion in misfortune back through the same rooms where the smoke left us more air to breathe. Back where we started from, we realized it would be impossible to stay there long. In another direction the heat of the burning buildings in the courtyard made all escape out of the question. What was to be done?

We resigned ourselves to await death bravely. Then Monsieur de Trassène had a good idea and made me remove the cover of the stove in order to find some air to breathe in the mouth of this stove; and in fact we received great relief in this way from the smoke which was choking us. Unfortunately the fire, spreading from the balcony to the front door, reached the door of our room, and the flames were about to scorch us. I sprang to the window, broke it low down, threw a mattress on the sheets of red-hot iron which had fallen from the roof, and having made Monsieur de Trassène promise to follow me, I jumped down and then caught him in my arms. What were we to do in this furnace? I ran towards the front door of the house, but I was barely half-way across the courtyard when Monsieur de Trassène shouted: 'It's impossible!' 'Where can we go, then?' I asked him. 'Into the thermolamp.'[1] 'Let's go.'

We soon reached it, built between the garden and the wooden wing in which I was living. We spent nearly an hour there, between the embrasure of two walls, continually pirouetting on our heels to find air to breathe in one direction or another. Our resources diminished every minute.

Convinced that we could not last long in this position, I wanted to go into the garden in search of shelter, but a blazing hedge put off my companion. I went over it and explored, and soon found that we should be safe there from the flames. So I went quickly back to my companion and despite his apprehensions made him go over the hedge. We lay down on the grass near the pond, surrounded by burning houses and fences. Thanks to God we were saved. Another misfortune: it began to rain. It was four o'clock in the morning, we were soaked to the skin and chilled to the bone. We returned to our thermolamp and spent the rest of the night there.

I was almost blind. My eyes had suffered so much from the smoke that I found it very painful to open them. Only Monsieur de Trassène distracted me from melancholy thoughts by his talk of the imminent danger to which we had been exposed.

'Tell me frankly,' he said, 'do you think we should have run greater risks at the battle of Mozhaisk [Borodino]?'

'Eh? No, certainly not,' I replied. 'You are a hero, especially in your hat torn by fire debris.'

[1] An eighteenth-century apparatus for heating and lighting rooms by means of inflammable gases.

Madame Louise Fusil, the actress, relates that by night she and her friends required no lights, because nearby fires lit up the area until it was as light as at midday. Four more people took refuge in the house, including a wounded officer who advised them to demand a guard. So he, Louise Fusil, and Madame Vandraminy decided to go to the Petrovsky Castle for this purpose.

The day we undertook this journey was a memorable one for me. When we left, our house was intact, and there was not even a suspicion of a fire in any of the nearby streets. Madame Vandraminy's daughter, a girl of thirteen, was with us. She had not yet seen the fires except from a distance. The first she met was at the Red Gate, the oldest in Moscow. We wanted to take the usual route along the boulevard, but it was impossible to get through. Fires blazed everywhere, so we went up the Tverskoe, but there the flames were even fiercer, and the Grand Theatre, where we went next, was nothing but an inferno. A year's timber supply had been stacked against the walls, and the Theatre, built of wood, fed this terrible fire. We turned right, as that seemed less on fire, but when we got half-way along the street the wind drove the flames with such violence that they joined the other side and formed a canopy of fire. This may seem an exaggeration, but it is nevertheless exactly what happened.

We could go neither forward nor sideways, and we had no option but to retrace our steps. However, the fire was gaining every minute, and sparks dropped just by our carriage. The coachman, sitting sideways, held the reins convulsively, and his face, turned towards us, expressed extreme fright. We shouted to him '*Nazad!*' ('Turn back!'). This was difficult, but impelled by fear he managed to summon up enough strength to turn his horses. He set them at a gallop, and we reached the boulevard once more. We took the route back to our district, looking forward to being able to rest our eyes which were sore with dust and the heat of the flames.

I shall never forget my impressions when I saw what awaited us. The house, to which we expected to return peacefully, and where, only an hour before, there had been no sign of a spark, was on fire. This can only just have happened, because the people inside had not yet realized the fact. It was the cries of Madame

Vandraminy's little girl which brought them running. This child had lost her head and was shouting: 'Save mama, save everything. Oh, my God! We are lost!'

[*Madame Fusil remained calm and with the help of some soldiers managed to save a great deal.*]

When I had had everything carried into the garden, I went and sat down beside the portrait of my daughter which I had not wanted to be parted with, and I had time to look at what was going on around me. As I no longer had either a droshky or a carriage, I stood in danger of saving nothing. I quickly made up my mind, bundled up a small parcel of the things I needed most, and placed it on the droshky belonging to one of our companions in misfortune. I made a smaller packet and put this on an officer's droshky which was driven by a soldier named Martinot, an excellent fellow and most obliging. Having done this I put my jewels and money into my handbag and waited quietly for whatever it might please God to ordain. 'Whose boxes are these?' said the officer commanding the district. 'Mine, sir,' I replied. 'Well, madam, are you abandoning them like this?' 'Where do you think I am going to put them? I have no carriage and no horses.' 'Well, to be sure! That officer will take some of them. Clothes are more use to a woman than a mattress is to a man. Besides, we must help one another.'

And so I saw myself half rescued, even though I was going to lose a good deal of furniture and some boxes filled with belongings. Everything else I left, and abandoned my daughter's portrait in the corner of a conservatory. I was in tears, because I foresaw that I should never set eyes on it again. How angry I felt that the portrait was not a miniature!

We left the house and were soon a prey to the soldiers. Nothing was more distressing than to see the women, children, and old men fleeing, just as we were, from their burnt houses. A numerous file of soldiers, on their way to camp, were marching by at the same time and we decided to follow them. After wandering for a long while, we found a street which was no longer burning. We entered the first house — they were all deserted — and threw ourselves down on couches, while the men guarded our horses and droshkies in the courtyard and looked to see that no flames took hold of the house. So ended a sad day which I can never forget.

Major Eugène Labaume records that the 4th Corps left Moscow on 17 September and spent four days at Petrovsky Castle, built in 1775 for Catherine the Great to commemorate a victory over the Turks.

Torrential rain fell, and the small number of houses available near the palace for the great multitude camped there made it very difficult to get any shelter. Consequently men, horses, and vehicles bivouacked out in the fields. The headquarters, installed round the castles in which their respective generals lodged, were established in English gardens, and the staff lived in grottoes, Chinese pavilions, kiosks, or green arbours, while the horses, tethered under acacia or lime trees, were separated off one from another by hedges or flowerbeds. This really picturesque camp was made even more so by the new costumes adopted by the soldiers, most of whom, as protection against the onslaughts of the weather, put on the same clothes which we had seen earlier in Moscow and offered the most intriguing variety in the bazaar. Thus one saw walking about the camp soldiers dressed in Tartar, Cossack, or Chinese style. One wore a Polish cap, another the tall hat of the Persians, Bashkirs, or Kalmucks.[1] In short, our army looked like a carnival, and this is why people said later that our retreat began with a masquerade and finished with a funeral.

Captain Boniface de Castellane was on duty at the Petrovsky Castle on 17 September and noted in his diary:

In the evening the view of burning Moscow presented a fine effect of light. I was sent with General Narbonne[2] to try and save the beautiful Yellow Palace of Catherine from the flames. We arrived there at ten o'clock after being obliged to make long detours, because the fires blocked our path. In the streets we saw

[1] A Mongol-speaking people who migrated from Turkestan to the region of the lower Volga in the seventeenth century.

[2] Count Louis de Narbonne was one of Napoleon's aides-de-camp.

many armed Russian soldiers walking about freely; others, who had been wounded, were trying to get away from the flames. We met a crowd of inhabitants who were taking away their most precious belongings on carts. As our troops were robbing them, we gave them an escort. A great number of these unhappy people were sitting about in groups on the outskirts of the city.

It was impossible to save the Yellow Palace. We removed several pictures, but I do not know what happened to them. We had time to admire the rich furniture.

18th. At daybreak we left after a sleepless night. I went to a new lodging, opposite the house which had been burnt the evening before. This belongs to Count Kamensky, judging by love letters left in his library. As I am unable to make myself understood to the serfs, it is very difficult to discover the owner's name. I spent my morning running around to save a droshky from the flames. I acquired several fur-lined cloaks. If one wants anything one is forced to buy it from a soldier. The troops snatch everything from the fire, and in some way this makes their pillage legitimate. The resources of Moscow were unparalleled. The houses had provisions to last eight months, and quantities of wine. Indeed, all our soldiers get drunk. One sees them in the streets, stretched out round large jam-jars. They have broken the rounded glass at the side, and eat as if out of a mess-tin. Surrounded by a host of bottles, they generously offer wine to passers-by. There is plenty of champagne and birch wine, which is a poor imitation.

Apollon Dmitrievich Sysoyev, a youngster living in Moscow at the time, relates how when the inferno began to rage, his family feared that their home would catch fire.

Grandfather said: 'Let us go to Bozhedomka, it will be safer there.' At Bozhedomka there was a large garden with a high fence — I do not recall to whom it belonged — and we hoped to reach it. . . . And so we left the house empty-handed. There was nothing to take. Grandfather walked ahead with me, Mother was leading Grandmother, and behind them went our woman-servant. We had gone only a few yards from the house when we looked round — our servant was not there. We stopped, and all four of us began calling her, but around us everything was crackling and falling in and the

The Battle of Borodino, from the painting by Baron Louis Lejeune at Versailles

Napoleon on the Heights of Borodino, from the painting by Vasili Vereshchagin

wind was howling so. We waited a short while and then went on our way. Thus we never discovered where our poor Malanya disappeared; whether she had rushed off in another direction or whether she had managed to escape or had perished.

. . . We reached the garden, and found many people sitting there with their possessions piled up — all kinds of things: chests, bundles, baskets, and various vessels. The garden was a large one and everyone was seated in small groups of fifteen to twenty, close to each other. They were sleeping side by side on the grass. . . . They wandered through the kitchen-gardens, ate vegetables, and sometimes found provisions in the cellars, though they rarely ate their fill. . . . From time to time Frenchmen would come up to us, go round everybody, and take anything they came across; and everybody gave away his property, if only to keep his head on his shoulders. You see, they had muskets and swords and we had our bare hands. Then again, on our side, nearly all the people were women, old men, and children, so we had perforce to bear it. However, when one of the French on his own or two of them together looked in on us, we received them in our own way. I recall seeing one dashing young lad going along in search of gain. He did not touch us, but went on and started to take someone else's things. All at once several men set on him and then the fun began: our people shouted and he shouted — begging for mercy. But how could he expect mercy when the people themselves were homeless and starving and were now, on top of everything else, being robbed. I saw them drag the wretched Frenchman off somewhere, and afterwards return without him. 'We finished him off,' they said. 'We strangled him and put him down a well.'

Many a French soldier who went pillaging on his own was attacked, especially if he ventured into a cellar in which the local inhabitants had taken refuge. A shopkeeper named Anna Grigorievna had this to say many years later.

My father stayed in our cellar alone with the women. As ill luck would have it, an enemy soldier forced the door. Over his shoulder he carried a huge cudgel. He brandished it in his left hand and with his right seized my father by the throat. I rushed at the brigand, snatched his cudgel, and caught him by the nape of the neck. He dropped, whereupon everyone fell on him, killed him in an instant, and dragged his body off to the pond. We had thrown quite a few uninvited guests into this pond and two wells. Sometimes four or five of them arrived together. They rummaged all over the place, but we did not move. They could see for themselves that there was nothing to take, and if they took it into their heads to do us harm, we knew how to bring them to reason. Not one of them went out alive. All this sickened me, but the instinct for self-preservation is uppermost. If we had let them go after beating them, you can see that they would have gone away in a fury and returned in a band to exterminate us to the last man. And so we had no pity. To the death!

I remember how one day a merchant named Zarubin came to find us. He had enemy soldiers billeted in his house and they were inquiring whether there was any means of procuring some fish. Zarubin knew that our pond — it belonged to General Kisselev's wife — had some carp in it. He said to my father: 'Is there no way of casting my net into your pond?' 'No need to ask permission,' my father replied. 'The pond does not belong to us. But what are you going to catch in your net, Gregor Nikich? A carp — or a trooper?'

Andrei Karfachevsky, the postal official, lived in the post office and saved the building from being set on fire by paying two hundred roubles to the French guard.

The fires went on for six whole days and nights, so that it was impossible to tell night from day. All that time pillage continued: the French entered houses and, committing gross acts of violence, took from their owners not only money, gold, and silver, but even boots, linen, and — most ludicrous of all — cassocks, women's furs and cloaks, in which they stood on guard and rode on horseback. It was not uncommon for people walking in the street to be stripped to their shirt, and many were robbed of boots, overcoats, frock-coats. Anybody who resisted was beaten savagely, often to death; and in particular many priests of the churches here endured severe tortures at the hands of the French seeking to extract from them information on where their church treasure was hidden. The French seized merchants and peasants, judging from their beards alone that they were priests. In short, their treatment of the inhabitants was most inhuman, and they made no distinction: any man they came across, whether official or peasant, they put to work. They made him carry sacks of stolen property and barrels of wine, dig potatoes in the vegetable gardens and then peel them, chop cabbage and drag from the streets the bodies of men and horses. . . .

After pillaging churches they stabled horses, slaughtered cattle, and lodged wounded soldiers there; and having stripped the sacred ikons of their frames they bayoneted them and poured filth on them; they also committed other abominations which the tongue cannot mention. In the houses of merchants and gentlemen property which had been placed in store-rooms and basements and cleverly walled up with bricks so that it was quite impossible to perceive that there was a hole was discovered by the French. Not even property buried in the ground escaped discovery; under vegetable gardens and courtyards they prodded the ground and pulled out chests.

An officer from Württemberg, possibly Captain von Kurz, spent days wandering about Moscow.

Many inhabitants who had fled to the woods believed, when they saw the fires die down, that they had nothing more to fear, and returned with their families. Some wanted to visit their churches and kneel down before the altars, but they found to their horror that these had been desecrated and turned into stables. Others searched for their homes and found ashes instead. The public walks in the city presented a terrible spectacle. At every step one trod on dead and scorched people, and the corpses of incendiaries hung from many half-burnt trees. Amid all this horror one could see the wretched inhabitants, who had come back and had no roof over their heads, collecting iron or lead which had once covered the roofs of palaces. They did this so as to build huts in the numerous gardens, and they stilled their pangs of hunger with raw vegetables which our soldiers had overlooked.

Besides the poorest class of Moscow's inhabitants, there remained behind a large number of prostitutes, because this class of person alone believed it could derive benefit from the downfall and plundering of the city.

Many took up these creatures, who then became housekeepers in houses which had been spared by the flames. Among them were girls who deserved respect and sympathy on account of their upbringing and, in particular, their misfortune. Hunger and want drove them to offer themselves.

Captain Vionnet also comments on the large number of prostitutes who had remained behind in Moscow.

They included some honest women who were nearly dying of hunger and obliged to surrender themselves at discretion to the first comers. As a result, one saw nobody except these creatures in every house which was still upright. They had installed themselves as if they owned the houses; they took possession of the ladies' adornments; and they accepted as presents, in payment for their favours — often very bitter ones — rich dresses which the army had pillaged, and silver bullion. This contrasted sharply with their figures, their manners, and their clothes. On my walks I often came across old men who were in tears at seeing this appalling disorder.

Friedrich Klinkhardt, a Westphalian bandmaster, paid his first visit to Moscow at the beginning of October, when he joined a detachment under orders to fetch provisions for the 8th Corps.

As we went through the city we found all the streets full of French soldiers, who had lit huge watch-fires by their muskets piled in pyramid formation. A regular camp life had developed. The streets and alleys were a mixture of splendid stone-built palaces, wooden houses, and thatched huts, and along every lane and alley blew dense smoke from the camp fires, so that it was seldom possible to get a view. We were sent from one duty picket to the next and nobody seemed to know what was what. Eventually I felt hungry, and turned to the commander of one picket and asked him to produce something to eat for me and my weary companions. Our request was granted in the most amiable fashion, and we received bread, meat, Dutch cheese, and wine in plenty. The copious meal and excellent wine worked wonders for our morale, and once again we felt proud to be soldiers of Napoleon's victorious army. The French regiments greeted us in a very friendly way and often called to us: '*Vive la bonne armée de Westphalie! Vive le roi Jérôme Napoléon!*' Furthermore, disorder reigned such as I had never seen before. Here a soldier was holding forth to a circle of attentive listeners; there an affair of honour was being fought out. Now a band played tunes, now one saw senior officers strolling arm in arm down the streets. Cheerful faces looked from palace windows, and some pretty women even nodded to us. Everything was full of life and bustle. We saw little of the hardships of war until we reached the foot of the Kremlin and saw quite a different scene. Large wide streets had been burnt to the ground. Wherever we walked we saw smoking ruins in which every gust of wind fanned a bright flame. Choking smoke blew in from all directions, and once again we were shocked to see the horrors of war.

Colonel de Fezensac rode through the ruins of Moscow for the first time at the head of the 4th Regiment of the Line.

The sight was at once horrible and bizarre. Some houses appeared to have been levelled to the ground, others still retained a few pieces of smoke-blackened wall. Rubble of all sorts cluttered up the streets. A fearful smell of burnt matter came from all sides. From time to time a cottage, a church, a palace stood out amid this great disaster. The churches in particular, by their multicoloured domes, by the richness and variety of their architecture, recalled Moscow's former opulence. Most of the inhabitants, driven by our soldiers from the houses which had been spared by the flames, had taken refuge in the churches. These wretched people, wandering like phantoms in the ruins, and dressed in rags, had recourse to the most melancholy expedients for prolonging their miserable existence. Now they chewed a few vegetables still to be found in gardens, now they tore strips of flesh from animals dead in the street. One even saw some people diving into the river and bringing up wheat which the Russians had dumped there and which was fermenting. During our march the thud of the drums, the sound of martial music added an even sadder note to this spectacle, recalling as they did the idea of a triumph amid a scene of destruction, misery, and death.

On 30 September Colonel François Parguez, aide-de-camp to General Count Morand, wrote to his wife Julie, living near the Tuileries in Paris. His letter was intercepted by the Russians.

It is a very ugly thing to see a large town burnt down. Picture to yourself Paris ravaged by fire, all the houses without a roof, door, or window, full of smoking debris, a few houses preserved and apparently intact, like the Cité or the Île Saint-Louis; you will see Moscow in deep mourning. . . . In general the big houses were roofed in iron and built of bricks, and very well at that. Few of the houses have two storeys, and that is why the town stretches such a long way.

Plundering by the rabble and the soldiers has been at its peak. People live off what they can retrieve from cellars that have not fallen in, and they live badly. All the wine has been drunk or destroyed. I ask for it from everybody I meet, but I am a voice crying in the wilderness. Those who have any wine keep it with thoughts of the winter; in a fortnight we shall be using sledges. There is no shortage of sugar and coffee. We have procured three cows, and the three of us drink down a strong bowl of coffee every morning. . . . You will see that we are not so badly off, but that things get steadily worse, and beware of the winter which starts well here. Rain, wind, snow, and frost — so much for the mild temperature in Moscow today. So that my bones shall not freeze this winter, I have prowled around among the troops and managed to buy, at not too unreasonable a price, a warm fur which I shall use to line my old greatcoat throughout. I had a soldier make me a pair of bearskin boots, with the fur inside, and I shall find a way of protecting my nose — yes, laugh! — protecting my nose.

A Muscovite named Sokolsky wrote a letter in particularly bitter terms about the conduct of the French soldiers, many of whom he thought brutal and cowardly.

The coarseness of the lower ranks was indescribable. There was no discipline, no respect whatever for their commanders. . . . The Germans too are stupid, but you will not find such ignoramuses, such barbarians, such slovenly brutes as these Frenchmen. . . . Their officers did not disdain to knead their loaves in the same trough in which a private soldier had just washed his underclothes, although the Russians had assured them that the trough was polluted.

If you ask about their cleanliness and elegance, I saw some who had not washed their ugly faces since their very departure from Paris. And what their allies — Germans, Italians, and Poles — have to suffer from them is impossible to describe. Us they called 'barbarians, devils', but their allies 'damned dogs'; and they teased and abused them exactly like dogs. The wretched allies, in fear of sabre or whip, looked round with trepidation as they dragged themselves along. Germans and Poles received neither forage, nor bread, nor meat, nor wine, and the most well-to-do of the Italians had to pay a thaler a day each to the Emperor. In general our Moscow visitors lived in such harmony that if a private soldier of Number 2 Company stole a scoop of flour from an officer in Number 1 Company, then the latter, if he caught the private, would break his back with a blow from his sword. That happened in our street.

In convents the older nuns trembled for the virtue of their young sisters, but these, torn between fear and curiosity, did not make things any easier by climbing on to roof-tops to catch a glimpse of uniforms and epaulettes or else pressing against the windows of cells in which they had been shut. Many years later a certain Antonina, who had been a novice in 1812, recalled her experiences.

We had all been crammed into the same room, and through the little windows we watched three officers walking to and fro with our almoner, our treasurer, and two aged nuns. Then they went to the other side of the church and we lost sight of them. We were overcome with an inordinate desire to see what they were doing, so we decided to go outside and have a look. We opened the door and advanced in single file. One of the old women spotted us and ran up. She was a good sort, but how she grumbled! 'Where are you going?' she cried. 'Get back inside this instant! Ah! You are keen to see the military? What shameless creatures you are! Look how flushed you look, when you ought to be pale with fright!' We replied: 'Not so fast, Axinia Nikitichna! How can we avoid having red cheeks? We are squashed like herrings in a barrel. One can scarcely breathe. If we died, we could not turn pale in here.' But she went on scolding, and shut us up in the cell again.

A number of accounts by Muscovites suggest that the French soldiers behaved a good deal better than did some of their allies from Bavaria and Württemberg. Here is what a shopkeeper named Andrei Alekseev recalled:

The first time they came to my house they examined the room and went straight to the image of the Protectress. They removed her halo and silver fittings. My mother greeted them and begged them to spare the holy ikon, but they only shouted and drew their swords on me when I tried to move them to mercy. As for my poor little sisters, they were so frightened that they ran out and hid in the courtyard. However, these soldiers were not *real* Frenchmen. How good the real Frenchmen were! When any of them came, we at once recognized them from their manners and way of talking. Then we were not afraid, because we knew that they had a conscience. But God preserve us from their allies! We nicknamed these *bezpardonnoe voisko* ('the army without pity'), because they were impervious to prayers or fears. The inhabitants even said that they were proof against bullets and that the Devil protected them. If they did not insult one by deeds, they did so in words. We could not understand what they said, but one was well aware that it was offensive. The French never permitted themselves such gratuitous insults.

Many of Moscow's churches were filled with people who took refuge in these temples of stone which had survived the flames. Napoleon's troops often entered them, not without profanity and sacrilege, as one Russian nun later recounted.

They slept in the sanctuary, they ate off the altar. In the hospital church there was a large ikon representing the appearances of the Mother of God, painted on wood and without fittings. One of our elderly sisters had bought it with her own money and presented it to the church. The French took it from the wall and used it as a table. When the donor saw how they laid their shakos and sabres on her ikon, she began to cry out: '*Bozhi moi! Bozhi moi!* (My God! My God!). What have they done, the pagans!' They heard her, but I do not know whether they understood. What I do know is that they began to mimic her; and thereafter, whenever they saw her, they amused themselves by shouting '*Bozi mo! Bozi mo!*' We were extremely upset to find that they had no respect for our churches, and our almoner said to us: 'How do you expect them to revere churches which have been turned into dwelling-places. If they sin through ignorance, God will forgive them, because they have not profaned the holy relics.'

The Abbé Adrien Surugue (1752–1812), the priest in charge of the Church of Saint-Louis des Français since 1808, was never summoned to meet Napoleon, nor did the Emperor ever visit the French parish. In a letter dated October, the sixty-year-old Abbé wrote to a friend:

During the six weeks the French spent here, I did not even see Napoleon's shadow, nor did I try to see him. I was told that he might send for me: I trembled at the prospect, but avoided it. He did not come to our church; indeed, I doubt whether he gave it a thought. Four or five officers, members of the ancient families of France, did come to services, two or three made their confession. Besides, you will be able to judge the Christianity of this army when I tell you that in a body of 400,000 troops who crossed the Niemen there was not a single chaplain. Nearly 12,000 men died during their stay here, yet I have buried with the ordinary ceremony one officer only and one of General Grouchy's servants. All the others, officers and soldiers alike, have been buried by their equals in the nearest garden. They seem not to believe in a life hereafter. I once visited a room full of wounded officers. They all talked about their physical needs, but not one about his spiritual weaknesses, and yet a third of them had death on their lips. I have baptized the children of a few soldiers: that is the only thing they still insist on; and I have been treated with respect. Otherwise religion is for them an empty word.

Paul de Bourgoing and General Delaborde took up residence in Count Rostopchin's enormous town house in Lubianka Street, with a garden full of kiosks, grottoes, and Greek temples.

I spent hours on end reading in the Count's splendid library. One day, while looking over the shelves of books, I came across a work my father[1] had had published in 1787 under the title *Tableau de l'Espagne moderne*. I wrote on a sheet of paper, which I inserted at the front of the first volume, the following sentence: 'The author's son was very pleased to find one of his father's books so far from his native land. He regrets that war should have brought him to this place.'

Captain Boniface de Castellane wrote in his diary for 27 September:

Snow is falling, but it melts immediately. I am on duty. These days I often go to the ante-room of the Emperor's study and talk to Angel, the usher and former valet to the Duchess de la Vallière. This man has befriended me and willingly talks about His Majesty. Among other things he told me: 'Since we arrived in Moscow the Emperor makes me put two candles by his window every evening, so that the troops exclaim "Look, the Emperor does not sleep by day or at night. He works continuously!"'

Here is something to convince the incredulous people who refuse to believe that Moscow was set on fire by men left behind

[1] Jean-François, Baron de Bourgoing (1748–1811).

deliberately. Monsieur de Longuerue, General Lauriston's[1] aide-de-camp, found some oil of aspic on the back staircases of his house. This train led to a wick which emerged on to the street by a lower window, through holes blown in the double glazing by pistol bullets. Had it not been for this discovery, the stairs would undoubtedly have been set alight as they have been in two other billets.

And on 5 October:

I rode with the Emperor in the most beautiful weather. There is great activity in the service. His Majesty attends to the artillery. He works all night. He sleeps, it is true, for part of the day. We anticipate leaving very soon. There is talk of going to India. We have such confidence that we do not argue about the possibility of such an enterprise succeeding, but instead discuss the number of months the march will last, or speculate on how long letters will take to reach France. We are accustomed to the Emperor's infallibility and to the success of his undertakings.

Baron de Bausset, Prefect of the Palace, found himself responsible for the members of the French theatre who had been in Moscow since 1807, when the Peace of Tilsit had eased relations between France and Russia.

The Company was under the direction of Madame Bursay,[2] a woman of between forty-five and fifty, who had a good deal of intelligence and a firm and courageous character. When the Russians evacuated their capital, they did not, as one might imagine, bother about what would happen to our unfortunate compatriots. They sacrificed their own wounded, and so sacrificed equally everything that was foreign to them; but as this easily understandable indifference was not limited to contempt, our poor actors were first of all pillaged by the Russians who were fleeing, and then again by our soldiers who had just arrived and took little trouble to discover their nationality. The fire put the finishing touches to their misery. I

[1] Jacques-Alexandre-Bernard Law, Marquis de Lauriston (1768–1828), had been French Ambassador in St. Petersburg before the war. Napoleon sent him on an abortive mission to Kutuzov's headquarters.

[2] Aurore Bursay had, according to Dedem van der Gelder, been mistress to the Duke of Brunswick prior to his death in 1806.

took the opportunity of mentioning the matter to the Emperor during lunch, and he distributed some immediate relief, appointed me to superintend them, and ordered me to find out whether, given their present composition, it would be possible to stage a few performances and so entertain a little the army lodged in Moscow.

. . . We drew up a sort of repertory. In the unhappy situation in which the actors found themselves, nobody had any pretensions. The distribution of parts was very easily done. Never was there a cast more united, more flexible, or easier to manage. Besides, Madame Bursay had a strong influence on them and knew their means and their talents well. I wasted no time in obtaining costumes and suitable premises for their performances. The military authorities had collected in the Mosque of Ivan everything that had been rescued from the flames, and thanks to the kindness of Count Dumas, the army's Intendant-General, I found all sorts of costumes in this mosque. The French actors took velvet dresses and clothes which they fitted to their figures and to which they fastened wide gold braid which was to be found in quantities in these stores. In fact, they were dressed in great style, but such was their distress that several of our actresses barely had the necessary linen to wear under these beautiful velvet dresses — at least, that is what Madame Bursay told me. I found an attractive little theatre in the Posniakov mansion which had been spared by the flames. . . . The opening took place with a performance of *Le Jeu de l'amour et du hasard*,[1] followed by *Amant, auteur et valet*.[2] This was a brilliant début. There was no intrigue either in the theatre which was packed with the military, or on the stage, where no rivalries of *amour-propre* existed. The pit was filled with soldiers, while the two rows of boxes seated the officers of all arms. The orchestra was excellent: they were bandsmen of the Guard. Only a small charge was made at the doors and this was shared among the actors, with nothing but the cost of lighting deducted. During our stay eleven performances were given.

[1] Pierre de Marivaux's famous comedy had been written in 1734.
[2] A one-act comedy by Céron.

Dr. von Roos and his regiment were in a camp outside Moscow, along with Poniatowski's corps and some cuirassiers.

It sometimes happened, though rarely, that one of the regiments in Moscow, knowing how short we were, would send us some tea, coffee, and sugar. A good brew, a pipe of tobacco, and conversation round a good fire made the nights more bearable, for they were too long to be spent entirely in sleep. The topics of conversation were very varied, but they were never gay. Reinhardt and several other officers, counting on Napoleon's genius, would bolster up the courage of those who assessed the future by our present situation.

'So long as his hand is on the rudder,' said Reinhardt, 'we must never despair.'

But most of the non-commissioned officers and soldiers replied: 'You do your duty in trying to show us the rosy side of the picture, but your words do not reflect what you really think.' The women who made our coffee went further and had their bitter say. 'When will he keep his word, he living as he does in comfort in Moscow with his Guard, and sending us here to die of cold and hunger?' 'Yes,' said another, 'Napoleon has never held up before our eyes anything but gilded mountains and beautiful countries where we shall have winter quarters. He has not kept his promises. He will do so when it is too late and we are all dead of want. As for him, he'll manage to get himself out of this tight corner all right,' and so on.

We allowed the women to let off steam by talking in this way, but none of us would have taken a similar liberty.

Count Soltyk spent most of his time in Moscow on statistical and topographical reports which were to affect Napoleon's planning.

I was charged with providing a description of the roads which led from Moscow into the interior of the Empire. By dint of a great deal of research, and with the aid of several foreign merchants who had frequently travelled to Kiev, Kazan, St. Petersburg, and Kaluga, I was able to furnish the Emperor with reasonably satisfactory reports on the main roads leading to these different places. General Sokolnicki[1] placed them before Napoleon who discussed

[1] He was responsible for providing the Emperor with intelligence about the enemy, for analysing captured dispatches, and for the work of spies.

in his presence the advantages there might be in going in one direction or another. While in Moscow the General assured me that at one moment Napoleon considered heading for Kiev, so as to crush the enemy forces occupying the Ukraine. He intended that our troops in Lithuania should co-operate in this operation. Then he wanted to establish himself on the right bank of the Dnieper and spend the winter in the fertile provinces in the middle of Poland, thus changing his line of operations from north to south but still drawing his supplies from his base on the Vistula. However, the reports I had given him on the considerable rise in the level of the Dnieper, which in October of a normal year flooded to a width of two leagues up as far as Kiev, and on the bad state of the roads at that season, made him alter his plans. This is another example of the uncertainty of human enterprises, which so often depend for success on causes which their wisdom cannot foresee.

Captain Fantin des Odoards wrote in his diary for 12 October:

In the heart of the great ruined capital, deserted and pillaged, in which we have been living for a month, our way of life cannot but be peculiar. As in camp, military industry has had to supply everything. I am billeted with several other officers of the Guard a short distance from the cathedral church, in a house which must have been lived in by priests, because from top to bottom there is nothing but priestly ornaments and canonicals. Pillage has provided our furnishings. Cushions, Orthodox Church cassocks, and altar cloths make up our beds. Grenadiers have picked up table linen for us, and household utensils. Others have supplied us with provisions of all kinds. Herds of horned beasts which have come up to the army give meat. Our bakers bake bread with flour found under the ashes. In fact, the army here has all the essentials, in spite of Rostopchin.

In the part of the Kremlin we occupy we have stored a six months' supply of wine from various countries, rum, coffee, sugar, chocolate, tea, meat, salted fish, and preserves. This last item seems to be very popular with the inhabitants, to judge from the prodigious quantities which are found. Among these preserves my favourite is that made from rose petals. I should like to have the recipe, for it is a real delicacy. Our soldiers share this temporary abundance. Hot wine and punch flow freely in silver and porcelain cups, and our barracks, as our camps, ring day and night with convivial shouts.

And again on 17 October:

In the Kremlin and nearby there is such a crowd of our soldiers that one scarcely notices the absence of the population. But when one gets away from this bustling centre one comes to certain districts which have been spared by the flames; and here one is struck by the funereal silence that reigns. Nobody in the streets, nobody in the houses, nobody in the churches. Everything is dead. These palaces, as empty of furniture as of occupants, give no sound but the echo of our footsteps. Herculaneum and Pompeii appear like this to the foreigner. Only now and then does one glimpse one of the Russians who remained in our midst in order to share in the plunder. Wearing tattered clothes, his beard matted, he wanders through these solitary places, and when a Frenchman approaches, he vanishes like an apparition, afraid of being robbed.

On 15 October Baron Louis Bacler d'Albe, director of the Emperor's topographical cabinet, wrote from the Kremlin to his wife. The letter was intercepted by the Russians.

My dear little glutton, you are probably eating good grapes from Fontainebleau, or rather from your garden, you are sorting your apples, your winter pears, etc., and here we are calculating how long we shall still have any potatoes and cabbage to help us get the beef down. Today there are three inches of snow on the ground. I won't say on the roofs: there it has gone. I have been fortunate enough to find a grenadier who kindly made new warm linings for my clothes. I have had an excellent, though antique, cloak altered so that I can ride in it; my summer hat has been cleaned by a very skilful hussar; a chasseur is mending my boots and has promised me a pair of fur half-boots to wear over them. I have had my Paris cap covered with miniver. Thus I am warmly re-equipped. Joson[1] is equally well off with a good wolf's fur, and we are pre-

[1] Bacler d'Albe's eldest son, who was aide-de-camp to General Philippe de Ségur.

pared for any eventuality. I have new *French* servants to replace the prisoners, and good local horses. Sappe can bake bread for a fortnight, we are collecting a little oats, packing up some rum and wine, some sugar, tea, even some coffee and chocolate.

I still have left over a few soup tablets and several hams. You can see that with all this we can travel 150 leagues in any direction. In two days' time we shall probably know what is in store for us. It is *very possible* that our move will be so arranged and so *unusual* that several days will go by without our receiving or dispatching any couriers. Knowing how your mind works, I must warn you of this, because I do not want it to get in a turmoil. We shall be in good and numerous company, so do not worry or be surprised at our silence.

On 12 September Countess Rostopchin had said goodbye to her husband and left Moscow with her two daughters, Natalya and Elisabeth, travelling first to the Convent at Troitskaya and then to Yaroslavl, which lies some 150 miles away to the north-north-east. There was no hotel, Natalya tells us, so they lodged in the house of a wealthy flour-merchant.

The days went sadly by in Yaroslavl. Not till the third day did a Moscow boyar [nobleman] named Tolbukin arrive to confirm the news that the capital had been destroyed — news which had been rumoured already. . . . It is hard to describe the extreme distress of the local inhabitants. Everyone dreaded the prospect of seeing the French extend their conquests far beyond Moscow, and each person made preparations to flee to the uttermost parts of our country. I fail to understand why Napoleon did not think to send detachments in our directions. Two rich convents, at Troitskaya and Rostov, were on the main road to Yaroslavl, and the French troops could not have failed to plunder them. Even the town of Yaroslavl itself could have provided an enormous quantity of hay, flour, and cloth. Fortunately the only enemies who visited us were poor prisoners sent to us by Headquarters. How many times, while walking along the banks of the Volga, was I saddened to watch these wretches, ill-clad, undernourished, half frozen. In fairness to the people of Yaroslavl, however, I must say that they behaved

Moscow in flames after the entry of Napoleon's forces, from the drawing by John Vedramini

A scene in Moscow, from a lithograph by C. W. von Faber du Faur

Generals Bennigsen (*top left*), Wittgenstein (*top right*), Miloradovich (*bottom left*), and Dokhturov (*bottom right*), from paintings by George Dawe

generously and charitably towards all these foreigners who fell into our hands.

I do not quite know why the carts always collected in the main square whenever the prisoners arrived and departed. Every day the people hurried there, some drawn by curiosity, others by better motives. Egoistic as usual, the nobility contributed little, but the merchants brought everything which might protect these men from cold and hunger — men who would have to remain exposed to the chill air for a long time yet: sheepskin pelisses, warm blankets and boots, bread, sugar, tea, and coffee cluttered up the miserable carts of these exiles. A few people obtained permission to cook meals for them at home.

On 13 October Joseph de Maistre, who in 1796 had made a wide reputation with his Considérations sur la France *and was now in St. Petersburg as Ambassador from the King of Sardinia, wrote:*

Here we continue to be on the go. Everything of any value is packed; all the stables are full of horses; my small packets have already been done up and their destination settled. It is now that one can repent at leisure over having wasted or lost money. In the past twenty years I have witnessed the obsequies of several dominions, but nothing has struck me so forcibly as what I see at this moment, because I have never seen anything so large trembling. Furthermore, one could retreat as far as this place, but at present we have nothing behind us except Spitzbergen. For my part, if pressed I should slip away and go to England; but I assure you I am very far from thinking the situation as desperate as that. . . .

This last month in St. Petersburg more paper has been burnt than would be required to roast all the cattle of the Ukraine. I have burnt all I could on my own account, and yet I am extremely encumbered, though not for myself, since I do not keep a line. . . . On all sides I can see boats and waggons loaded. I hear the voice of fear, resentment, and sometimes malice. I see more than one terrible sign. In truth, Sire, all this is not rosy.

On 13 October General Wilson wrote in his diary:

The bearded warriors of the Don (being chiefly veterans and fathers of families, who are distinguished by bearded honours) continue to arrive, and 'General Winter', who is our most powerful ally, has already presented the torrents of his advanced guard. . . . While I was dining with Platov[1] and a great party of general officers the day before yesterday, Platov received a letter from one of the Tartar regiments informing him that they had made prize of a considerable sum of gold and silver which had been melted by the enemy from church ornaments; but that they placed their prize at his disposal, as though they thought it a sacrilege to take it from their country. . . . It is true the light troops have no want of unrighteous gold; they have taken so many horses, watches, Louis-d'or,[2] &c., that one Cossack regiment has divided booty that gives every man eighty-four pounds sterling.

. . . The Don regiments continue to pour in. Such a reinforcement of cavalry was perhaps never equalled. . . . They bring us the most agreeable wines, sturgeon, caviare, and large barrels of red and white grapes, of which Platov has given me a superabundant share.

Four days later he wrote:

I passed a delightful night. The Cossack chiefs fêted me with all their luxuries, amusements, honours, &c. The enemy were not distant more than six hundred yards, and grouped to hear the music. The singers gave me their famous boat song, and the enemy having recognized my vessel, the answer to the hail was: 'She is charged with Spanish victories.'[3]

[1] Matvei Ivanovich Platov (1757–1818) had been Hetman of the Cossacks of the Don since 1801.

[2] A gold coin worth just under a guinea.

[3] Wellington's victory at Salamanca and entry into Madrid.

All this time the partisans had been active against Napoleon's lines of communication and outposts. One of the leaders was Colonel Denis Davidov, and these are his instructions to a group of villagers as to how to deal with bands of French marauders.

'Receive them,' I told them, 'in friendly fashion, offer them with bows (since in their ignorance of the Russian language they understand bows better than words) all you have in the way of eatables and especially drink, put them to bed drunk, and when you perceive that they are really asleep, all of you pounce on their weapons which are usually to be found in a heap in a corner of the cottage or piled in the street. When you have exterminated them, bury their bodies in the pigsty, in the forest, or in some impenetrable place. Take care at all costs that the spots where the bodies are buried are not given away by freshly dug earth; for this purpose scatter a pile of stones or logs over the spot. All military booty such as uniforms, helmets, straps, etc., you must either burn or bury in the same places as the bodies of the Frenchmen. This precaution is necessary because another band of infidels will very likely dig in the fresh earth, thinking to find money or your possessions there; but when instead they unearth the bodies of their comrades and objects belonging to them, they will kill you all and burn down the village. And you, friend headman, must supervise the carrying-out of all my instructions and give orders for three or four lads to be always ready in your yard, so that the moment they catch sight of a very large number of Frenchmen they can mount their horses and gallop in different directions in search of me — I shall come to your aid.'

Retreat to the Dnieper

ONCE they had ascertained the Grand Army's route, the Russians decided to head off Napoleon at the steep defiles of Malo-Yaroslavets. Fighting went on through most of 24 October in and around the burning town, Prince Eugène's Italians bearing the brunt of the struggle; and though the French evicted their opponents and retained possession of the place after it had changed hands seven times, Kutuzov succeeded in barring the road to Kaluga, his troops drawn up in positions which Marshal Bessières declared to be unassailable. Napoleon's manœuvre had been frustrated. Now the French would have to fight their way through to the south — if they could — or move westwards through Medyn and Elnya, or else retreat north to Mozhaisk and there pick up the Smolensk high-road and the devastated line of their advance.

Not without prolonged hesitation and consultation, Napoleon opted for Mozhaisk, which was reached on 28 October. Here Mortier and the Moscow garrison rejoined the Emperor. As the army was clogged with stragglers and lagging guns, waggons, and horses, all of which had, on Napoleon's orders, to be herded along by the rearguard, progress was slow, but no more so than the Russian pursuit. Kutuzov had been urged to fight a decisive battle, or else to cut off Napoleon's retreat by a swift march on Viazma, but he declined. He was prepared to get the Grand Army off Russian soil, but was not convinced that its destruction would benefit Russia as much as England. In any case, he did not believe that Napoleon could hold his empire after a failure in Russia, and he was reluctant to shed Russian blood to achieve a result which he deemed inevitable. He had been ready to retreat had the French renewed their attacks at Malo-Yaroslavets. Now, by operating along the southern flank, he could threaten constantly to intercept the enemy's line of retreat without, in his view, exposing his own troops to any sudden onslaught. Let the Grand Army be further weakened by a long march, and then Admiral Chichagov's Army of the Danube, veterans of the war against Turkey, could intervene. Accordingly, Kutuzov followed at a safe distance, yet even so his army was to lose nearly half its effective strength while advancing from Tarutino to Krasnyi and the region south of Smolensk.

Elsewhere Russian offensives were being set in motion. Troops came down from Finland; Wittgenstein prepared to drive Saint-Cyr from Polotsk; and Chichagov advanced northwards from Moldavia across the River Styr, then skirted the western side of the Pripet Marshes, whereupon Schwarzenberg and Reynier retired a little way towards Belostok.

Meanwhile Napoleon's own motley force, strung out along bad roads, was in difficulties: exhaustion, inadequate provisions — the men were already eating horseflesh — frosts, sickness, increasingly bold Cossack attacks, and, as the army approached Viazma and then Smolensk early in November, heavy pressure from flanks and rear. Indeed, Eugène and Poniatowski had to turn back to aid Davout's corps, and a hard action was fought on 3 November. Marshal Ney, commanding the rearguard, was under attack, but a sharp repulse of Miloradovich at Dorogobuzh eased the pressure.

Officers and men who had campaigned in Spain were loudly stating that the Peninsula was a bed of roses in comparison with the present hardships. Larrey, the chief surgeon who had performed two hundred amputations in twenty-four hours at Borodino, wrote to his wife: 'I have never suffered so much. The campaigns in Egypt and Spain were nothing when compared to this one; and we are by no means at the end of our troubles.' How right he was to be proved! By this time, before any snow or unduly severe cold had set in, that portion of the Grand Army under the Emperor's command had been reduced to about 55,000 men and 12,000 horses fit for active service.

The first heavy snowstorm occurred on 6 November, on which day Napoleon, while at Dorogobuzh, received news from Paris of an attempt *coup d'état* by General Claude de Malet, who four years earlier had been arrested for his part in a republican plot to overthrow the Emperor. Recently released from prison into a clinic for mental patients Malet had organized a new conspiracy and had arrested two Ministers and the Prefect of Police, only to be thwarted by the general commanding the Paris garrison. Though abortive, even farcical in some aspects, the *coup* underlined the weakness of Napoleon's regime and still more the ready acquiescence with which responsible officials had, on being told the false news that Napoleon had perished in Russia, accepted a change, and one which ignored both the Empress and his son, the King of Rome.

Napoleon also heard, from closer at hand, that Saint-Cyr's evacuation of Polotsk on 19 October had induced Marshal Victor to leave Smolensk and hasten to his aid, but after encountering Wittgenstein in an indecisive battle, Victor had retired to a point between Vitebsk and Orsha, and Saint-Cyr himself had been obliged by a wound to give up his command. It cannot be said that during this stage of the retreat Napoleon did much either to warn his subordinates of his own grim situation or to co-ordinate their operations.

Napoleon, with the Guard and the Westphalian regiments, reached Smolensk on 9 November. His original intention had been to retreat no further, but to remain here and in the region of Mogilev and Minsk for the winter had now been rendered impossible by the convergence of hostile armies, the impending onslaught of icy conditions, and the disappointingly small amount of supplies available in the town. Hopes which had buoyed up many a weary soldier were dashed abruptly. Reduced rations for two weeks might have been provided for everyone had methodical distribution been effected, for the magazines contained bread, flour, salt, and spirits; but few men received very much in spite of Napoleon's orders that the Guard be given food for fourteen days and the other troops for six. As for the horses, many more died for want of fodder or because, through lack of foresight, they had not been rough-shod. Despite these serious handicaps, Napoleon managed to assemble some 50,000 men and, in the hope of establishing a winter line along the Dvina and Dnieper Rivers, sent the Poles and Westphalians ahead to Krasnyi.

The Emperor's five-day halt in the burnt-out shell of Smolensk gave the Russians, who had not followed him to the town but had kept south for Krasnyi, hoping thereby to intercept Napoleon's route to the Berezina, a chance to overtake on a parallel course, but Kutuzov delayed to give his troops a day's rest. At Krasnyi Napoleon halted in the resolve to attack Kutuzov and gain time for, and reduce pressure on, Eugène, Davout, and Ney, who were still coming up. On 16 November Eugène de Beauharnais managed to by-pass Miloradovich and so rejoin the Emperor, who sent him on to hold the bridges at Orsha forty miles away. Next day Napoleon's attack on the Russian centre, this time committing the Guard who had stood idle at Borodino, enabled Davout's corps to slip past to safety, but it was then considered too dangerous to wait for Marshal Ney and the rearguard, who had still not appeared in spite of warnings to hurry. Instead, Napoleon ordered the retreat to be resumed to Orsha.

What had happened to Ney? After blowing up some of the ramparts, he left Smolensk on the 17th, unexpectedly bumped against Miloradovich, tried to force his way through, but was thrown back with heavy loss. He refused a summons to surrender, and, leaving his camp fires burning deceptively, led his men north through snowbound forests to the Dnieper, which, so he assured his followers, would be frozen; but when three thousand arrived there only a thin coating of ice covered the water. Ney led the way across by night, but far too many of his corps fell through the ice and were drowned, while the guns and waggons had to be abandoned. When the Marshal, already being mourned as dead by an anxious Emperor, who talked of him as 'the bravest of the brave', rejoined the main body at Orsha with assistance from Eugène, he had barely nine hundred survivors. His salty comment on the retreat ran through the Army: '*Ceux qui en reviendront auront les c . . . attachées avec du fil de fer.*'

On the Russian side Kutuzov was again severely criticized for failing to provoke a decisive engagement.

Captain von Kurz recalls the morning of 19 October — a bright autumn day — when Napoleon left Moscow with his army.

Although the march-out of the army had been going on since two o'clock, at midday crowds were still pushing their way out through the gateways of this half-ruined city; and in countless columns they moved along the broad high-road.

It was not only the number of fighting men who made up the endless procession, but the innumerable waggons, carts, droshkys, chaises, often laden with booty. And the number of guns, ammunition waggons, vans, and the like, moving in eight or ten parallel columns, took up an incalculable stretch of the road. Besides the artillery, powder-waggons, and carts, the rest of the many vehicles were loaded with provisions of all sorts: wine, brandy, sugar, coffee, tea, tobacco, salt meat, dried fish, etc. Other waggons contained booty in the form of gold, silver, precious stones, and valuable furs. Whereas most officers owned a cart, the generals had half a dozen. Supply officials and actors, women and children, cripples, wounded men, and the sick drove in and out of the throng in kibitkas and droshkys; countless servants and maids, sutlers and people of that sort accompanied this march. In short, the whole thing presented such a peculiar and astonishing appearance that no pen can describe it adequately. From both sides the columns of horsemen and pedestrians broke out and went wherever the ground allowed, across the fields beside the road, so as to leave the paved road free for those on foot. Nevertheless the enormous clutter of transport became jammed, and it was impossible for individuals to find room. The great crowd had become so intermingled that to make one's way forward required a tremendous effort.

The great congestion of waggons and troops poured through the fields in three wide columns. Inexhaustibly they seemed to press out from the ruins of Moscow, and the heads of these columns vanished far away on the horizon.

Lejeune recalled bitterly the burdensome number of carts and carriages which, on the road to Kaluga, slowed up the early stages of the retreat, just when an attempt should have been made to steal two or three marches on the Russians.

All these vehicles, laden with the food and booty which were to sustain us against cold and hunger, still assumed enormous proportions, and I am going to give you an idea of my own position in this respect — I who was one of the officers most interested in travelling without impedimenta. I still had: (1) five riding horses; (2) a carriage drawn by three horses and carrying my belongings, as well as furs to wrap round me in camp; (3) the waggon laden with staff documents, maps, and the kitchen utensils for the officers and clerks — this was pulled by four horses; (4) three small carts, each drawn by three little Russian horses and weighed down by the clerks, the cook, the oats, sugar, coffee, flour, and some scarce bales of hay; (5) the secretary's horse; (6) lastly, the three horses which I had harnessed to my sister's carriage: she had gone ahead. All this made a clutter of six vehicles and twenty-five horses, which scarcely carried the essentials. The traces kept on breaking; halts held up the march; sand, defiles, marshes all caused delays, and the army took twelve hours and often longer to cover the distance that one vehicle on its own would have covered in two hours.

The Emperor was very upset by these delays, and ordered that every vehicle not essential for transporting the few provisions we carried should be burnt and the horses used to pull the guns. This very wise step was feebly put into force, such was the number of people who had an interest in evading this severe measure. The Emperor had one of his own carriages burnt, but the example was not compelling enough and found no imitators. Consequently the army, which still numbered about 105,000 combatants and five hundred guns at the time, took six days to cover eighty miles.

On the evening of 19 October Colonel Count Roguet left Moscow, escorting the treasure and the Intendant-General's headquarters.

I carried away trophies from the Kremlin, including the cross of Ivan, several ornaments used at the coronation of the tsars, all the colours captured from the Turks in the past hundred years, and a madonna enriched with precious stones, which had been given by the Tsarina Anna in 1740 in memory of the victories won over the Poles and of the capture of Danzig in 1733. The treasure comprised silver coins or bullion melted down from the large amount of silverware found in the ruins of Moscow. For nearly forty miles I had to pick my way through the army's procession of horse-drawn vehicles. Every one was laden with useless baggage.

Captain Thomas-Joseph Aubry, commanding a squadron in the 12th Regiment of Chasseurs, *had been wounded in the battle of Borodino and taken to a Moscow hospital for officers. Here he was fairly well looked after,*[1] *but had to be left behind when the Grand Army departed.*

I remained there almost the whole time the French stayed in Moscow. I had a severe bout of the illness and in particular suffered from lack of sleep. When it became a question of our troops leaving, I was evacuated to the Foundlings' Hospital — a superb and enormous building which held about two thousand of us. . . .

The Young Guard were the last to leave Moscow, and as soon as they had gone, the Russians — a few inhabitants, some peasants, and the Cossacks — went in all directions. They began by killing all the Frenchmen still in houses and throwing them into the Moskva. The population were unrestrained, but we all had weapons and we fired out of the windows. We were led, sword in hand, by three wounded Russian generals who had been picked up by our men and very well looked after. Soon our refuge became unapproachable, and eventually, when Russian line regiments arrived, they set up posts and we were respected. I had had myself carried into one of the soldiers' rooms and there, sword in hand, I

[1] A report drawn up in October for Napoleon revealed that Moscow contained about 12,000 French and allied sick and wounded, few of whom were fit enough to stand the rigours of a road journey.

gave the fire orders. My illness was at its height, and I was delirious. . . .

After this the typhus made appalling inroads in our ranks. We were forty-three officers in our ward. All of them died, one after the other, and delirious from this dreadful disease, most of them singing, some in Latin, others in German, others again in Italian — and singing psalms, canticles, or the mass. When this happened they were nearly always in their death agony. Only three of us survived, and we included a cuirassier officer who had had a leg amputated at the thigh. Among the soldiers the proportion of deaths was similar, and more than 1,800 out of the 1,850 in the hospital died. In the end we were taken elsewhere and the deaths stopped at once. After the winter we were sent to Siberia, and this restored us to health.

Colonel Griois, commanding the artillery of Grouchy's 3rd Cavalry Corps, has a description in his memoirs of how the retreat began for troops who were already outside Moscow.

The hopes we had entertained of peace gradually faded. Cossack officers with whom we talked at the outposts said quite frankly that peace was impossible, that the Russians would never make peace so long as we stayed in their country, that a new campaign was going to open with the arrival of winter. And each day we could hear section and platoon musketry which told us of the arrival of numerous recruits whom the Russian Army was hurriedly training. For three days past the King of Naples, no doubt warned that the Russians were preparing a general offensive, had ordered that every evening all baggage waggons, horses, and anything else which might hinder a battle at night should be sent back to a village known in our camp by the name of 'Trois Clochers', less than a league to the rear. They were to be sent forward again next morning if nothing had happened meanwhile. This order was punctiliously obeyed for the first few days, but when people saw that the enemy launched no attack and that this precaution served merely to exhaust the men and horses, it was relaxed, and we were living in perfect security on 18 October, which was in truth the first day of our retreat.

. . . Alone in our smoky room, stretched out on a bench, I was fast asleep when at first light on 18 October I was woken by the noise of firing. To begin with I thought this must be the recruits practising in the Russian camp, but soon the noise seemed to be closer than usual. I opened the window beside me; that is to say, I pushed up a small wooden shutter like those used in hen-cages, and on the far side of the ravine I saw our sentries exchanging shots with enemy sharpshooters. Everything lay in a thick mist, and I thought it was merely a question of some Russian patrols which had approached. But the firing could be heard from other points too, and all over the camp trumpeters were sounding 'To horse!' So it must be a serious attack.

I ordered the artillery to harness up immediately. I sent my servant and vehicles to the rear, and went with my adjutant and orderly officers to the forward edge of the camp. Our pickets were already withdrawing on their regiments which had formed into battle order. We stayed watching for some time. Eventually the Russians moved off, and the lifting mist enabled us to see their masses advancing towards us, manœuvring as they came. I aimed my artillery fire at them, the Russian gunners replied, and the battle raged all along the front.

Luckily for us, General Lahoussaye,[1] who had been ill for several days, was not fit to mount his horse, so he withdrew to the rear in his carriage, and the command devolved on General Chastel,[2] an excellent soldier who combined great gallantry, experience, and coolness. He took the steps he judged most suitable to repulse the attack. He even had our cavalry make several charges, but the forces were unequal, so he restricted himself to withdrawing without being mauled in the process. We formed the extreme right of the line, and the enemy could easily have turned this flank if he had not directed his opening effort against the left of our front which was held by the 2nd Cavalry Corps. At first several regiments there had to fall back, and a large part of the artillery was captured by the Russians, but Murat went over with reinforcements, restored the situation, held the Russians at bay, and the retreat was carried out in good order.

[1] Armand Le Brun, Baron de Lahoussaye (1768–1846), commanded a division of dragoons.

[2] Aimé-Pierre Chastel (1774–1826) had command of a light cavalry division (*chasseurs* and hussars).

For some time the guns had been roaring behind us, the enemy having penetrated our line and seized a defile through which we should have to pass in order to retire on Moscow. After a hard struggle the Russians were driven off by a Polish division and by General Friederichs's[1] division, which were bivouacked nearby. . . .

The battle had started at daybreak and barely stopped at day's end. Having withdrawn three or four leagues, we took up positions behind a stream near a large village called, I believe, Voronovo, and there we bivouacked, rather anxious about the result of this action, but very far from foreseeing the long series of misfortunes in store for us. Alas! This day was only the prelude to our troubles: the disastrous retreat was about to begin.

On the 19th we saw no enemy troops and we moved to the village of Krasnyi-Pakhra, a few leagues nearer to Moscow. Next day we were expecting to continue our march when we spotted the long columns of our army which had left Moscow the previous evening on receiving news of our battle and were on their way to join us. When the army reached our ridge, it moved away to the right along cross-country tracks so as to pick up the new road to Kaluga.

General Wilson was at Kutuzov's headquarters in Aristovo, twelve miles west of Tarutino, when on 23 October messenger after messenger came in from all quarters to confirm that the French Army had evacuated Moscow and was on the march to Fominskoye, having already entered Borovsk.

It was clear that Malo-Yaroslavets was the point on which the enemy was moving; and whilst the corps was getting under arms, advice was received that the enemy from Fominskoye was already on the march in that direction. Not a moment was lost: by seven o'clock the corps of Dokhturov was straining every nerve to reach Malo-Yaroslavets before the enemy, whose lights were frequently visible during the night, as the columns occasionally approached within a mile or two of each other.

. . . Kutuzov was in full possession of the requisite information

[1] Jean-Parfait, Baron Friederichs (1773–1813), had replaced the wounded Dessaix in command of the 4th Infantry Division. He was killed at Leipzig.

for the government of his proceedings by nine o'clock in the evening, and his army had but to march ten miles, whereas Dokhturov, when at Aristovo which he left at seven, was distant from Malo-Yaroslavets twelve miles, without any regular road, but having to wind and make his way through a flat meadow-country full of streamlets and large ditches, unprovided with any bridge for the passage of his artillery, without any pontoons or means except such as could be found on the spot; and yet before day dawned he had crossed the Protva at Spasski, and gained the plain which lay in front of Malo-Yaroslavets [thirty miles north-east of Spasski].

Everyone was ignorant of the locale, and therefore the only disposition that could be made during the imperfect light was to post columns on the different roads leading from the town, and of which there were, including the Spasski road, five principal ones, to resist the egress of the enemy (who it was supposed would endeavour to move forward at daybreak), and to confine him within the town until the main Russian army or sufficient reinforcements could arrive to frustrate his project. Dokhturov then ordered two regiments of *chasseurs*, supported by two more, to dash into the town, and drive the enemy (whom some fugitive inhabitants reported to have reached and entered it) out of the place, and over the River Luzha, which ran immediately below, and to destroy his bridge.

Malo-Yaroslavets is built upon the side and summit of a lofty hill, rising immediately above the Luzha (which the enemy called the Lutza), and over which river is a bridge distant about a hundred yards from the ravine. The ground on both flanks of the town, ascending from the river, is woody and steep, and the ground on the left is intersected with very deep fissures and ravines, so as to be impracticable for artillery movements from the bank of the river. The whole town is built of wood; near the summit of the hill there is an open space like a *grande place*; and near the ravine, at the bottom, are a church and a couple or more of houses that command the approach.

. . . The *chasseurs* charged forward and quickly dislodged the enemy in the town; but at the bottom of the hill on which it is built ran a deep ravine, the opposite side of which covered the bridge, and behind this ravine the enemy found unassailable shelter.

The English General [Wilson himself] having gone upon the right flank of the town to reconnoitre this embankment and the position of the bridge, perceived, as day dawned, a large body of the enemy descending the lofty hill on the left bank of the river to pass the bridge and enter the town: this dense body was flocking forward as if quite at ease and unconscious of any serious opposition being designed to the passage and occupation.

The English General, having reported this incident to Dokhturov, galloped with a battery of light artillery placed under his directions to an elevation which he had selected for its site, and opened its fire almost within grapeshot of the mass. At the first discharge there was a general halt, on the second a wavering, on the third a total dispersion, and every one flew forward or scrambled up the hill to get out of the reach of this unexpected cannonade. The movement of the advanced guard was thus checked, and nearly an hour gained before the Viceroy [Eugène] could arrive in person, bring up his artillery, and re-establish order: an essential hour for the Russians.

In about an hour the enemy (Delzons's division),[1] under cover of a heavy fire, recommenced the descent of the hill; and joining the two battalions defending the bridge, pushed up through the streets of the town to the skirts, when the battle began with a violence which corresponded with the magnitude of its objects and the resolute determination of each party to achieve its own.

The enemy was infuriated by despair; the Russians by 'the Moscow cry of vengeance'.

The very militia who had just joined (and who, being armed only with pikes, formed a third rank to the battalions) not only stood as steady under the cannonade as their veteran comrades, but charged the sallying enemy with as ardent ferocity.

Dokhturov, under cover of his powerful artillery, which poured shot, shells, and grape on the advancing columns, re-entered and repossessed himself of the whole town as far as the ravine, except the church and adjoining houses which the enemy had garrisoned, and which commanded the ground beyond, so that the Russians could not remain under their fire to contend for the ravine and

[1] Alexis-Joseph, Baron Delzons (1775–1815), commanded the 13th Division. His long fighting career included the battles of Lodi, Rivoli, the Pyramids, and Wagram.

seizure of the bridge. In this attack Delzons was killed, and fell into the arms of his brother,[1] who also received a mortal wound.

Guilleminot[2] succeeded to the command, and resumed the offensive. After various attempts he at last regained the *grande place*; but, though reinforced by the division Broussier,[3] he could not establish any lodgment beyond. About ten o'clock the corps of Davout and Ney had reached the heights opposite Malo-Yaroslavets; and every instant it became more manifest that the enemy had resolved to force his passage through the Russian circumvallation.

Officer after officer had been dispatched to hasten the arrival of the reinforcements, and of the main army under Kutuzov. Every regiment of Dokhturov's corps had been already engaged, and the killed and wounded exceeded five thousand. The troops, exhausted by their previous marches and seven hours' combat, could scarcely continue the action.

At that anxious moment the corps of Raevsky arrived within view; and, as soon as it reached the position, was ordered to penetrate into, and carry the town by storm. The 'huzzas' of the columns announced to the enemy that they were about to be assailed by fresh troops, whose impulse they quickly found they were unable to resist. The Russian grenadiers carried all before them; and for the sixth time the Russians became masters of every post but the fortified church and buildings adjacent.

The Viceroy, alarmed for the safety of the troops left within them and in the ravine, as well as for his bridges, a second one having been constructed, urged forward the division Pino to rally the fugitives and lead to another onset. . . . The Russian grenadiers, notwithstanding its impetuous efforts and the flames raging around them (for the town was on fire in all parts), tenaciously maintained their position: and the Viceroy was compelled to send across the river all his corps except the cavalry to preserve his *têtes de pont*.

The Russians in their turn, yielding to the new pressure, retired from the town, and took post at half-cannon shot distance from the

[1] Jean-Baptiste Delzons, a major, born in 1787.

[2] Armand-Charles, Count Guilleminot (1774–1840), was chief of staff to Eugène's 4th Corps.

[3] Jean-Baptiste, Count Broussier (1766–1814), commanded the 14th Infantry Division.

outskirts. The enemy, elated, presented heads of column at the several outlets, as if they were about to advance on the Russian alignment; but they were unable to face the artillery that swept the esplanade in front, and the Russian *chasseurs* repossessed themselves of the nearest houses yet unburnt. . . .

. . . Kutuzov had perseveringly turned a deaf ear to every messenger and entreaty, founding excuses for delay on the absence of foragers, and other frivolous pretexts. The thunder of the cannonade had shaken the very windows of his quarters; but it was not until after his dinner meal that he ordered his droshky, and five o'clock had passed before the army occupied its already selected stations.

. . . The army of the Viceroy had been so reinforced within the town, and the flames of the burning houses had so extended and raged with such violence, that retention of any portion but the skirts was impracticable. The enemy had also established considerable batteries that swept the whole interior. The Russian *chasseurs* however continued to occupy the gardens, hedges, and ruins, whence they kept up an active musketry fire till eleven at night. The vigour of the cannonade had ceased at nine, but shells were thrown till nearly midnight. . . . The town had been consumed to ashes, and with it all the severely wounded.

After sunset the spectacle had been indescribably magnificent and interesting. The crackling flames — the dark shadows of the combatants flitting amongst them — the hissing ring of the grape as it flew from the licornes[1] — the rattling of the musketry — the ignited shells traversing and crossing in the atmosphere — the wild shouts of the combatants, and all the accompaniments of the sanguinary struggle formed an ensemble seldom witnessed.

Löwenstern, now promoted to lieutenant-colonel and on Kutuzov's staff, found himself out with the Russian advance-guard early in October and was disgusted by several instances of ill-treatment of prisoners.

Hitherto the French prisoners had always been very well-treated. I even remember that, when the campaign opened, the

[1] A kind of howitzer, though at the time it was more like a mortar fitted on a field-carriage.

Commander-in-Chief distributed two ducats to every captured officer, and that Count de Ségur,[1] to whom I had been instructed to make this present, was very offended at the idea and gave the ducats to the Cossack escorting him. Later the distribution of money was neglected, but several prisoners did receive it and expressed their gratitude.

General Yermolov, I don't know from what motive, had the prisoners ill-treated and almost done to death. He had a particular grudge against the Poles, and I shall always remember the revolting way in which he treated Count Plater. He spat in his face, and when handing him over to the escort he told the Cossack officer who was to go with him to help the Count on his way with strokes of the whip. I do not know whether this barbarous order was carried out, but I thought the whole idea atrocious.

Moreover, I could not refrain from saying to several youngsters who applauded this order that it ill became a brave man, as General Yermolov undoubtedly is, to issue such an order, because to be captured did not mean that one stopped being brave, and cowards were seldom taken prisoner. General Yermolov believed he was exalting the army and the nation by such atrocities. If such was his aim, he succeeded, and success justifies everything.

I shall always praise a nation which assassinates an enemy who invades its country and destroys its homes and its very existence, but I shall never stoop to heap praises on soldiers who ill-treat prisoners who surrender and, asking for their lives to be spared, trust the victor's good faith.

Figner[2] and others thought they were acting heroically by massacring all their prisoners. Fortunately their ferocity had no imitators, and almost nobody except a few young men, as inexperienced as they were unprincipled, committed acts of cruelty in a mood of exaltation. General Yermolov encouraged them, but I must say, for the honour of our army, that few officers were eager to earn praise at such a price, and the soldiers continued to be good and loyal fellows, because in general Russia acts generously towards a vanquished foe.

In the heat of battle the Russian soldier kills his men without

[1] Captain Octave de Ségur (1779–1818), the brother of Philippe, was wounded near Vilna at the end of June.

[2] A particularly bold and ruthless partisan leader.

fear or compunction, but once his opponent has surrendered I have more than once seen the Russian share his bread and his brandy with the enemy he would unhesitatingly have killed a moment before.

In fact, Figner and his associates had difficulty in finding in their units men willing to undertake these massacres, and it was usually the Cossacks of the Bug who did so, being fiercer than the rest and eager for the booty they received.

Baron Antoine-Baudouin-Gisbert van Dedem van der Gelder, son of a former Dutch Ambassador in Constantinople, was commanding a brigade in the 2nd Division of Davout's corps.

In Moscow I had taken into service as stable-boy a child who appeared to be full of zeal, drove my carriage, went off foraging without fear of the Cossacks and with a rare boldness, and sometimes cooked my supper. Everybody admired the intelligence and energy of my little gunner. It was only at Smolensk, where in a moment of impatience I struck him, that he revealed his identity. It was a girl aged fourteen or fifteen, who had left her parents' home to go off with a French artillery officer with whom she had fallen in love. He had been killed at the battle of Borodino. She had hidden her sex so cleverly that for a month she had lived with my staff without one of them becoming suspicious. Her parents were of good family, she herself had received a good education, but she had a marked taste for horses.

One circumstance should have betrayed her secret earlier: in Moscow she picked up all the pretty women's clothes, on the pretext that she was taking a few souvenirs back to a young sister who, she said, lived at Jauer in Silesia. We were none of us Ulysses, and after the event we were all amazed at our stupidity, in particular several aides-de-camp who, in addition to my own, stayed with my train as long as they could find subsistence there. My little female jockey was as well treated as circumstances allowed. I bought her a horse, and not until the crossing of the Berezina did she get lost; I was never able to discover what happened to her. When at Krasnyi I lost what remained of my waggons, none of my staff gave a thought to saving anything; she alone forced a Cossack to give back a pair of epaulets. Furthermore, she arrived with a bottle of rum, and some sugar and coffee.

Louis-Vivant Lagneau, surgeon to the Fusilier Grenadiers of the Old Guard, tells us that while in Moscow he and his general had the foresight to have a tent made out of striped canvas. Pegs and poles had been made by the soldiers. Towards the end of October Lagneau recorded:

My ambulance waggon was large and very heavy. We loaded it with wine, rice, biscuits, sugar, coffee, and many other provisions, either in little casks as carried by our *cantinières* or else in big sacks, all of it comprising our viaticum for the retreat. We were obliged to abandon and burn it.

So as not to lose the provisions, we loaded them on the backs of our ambulance horses, in sacks suspended on either side in the form of a double bag, and in this manner we managed to subsist very well as far as Vilna without experiencing any serious privation.

One thing above all else turned out very advantageous in this sad loss of the waggon: we were able to keep our tent which hitherto had travelled on the waggon. Now it was loaded, along with its pegs, etc., on a little Cossack horse which was very gallant, and lived on pine bark or willow bark and went up and down ravines just as a little dog would have done. He was not shod and the hoof had grown down so much that it gripped very well on the ice. . . .

Whenever we reached a bivouac area our first job was to pitch the tent, which was about the only one in the army. Each member of our little group lent a hand: the general, Simon Robert; Major Guillemin, the adjutant, an excellent fellow and a real friend to me; Desprès the quartermaster and paymaster; and myself. We soon had our shelter up against the evil north wind which took our breath away if we could not get out of its blast. This done, we unloaded the provisions and stored them in the tent. We prepared soup, because we had some sappers under command and for soldiers they cooked very well. While they looked after their soup (because they always had their share of this as well as of the other food we carried with us), we sheltered in our tent, and were soon as warm as in some billet in Germany.

When dinner was ready we ate it and then went back into the tent, in front of which a good fire blazed. We could do without this, but it served our excellent soldiers.

Colonel Griois had been commanding the artillery in the 3rd Cavalry Corps, but after 3 November at Viazma his batteries no longer existed, so on his own authority he followed Prince Eugène's 4th Corps, and was soon appointed to command its artillery.

I left Dorogobuzh with my guns, on 6 November, crossed the river [Dnieper] by a ford, and established myself some distance from the right bank where the 4th Corps had taken up positions.

The only shelter near the place I had halted in was a sort of barn open to all the winds and its roof supported by four posts. This lodging seemed to me excellent by comparison with those I had had for a long time past. I had a large fire built in the centre and lay down to sleep beside it, surrounded by my horses. But during the night snow began to fall heavily, and the wind blew it under the roof with such force that when I woke up at daybreak I was covered in snow, as was the whole landscape. The snow had stopped falling, but the cold was icy, and the snow had hardened and was all frozen. Winter had just fallen on us with full severity and was not going to leave us.

. . . My guns were harnessed and we had to get them moving. This was not easy. The previous day the ground where I had parked them had been soft and rain-sodden, but this mud froze during the night and our poor exhausted horses tried in vain to pull them clear. It was not until they had doubled the teams of horses, dug out the wheels with spades, and added their own efforts to those of the horses that my gunners and waggon-train soldiers succeeded in getting part of the artillery moving. We now encountered a new difficulty: the slippery surface of the hardened snow offered no purchase to the horses' feet. We had reserves of ice-nails all right, but we had not yet used them for shoeing the horses. Even this would not have sufficed, because after several hours' march their diamond-sharp heads were worn and they became absolutely useless, as we discovered later. Iron crampons are much better, but we should have needed more time and resources than we had to shoe our horses in this way. Eventually we managed to tow all our vehicles out of the park, one by one, by means of doubling, even trebling, the teams of horses. But it was quite impossible that four horses to each vehicle — we were obliged to reduce most of them to that number — could manage on the slippery tracks we had to move along. After several vain attempts I had to resign myself to further sacrifices and I decided to leave behind two guns and two ammunition waggons.

But first of all I had the ammunition spread out on the snow and the waggons and guns collected under a nearby barn. There we set fire to them. Gun-carriages and waggons were reduced to ashes and the guns buried under the ruins. This was a precaution that had been taken hitherto so as to prevent the enemy from profiting by our artillery. Later on too much time and trouble would have been required for destroying such guns as we left behind. We no longer bothered.

During the campaign and since the retreat began I had already been compelled to abandon some empty waggons in order to reinforce the teams pulling other vehicles. But this was the first time I had left loaded waggons and guns. I was sad at heart when we set off again on 8 November to rejoin the 4th Corps.

Sir Robert Wilson returned to Viazma on 5 November:

The shells that the enemy had buried in the different houses then burning were continually exploding, and the passage through the streets was very dangerous. This thoughtless conduct of the enemy was the death-warrant of many an unfortunate wretch. I had the satisfaction, however, of seeing a very interesting Swiss family saved. The two daughters were as beautiful young women as I ever saw in my life. The first day I proceeded forty versts, the next seventeen, the next twenty-five, when we entered Dorogobuzh by force, the enemy having two divisions in the town who attempted some resistance. The marches were very severe, as the weather was of the most desperate character; but the scene for the whole route represented such a spectacle that every personal consideration was absorbed by the feelings that the sight of so much woe excited.

The naked masses of dead and dying men; the mangled

carcases of ten thousand horses, which had, in some cases, been cut for food before life had ceased, the craving of famine at other points forming groups of cannibals; the air enveloped in flame and smoke; the prayers of hundreds of naked wretches, flying from the peasantry whose shouts of vengeance echoed incessantly through the woods; the wrecks of cannon, powder-waggons, military stores of all descriptions, and every ordinary as well as extraordinary ill of war combined with the asperity of the climate, formed such a scene as probably was never witnessed to such an extent in the history of the world.

At Viazma, fifty French, by a savage order, were burned alive. In another village fifty men had been buried alive; but these terrible acts of ferocity were minor features — they ended in death with comparatively little protracted suffering. Here death, so much invited, so solicited as a friend, came with dilatory step; but still he came without interval of torturing pause.

I will cite three or four of the most painful incidents that I witnessed.

1. A number of naked men, whose backs had been frozen while they warmed the front of their bodies, sat round the burning embers of a hut. Sensible at last to the chill of the air, they had succeeded in turning themselves, when the fire caught the congealed flesh, and a hard burnt crust covered the whole of their backs. The wretches were still living as I passed.

2. Sixty dying naked men, whose necks were laid upon a felled tree, while Russian men and women with large faggot-sticks, singing in chorus and hopping round, with repeated blows struck out their brains in succession.

3. A group of wounded men, at the ashes of another cottage, sitting and lying over the body of a comrade which they had roasted, and the flesh of which they had begun to eat.

4. A French woman, naked to her chemise, with black, long, dishevelled hair, sitting on the snow, where she had remained the whole day and in that situation had been delivered of a child, which had afterwards been stolen from her. This was the extreme of mental anguish and bodily suffering.

I could cite a variety of other sad and sorry calamities, but the very recollection is loathsome.

As a man and as an Englishman, I did all in my power to mitigate their griefs. I saved the woman; I gave what little bread I had to the famished; but my all was a mite, and my aid to the afflicted was, from a combination of controlling circumstances, but very inadequate to my desire. Even lives that I preserved were probably but prolonged for a very short date. One anecdote of a veteran French grenadier I, however, must notice. I was just putting a bit of biscuit into my own mouth, when I turned my eye upon his gaze. It was too expressive to be resisted; I gave him what I designed for myself. The tears burst from his eyes, he seemed to bless the morsel, and then, amidst sobs of gratitude, expressed his hope that an Englishman might never want a benefactor in his need. He lived but a few moments afterwards.

In his historical work Narrative of Events during the Invasion of Russia by Napoleon Bonaparte, and the Retreat of the French Army, 1812, *which was not published until after his death, Wilson, referring to himself in the third person as 'the English General', gives additional sidelights.*

On coming to the first enemy's bivouac on the morning of the 5th, some Cossacks accompanying the English General, seeing a gun and several tumbrils at the bottom of a ravine, with the horses lying on the ground, dismounted, and taking up the feet of several, hallooed, ran, and kissed the English General's knees and horse, danced, and made fantastic gestures like crazy men. When the delirium had somewhat subsided, they pointed to the horses' shoes and said: 'God has made Napoleon forget that there was a winter in our country. In spite of Kutuzov the enemy's bones shall remain in Russia.'

It was soon ascertained that all horses of the enemy's army were in the same improperly-shod state, except those of the Polish corps, and the Emperor's own, which the Duke of Vicenza,[1] with due foresight, had kept always rough-shod, as is the usage of the Russians.

From that time the road was strewed with guns, tumbrils, equipages, men, and horses; for no foraging parties could quit the high-road in search of provisions, and consequently the debility hourly increased.

[1] Caulaincourt, the Grand Equerry.

Thousands of horses soon lay groaning on the route, with great pieces of flesh cut off their necks and most fleshy parts by the passing soldiery for food; whilst thousands of naked wretches were wandering like spectres, who seemed to have no sight or sense, and who only kept reeling on till frost, famine, or the Cossack lance put an end to their power of motion. In that wretched state no nourishment could have saved them. There were continual instances, even amongst the Russians, of their lying down, dozing, and dying within a quarter of an hour after a little bread had been supplied.

All prisoners, however, were immediately and invariably stripped stark naked and marched in columns in that state, or turned adrift to be the sport and the victims of the peasantry, who would not always let them, as they sought to do, point and hold the muzzles of the guns against their own heads or hearts to terminate their suffering in the most certain and expeditious manner; for the peasantry thought that this mitigation of torture 'would be an offence against the avenging God of Russia, and deprive them of His further protection'.

When General Bennigsen and the English General, with their staffs, were one afternoon on the march, they fell in with a column of seven hundred naked prisoners under a Cossack escort; this column, according to the certificate given on starting, had consisted of twelve hundred and fifty men, and the commandant stated 'that he had twice renewed it, as the original party dropped off, from the prisoners he collected en route, and that he was then about completing his number again'.

Amongst this wretched convoy was a young man who attracted notice by his appearance, and by his keeping a little aloof from the main group. One of General Bennigsen's staff, of high titular rank,[1] after entering into some conversation with him about his country, rank, and capture, asked him 'if he did not under present circumstances wish for death?' 'Yes,' said the unhappy man, 'I do, if I cannot be rescued, for I know I must in a few hours perish by inanition, or by the Cossack lance, as I have seen so many hundred comrades do, or being unable from cold, hunger, and fatigue to keep up. There are those in France who will lament my fate — for their sake I should wish to return; but if that be impossible, the sooner this ignominy and suffering are over the better.' The

[1] The Grand Duke Constantine.

questioner then said that 'from the bottom of his heart he pitied his fate, but that aid for his preservation was impossible: if, however, he really wished to die at once, and would lie down on his back, to give proof of the interest he took in him, he himself would inflict the death blow on his throat'.

General Bennigsen was some little distance in advance, but the English General, who had stopped to hear the conversation, on finding that such a cruel issue was proposed, remonstrated against the idea, urging the necessity 'of saving the unfortunate officer' — for so he proved to be — '*coûte que coûte*', after having excited hopes by engaging in a discourse with him.

Finding that there was no inclination to abandon the intention, the English General spurred forward to overtake and bring back General Bennigsen; but happening to turn round before he could reach him, he saw the Russian officer, who had dismounted, strike with his sabre the fatal blow that severed the head nearly from the body! Nor could this officer afterwards be made to think that he had done a reprehensible act. He defended it 'by the motive, and the relief afforded to the sufferer, there being no means to save him, and if there had been, no one daring to employ them'.

The slaughter of the prisoners with every imaginable previous mode of torture by the peasantry still continuing, the English General sent off a dispatch to the Emperor Alexander 'to represent the horrors of these outrages and propose a check'. The Emperor by an express courier instantly transmitted an order 'to prohibit the parties under the severest menaces of his displeasure and punishment'; at the same time he directed 'a ducat in gold to be paid for any prisoner delivered up by peasant or soldier to any civil authority for safe custody'. The order was beneficial as well as creditable, but still the conductors were offered a higher price for their charge, and frequently were prevailed on to surrender their trust, for they doubted the justifiable validity of the order.

Famine also ruthlessly decimated the enemy's ranks. Groups were frequently overtaken, gathered round the burning or burnt embers of buildings which had afforded cover for some wounded or frozen; many in these groups were employed in peeling off with their fingers and making a repast of the charred flesh of their comrades' remains.

Innumerable dogs crouched on the bodies of their former

masters, looking in their faces, and howling their hunger and their loss; whilst others were tearing the still living flesh from the feet, hands, and limbs of moaning wretches who could not defend themselves, and whose torment was still greater, as in many cases their consciousness and senses remained unimpaired.

The clinging of the dogs to their masters' corpses was most remarkable and interesting. At the commencement of the retreat, at a village near Selino, a detachment of fifty of the enemy had been surprised. The peasants resolved to bury them alive in a pit: a drummer boy bravely led the devoted party and sprang into the grave. A dog belonging to one of the victims could not be secured; every day, however, the dog went to the neighbouring camp, and came back with a bit of food in his mouth to sit and moan over the newly-turned earth. It was a fortnight before he could be killed by the peasants, afraid of discovery.

General Count de Langeron, commanding a Russian infantry division in Chichazov's army, was also appalled at Russian treatment of some French prisoners, and says that the officers did their best to stop such revengeful atrocities.

Soon pity took the place of this thirst for revenge, which was certainly cruel and unjust but was perhaps excusable in view of the evil inflicted on their country and of memories of an invasion reminiscent of the most barbarous times. Soon they looked in silence and with indifference on the victims offered to them by fate, and then they shared their bread with them — a useless, even a cruel act of humanity, since it served merely to prolong the frenzied agony of these wretches.

Between the Vilya and Molodechno, where we arrived on 22 November, the road goes through an immense forest. It was so blocked with corpses that the Pavlograd Hussars who formed the advance-guard and moved on foot were obliged to lift these bodies and throw them aside in order to clear a path for the column. . . . In this forest I saw a woman who had just given birth to a child and had then died beside her dead baby. One cannot imagine the number of women the French army dragged along, and I noticed that they stood the cold better than the men did.

I asked several of these poor creatures who walked with us

where they were heading. They all replied: 'To Vilna, sir, to take up winter quarters. Napoleon promised us that.' I said to them: 'But you are no longer with him, you are in the midst of your enemies. What winter quarters can you hope for?' They answered: 'Sir, it's all the same. You don't harm us, you feed us, and we are going to Vilna to find winter quarters.' One could not deflect them from this notion and hope, which Napoleon had inspired in his entire army.

I saw a dead man, his teeth deep in the haunch of a horse which was still quivering. I saw a dead man inside a horse which he had disembowelled and emptied in order to crawl inside and get warm. I saw another man tearing with his teeth at the entrails of a dead horse. I did not see the wretched French eating one another, but I did see corpses from the thighs of which strips of flesh had been cut for eating.

Sergeant François Bourgogne of the Guard writes that on 5 November they set off early in the morning.

Before leaving, each regiment of the Guard made an issue of hand-mills to grind corn, provided we found any. But as there was nothing to grind and as these articles were heavy and useless, we got rid of them within twenty-four hours. This was a sad day, because some of the sick and wounded died. Hitherto they had made superhuman efforts in the hope of reaching Smolensk, where it was expected that food and lodging would be found.

That evening we halted near a wood and orders were given for shelters to be built for the night. A moment later our *cantinière*, Madame Dubois, wife of our company barber, was taken ill, and almost at once gave birth to a large baby boy. Snow was falling, and there were twenty degrees of frost: a wretched situation for a woman. I must say that in these circumstances Colonel Bodelin,[1] who commanded our regiment, did all he possibly could to help this woman, and lent his coat to cover the shelter in which Madame Dubois was bearing her pain with courage. The regimental surgeon also spared no effort, and in the end everything turned out well.

[1] Pierre, Baron Bodelin (1764–1824), had been in the battle of the Pyramids and at the siege of Acre. In Russia he was with Roguet's 2nd Division of the Young Guard, and in 1813 was promoted general.

That same night our soldiers killed a white bear which was eaten at once.

After spending a very painful night because of the extreme cold, we set off again. The Colonel lent his horse to Madame Dubois, who held her new-born baby in her arms and wrapped in a sheepskin. She herself was covered with the greatcoats of two men who had died during the night.

[*Bourgogne's account continues two days later.*]

We had been on the march for about an hour when day broke, and as we had caught up the corps ahead of us, we made a short halt. Our *cantinière*, Mother Dubois, wanted to use this rest to breast-feed her baby, but all of a sudden she gave a wail: her child was dead and as hard as wood. Those round her gave what comfort they could, saying that this was a good thing for her and the child; and in spite of her wailing and tears they pulled away the baby which she was hugging to her breast. It was handed to a sapper who went a few yards from the road with the child's father. The sapper dug a hole in the snow with his axe; meanwhile the father knelt, holding his child in his arms. When the hole was finished, he kissed the child and laid it in the grave. They covered it, and all was over.

Henri Beyle, who was later to write Le Rouge et le Noir *and* La Chartreuse de Parme *under the pseudonym Stendhal, was serving in the war commissariat and as an auditor in Paris. Then in July he was sent to join the Grand Army, carrying documents for the Emperor. On 9 November he wrote a letter to the wife of Count Pierre Daru, who had accompanied Napoleon as a Secretary of State and had just replaced the ailing Count Dumas as Intendant-General. Beyle's own appointment was* Directeur-général des approvisionnements de réserve.

Madame, here I am again in attractive Smolensk, which is this time a trifle spoilt by snow. I have just made a sentimental journey here from Moscow, and beg leave to give you some account of it. I can think of nothing more insipid than to praise something when one knows all the circumstances in advance. One travels from Paris to Strasbourg, one knows the name of nearly every post, one will grumble at a few postilions, and one will tell several innkeepers that they are rascals. This is all very true, but what could be more tedious? One is almost pleased when a wheel breaks and so provides some excitement.

Instead of this, I have just made a charming journey. Three or four times a day I swung from extreme boredom to extreme pleasure. I must admit that these pleasures were by no means subtle; for instance, one of the keenest occurred one evening when I found a few potatoes to eat without salt and with my mouldy ration bread. You can see the depths of our misery. This state of affairs lasted eighteen days: I left Moscow on 16 October and arrived on 2 November. Count Dumas had given me orders to leave with a convoy of 1,500 wounded, escorted by two to three hundred men. You can picture the huge number of little vehicles, the curses, the endless arguments, and all these carriages cutting in on one another and sinking into quagmires of mud. Regularly each day we spent two or three hours in a muddy stream, short of everything. That was when I cursed the ridiculous idea of coming to Russia. When we arrived in the evening after travelling all day and covering three or four leagues, we camped and slept a little, freezing the while.

On 24 October, as we were lighting our fires, we were surrounded by a swarm of men who opened fire. Complete confusion reigned. The wounded cursed. We had the greatest difficulty in making them take up their muskets. We repulsed the enemy, but we believe we are destined for great adventures. We had a gallant wounded general named Mourier[1] who explained the affair. Attacked as we were at that time of evening by a horde of infantry, it seemed probable that we were facing four or five thousand Russians, partly soldiers of the line, partly indignant peasants. We were surrounded and it was no safer to retreat than to advance. We decided to spend the night on our feet and next day, at first light, to form square, put our wounded in the centre, and try to break through the Russians. If hard-pressed, we would abandon our vehicles, form a small square, and fight to the last man rather than let ourselves be captured by peasants who would kill us slowly with knife-stabs or in some other pleasant fashion.

[1] General Pierre, Baron Mourier (1766–1844), commanding a light-cavalry brigade in Ney's corps, had been wounded at Borodino.

Having made this resolve, we took the necessary steps. Each man made up a bundle of what he regarded as his least essential belongings, ready to jettison them at the first attack so as to lighten the vehicle. I shared a room with five or six wounded colonels, who had been unknown to me a week earlier but who had become intimate friends on the march. . . .

All these men agreed that we were done for. We distributed our napoleons to the servants in an attempt to save a few of them. We had all become close friends. We drank what wine we had left. Next day, which was to be such a great day, we set off on foot, walking beside our carriages and armed from head to toe. There was such a mist that one could see less than four yards, and we kept on stopping. I had a book by Madame du Deffand,[1] and read almost all of it. The enemy did not consider us worthy of their anger, and we were not attacked until the evening, and then by some Cossacks who stabbed fifteen or twenty wounded men with their lances.

There, Madame, is the best episode of our journey. It was proper that I should render you an account of it. Although I always remain hopeful, during the night I did what I believe everyone else did: I drew up the balance-sheet of my life and reproached myself bitterly for not having had the sense to tell you just how devoted to you I am.

[*Beyle wrote again next day to the Countess, who was living in Paris.*]

The physical difficulties we met with on the journey from Moscow were diabolical. There is not a market porter who is as exhausted at the end of his day's work as we were each evening when we came to build our little hut of dry branches and to light our fire. I am still frozen, and no doubt you can see this from my scrawl.

My dear cousin, you would not recognize us, except for the Marshal, whose vehicles have held out, thanks to the kindness of his servants and of fifteen horses. We all look frightful. We re-

[1] Marie de Vichy-Chamrond, Marquise du Deffand (1697–1780), known for her brilliant Paris *salon* and her correspondence with, among others, Horace Walpole.

semble our lackeys. Quite literally, the first of us to arrive in Smolensk was taken for an insolent lackey, because he stepped forward to shake hands with the master of the house. We are far removed from Parisian elegance. I am reckoned to be the most fortunate because I saved my carriage by means of money and flying into a rage with any waggons which came near. If one can call 'saved' having only four shirts and one greatcoat. The trouble is, not everyone else takes this so cheerfully. A little gaiety would save the appearance of our misery, but those who are not fairly stout-hearted are full of bitterness.

Besides, all these unpleasantnesses are for the rich members of the army. The soldier lives well, he has cups full of diamonds and pearls. They are the happy ones in the army, and as they are in a majority, that is as it should be.

Amédée de Pastoret, Intendant of White Russia for two months, found himself caught up in the disasters of the Grand Army and obliged to retreat from his headquarters in Vitebsk. He reached Smolensk on 10 November.

Our troops, in particular the Grenadiers of the Old Guard, had set up a veritable bazaar at a main crossroads in the town. There one could find an incredible number of things: everything that luxury can desire or want require. In one place a *vivandière* would be offering watches, rings, necklaces, silver vases, and sometimes precious stones. Elsewhere a grenadier was selling brandy or furs. Further on a soldier of the train offered the complete works of Voltaire or the letters to Émilie by Desmoustier.[1] A *voltigeur* had horses and carriages on show, and a cuirassier had set up shop with shoes and clothing. It would be hard to imagine a more curious spectacle, and at this period, when hope was still alive, we retained enough composure to visit the bazaar frequently, and to listen to the shouts, arguments, and speeches of buyers and sellers alike.

That this abuse should have been tolerated was most unfortunate. The officers, whose needs were as numerous as anyone else's, went looking for everything they needed in these markets, or else to exchange whatever they had no more use for. They

[1] *Lettres à Émilie sur la mythologie*, by Charles-Albert Desmoustier (1760–1801).

treated those they did business with as equals, and henceforth the soldiers lost all respect for men with whom they had bargained or shared profit and loss. If a remnant of discipline survived we shall soon see what circumstances weakened it and then how it disappeared altogether.

In his letter-journal written for his wife in Westphalia, Major von Lossberg describes the scenes in Smolensk on 12 November:

Had order prevailed in Smolensk when all the corps were allowed into the town, the Army, as I saw to my own satisfaction in several magazines, would have found enough flour and fodder for a fortnight; but the right of the strongest often dislocated the distribution queue and anyone who failed to stand firm received nothing. If proper measures had been taken there should have been no shortage of meat either, since 1,000 cattle fell into the hands of the Cossacks not far from the town, and these could well have been protected.

. . . I cannot leave Smolensk without mentioning a regular fair which I found in the square where stood the magazines that issued rations. Hundreds of soldiers, most of them from the French Guard, were dealing in plunder they had obtained during the campaign, particularly in Moscow, and this largely comprised clothing, women's shawls, and scarves of all kinds, as well as articles stolen from churches. A non-commissioned officer in a green uniform — from his looks and manner of talking French he was probably Italian — asked 2,000 francs of me for a church ornament which, if he was speaking the truth (he talked with great knowledge about diamonds and explained the value of the different stones), was worth at least ten times that price. The throng of soldiers of all nationalities — they included many buyers too — was so great that one had difficulty in making one's way forward. For twenty francs I bought a yellow-brown beaver cloak with a double collar, and this I put on straight away. Smolensk Jews, who pushed in with great impudence and bought as well as sold, did a considerable trade here, but will they be able to retain their profits? From one of them I bought half a pound of coffee for a five-franc piece.

On 14 November General Compans wrote from Smolensk to his wife Louise:

I owe you a description of my costume which has led several of my companions to nickname me 'the Tartar'.

A cap of crimson velvet edged with the sable you gave me in Hamburg. A dress coat without embroidery or epaulets, though none of this is visible and my right shoulder requires no epaulet.[1] Blue breeches. Top boots. And over the top of all this, a roomy greatcoat lined with very good fox fur and trimmed with sable tails.

This fur, the collar of which covers my ears, reaches down to my ankles and lets nothing be seen except my cap and the feet of my boots.

Over this fur I wear my sword, hanging from a belt of gold-embroidered crimson velvet. The three stars on the sword-knot are the only indications of my rank. I have allowed myself the cap instead of a hat so as to protect my neck from the cold, as this would have hindered my wound from healing — that is, the recovery of my right arm. There, my dearest, is the full-length portrait of Compans the Tartar who sometimes goes for a fortnight without shaving.

General de Caulaincourt relates how Napoleon, in the belief that Kutuzov was trying to steal several marches on him and that he must quicken the pace of retreat to avoid being cut off, joined the Guard and Headquarters at Lyadyi, west of Krasnyi, on 17 November.

Here we found inhabitants and some provisions; hens and ducks wandered in the yards, to everybody's astonishment, because we had seen nothing like this since crossing the Niemen. These tokens of plenty relaxed every face, every man thinking our privations were over. I record these details among the grave events which threatened us, because these little things explain the situation in which we found ourselves, and because they have a strong influence on Frenchmen, who are cheered up by the least thing. For men accustomed, since leaving Moscow, to finding nothing but uninhabited places, devastated houses, corpses instead of living

[1] He had been wounded on the shoulder at the battle of Borodino.

human beings, it was a great event to see people in their houses and to find a meal there. The very modest resources of Lyadyi, added to those purchased in the neighbourhood, allayed the hunger of many who were accustomed to scorn all dangers but did not want to die of hunger, even if they merely went on living in order to brave new dangers.

The Cossacks continually raided our line of march, which they crossed whenever there was a gap, riding between divisions, even between regiments. However, three resolute men armed with muskets were enough to keep the enemy at a respectful distance. But where they had no bullets to fear, or where horse-drawn waggons were moving in disorder, or where unarmed soldiers had become isolated, the Cossacks charged down unexpectedly, killed some, wounded others, robbing those whose lives they spared, and plundering any waggon or carriage they came upon.

You can easily imagine the anxiety caused by such activities and the effect on the army's morale. More serious still, communications were made very difficult, not only from one corps to another, but even between divisions. The staff did not receive any reports, and their orders either failed to arrive or else travelled so slowly that they arrived too late.

Sergeant Bourgogne tells us that as far as Krasnyi he managed to keep fairly cheerful and patient, but then he became sad, a prey to sinister forebodings, and feverish.

The days were so short that it only got light at eight o'clock and darkness fell before four in the afternoon. That is why so many unfortunate soldiers strayed or got lost, because it was always dark by the time we reached our bivouacs, where the remnants of every corps mingled. All night one heard men arriving and calling out in a weak voice: 'Fourth Corps! . . . First Corps! . . . Third Corps! . . . Imperial Guard! . . .' And other men, already lying down and without strength, thinking they might get some help from those who had just come in, made an effort to call back 'Here, friends!', because people were no longer searching for their regiments but for the army corps to which they had belonged and which now mustered the equivalent of at most two regiments whereas a fortnight earlier there had been thirty.

Nobody could get his bearings or indicate which regiment he belonged to. There were many soldiers who, at the end of a whole day's march, had to wander about for part of the night in search of their particular corps. They rarely found it; and then, not knowing the hour of departure for the morning, they fell asleep too late and woke up to find themselves surrounded by Russians. How many thousands of men were captured and perished in this way!

[*Bourgogne bivouacked for the night a few miles west of Krasnyi.*]

It was about midnight when a sentry warned me that he could see a horseman who appeared to be coming towards us. I ran out with two armed men to see who this could be. After a little way I could clearly make out a rider, but he was preceded by a man on foot who looked as if he were being driven forward by the man on horseback. When they came close the horseman identified himself. He was a dragoon of the Guard and in order to procure food for himself and his horse he had slipped into the Russian camp during the night and, so as to avoid notice, had put on the helmet of a Russian cuirassier he had killed that same day. In this way he had gone through part of the enemy's camp, had taken a truss of hay and a little flour, had wounded one sentry with his sword, and had knocked down another one whom he was bringing in as a prisoner.

This brave dragoon's name was Melet, a native of Condé.[1] He spent the rest of the night with us. He told me that he did not take risks on his own account, but for his horse, for poor Cadet as he called him. He told me that he wanted at all costs to obtain food for the horse 'because if I save my horse, he in turn will save me'. This was the second time since Smolensk that he had penetrated a Russian camp. On the first occasion he had brought off a horse ready harnessed.

He had the good fortune to reach France with his horse Cadet, with whom he had already made the campaigns of 1806–07 in Prussia and Poland, of Spain in 1808, Germany in 1809, Spain again in 1810–11, and 1812 in Russia. Later he served in Saxony in 1813 and in France the following year. His poor horse was killed at Waterloo after taking part in more than a dozen major battles under the Emperor's command and in over thirty actions.

[1] Bourgogne also came from Condé-sur-l'Escaut, near Valenciennes.

In the course of this miserable campaign I met Melet once more, making a hole in the ice with an axe, in the middle of a lake, so as to get water for his horse. One day I spotted him on top of a barn which was on fire: at the risk of being caught in the flames he was trying to pull straw from the roof to feed the horse, because there was no more for the horses to eat than there was for us.

Eugen von Württemberg relates that in a village between Krasnyi and Orsha he encountered Prince Kutuzov for the first time since meeting him near Tarutino.

After welcoming me in the friendliest possible manner, a few words of reproof did not fail to appear in what he said. This went approximately as follows: 'Our young hotheads are angry with the old man for curbing their desires. They do not reflect that the circumstances alone are achieving more than our weapons. However, we ourselves must not knock at the frontier like haggard tramps.'

Colonel Hermann von Boyen of the Prussian Army was on a secret mission in St. Petersburg when news arrived of the Russian victory at Krasnyi, and he attended the thanksgiving service.

That afternoon there was a public riot in St. Petersburg which I feel I should mention as an evident contribution to the prevalent mood. At the end of the service the public had been granted permission to see the captured French eagles and Marshal Davout's baton which were on display in the church. This naturally attracted an exceptional crowd, and in the mêlée the Marshal's baton suddenly vanished. How this happened is frankly still a mystery as far as I am concerned, because when I saw these trophies they were placed so high that a person could not reach them except with difficulty. Enough that this baton captured in the baggage was gone, and at once word went round that it had been found with a member of the company of French actors then in St. Petersburg. For a long while these Parisian artists had been a target for public hatred, and only the Tsar had kept them there out of an untimely fancy. But now, once public opinion had been won over by this real or maybe fictitious stain on a member, even the imperial will had to give way to steadily increasing public disapproval. That same day every member of the company was embarked for their own safety, taken to Kronstadt, and from there sent on via Finland to Sweden.

Baron Larrey, Surgeon-in-Chief of the Grand Army, gives us some of his physiological observations.

I noticed that people with dark hair and an emotional, labile temperament, mostly from the countries of southern Europe, stood up better to the severe cold than did fair-haired men of phlegmatic temperament and coming for the most part from northern countries. This is contrary to the view usually held. The circulation of the first group is no doubt more active; their vital forces have more energy; it is likely, too, that, even in conditions of extreme cold, their blood retains much better the principles of animal warmth identified with their pigmentation. From the same cause their morale remains higher; they do not lose heart; and thanks, of course, to a care for their self-preservation, they know better how to avoid dangers than do the usually apathetic inhabitants of cold, damp climates.

. . . It is evident that the cold exercises its sedative effects chiefly on the brain and the nervous system. One fact goes far towards proving this: on our return from Moscow those people who had worn no fur hat or who had little hair were more susceptible to the cold; their heads lost more readily the heat they require.

The snow and icy water that the soldiers swallowed, hoping thereby to allay their hunger, or to quench the thirst produced by irritation of the mucous membrane in the stomach, largely contributed to the death of these individuals, since the little heat left in the viscera was absorbed. In particular they killed those who had grown thin from abstinence and the lack of nourishing food. In such people death was preceded by constrictive pains in the epigastric region, by sudden fainting fits, by a painful contraction of the throat, and by obvious anxiety — all symptoms of hunger.

I noticed from experience that a little good wine or coffee eased the hunger and stopped its painful effects. I remember how I had gone three whole days without taking anything except for two or three cups of pure coffee without sugar, when a friend gave me a glass of Bordeaux wine which I drank with indescribable pleasure. From that moment the symptoms of hunger to which I had been a prey for several hours vanished.

Horses in particular died very quickly from eating snow. To keep them alive one used to melt snow or ice over a camp fire if one had a suitable receptacle, and make them drink a small quantity of this water.

Sergeant Auguste Thirion of the 2nd Cuirassiers had been given the honourable but heavy duty of carrying the standard.

I marched with an escort provided by the few cuirassiers who still had horses, and every day, every hour, the number decreased. . . . My own horse's turn came, and the poor animal which I was tugging behind me, having gone two nights with nothing to eat except the bark of trees to which it had been tethered, dropped from exhaustion and hunger. I cut short the agony of this good companion by shooting it in the head. I threw my cuirass and sabre under a bridge, not wishing to leave my arms to the enemy. I shouldered the standard and a double-barrelled gun which I had bought in Moscow and which one of my dismounted cuirassiers was carrying, and continued the retreat on foot.

I must confess that I found the standard extremely heavy. At the end of a fairly long staff was a bronze eagle with open wings. Under the eagle, and nailed to the staff, was a square flag of white satin surrounded on three sides by a gold fringe made out of bullion the length and thickness of one's finger.

On this flag had been embroidered in large letters of gold: *The Emperor to his 2nd Regiment of Cuirassiers.* The reverse side bore the names of all the battles in which the regiment had taken part, and on every square inch of satin left blank by these inscriptions was a swarm of bees half the size of one's thumb.

To the eagle's feet was tied a white satin cravat which hung double for a yard and had at each end a tassel made from twisted fringes larger than a finger, all in gold. The whole thing was furled in a morocco sheath.

This enormous weight, to which was added that of my double-barrelled gun, was crushing my shoulder, and I looked for some way of getting rid of it, because quite apart from the fatigue, I felt a large burden of responsibility, if one bears in mind the dishonour attached to losing a standard.

Eventually, by dint of representing to my colonel first the state of exhaustion I was in, secondly the danger that, during the constant Cossack raids to which we were subjected, the standard might find itself undefended and be captured as a result, and thirdly the fact that my death would not save the standard, because my duty was to defend it as long as I had a spark of life in me — all these considerations decided the colonel to conceal it.

I unscrewed the eagle, which was placed in the portmanteau belonging to Millot, the adjutant; the flag and cravat were folded and put in the colonel's portmanteau; and the staff was burnt. Once this had been done, I felt very relieved, both morally and physically.

One eyewitness who comments on the revolting egoism inspired by an individual's desire to save his own skin is G. Lecointe de Laveau, who had been living in Moscow before Napoleon's arrival there.

Men curtly refused others a place by the fire, or charged up to one louis for the privilege. People declined to give a piece of bread or to lend a water-bottle. Beside a bivouac where the owner, who still had some rations, was boiling meat or taking coffee or drinking liquor, an unfortunate man, without shelter, would be roasting a piece of horse that he swallowed half cooked. Others had nothing to eat except a few handfuls of barley which they grilled. There were soldiers who prolonged their existence only by munching raw peas which they found in the horses' forage.

I have seen a senior officer reserve a stable for his horses, and prevent anyone pulling it down for firewood, even while men bivouacked nearby were dying of cold, and while women were obliged to keep their children warm by covering them in a pelisse, and wept tears of despair.

. . . It was this egoism which compelled the soldiers to throw down their arms when they no longer received any rations. Having no restraining hand, these men had ceased to obey their officers and become guilty of all the crimes that are begotten by disorder and licence. Theft was committed openly, and one even saw people barbarous enough to rob their comrades just when these wretches were in their death agony. 'Why wait?' they said with cruel composure. 'He is going to die anyway.'

It seemed as though the men had lost all feeling. I saw four waggons pass in single file over a soldier of the train who had just slipped, even though the drivers were ordered to stop. The fifth eventually obeyed, and the poor fellow was extricated and laid beside the road. He had his legs and thighs crushed.

One man was telling his companion that he had given a place on his sledge to a woman and that during a Cossack *hourra* she had fallen off. 'Did she really think,' added the barbarian, 'that I was going to stop and pick her up?'

On the roadside a medical officer, who had his hands and feet frozen, lay in the snow, imploring pity from passers-by and offering a very large sum of money to anyone who would take him to the next village. A man who had room for him on his sledge heard this proposition, went over, searched him and then, finding no money, abandoned him.

Dr. Heinrich von Roos found himself west of Krasnyi on 19 November.

On this day we were made particularly aware of the fact that soldiers were becoming weak-sighted and, indeed, many had gone totally blind. One saw men dragging their comrades along by sticks, like beggars. Massage with snow improved the condition for a while. Some were cured by this means, others remained blind; and to add to their misfortune, they often had the hard luck to be left behind by their companions.

The chief cause of this eye disease was the smoke of camp-fires, because in order to warm themselves as best they could, people used at night to put their head and hands over the flames. In addition, the snow wastes across which we struggled during the day were extremely injurious to many eyes. If one adds this combination of harmful influences to our general physical weakness, one can understand the eye trouble.

. . . The necessity for sleep had cost us many companions, especially youngsters, who required sleep more particularly. Some, when they slept alone, failed to hear the camp break up next morning, were left behind, and got lost; others lay down as soon as they arrived somewhere, omitted to take the food, little as it was, and early in the morning had to march on an empty stomach.

In earlier campaigns as well as this one I often saw young soldiers sleeping so soundly that they could not hear the cannon firing, even when balls flew over our camp. In such cases the corporal's cane was essential, because the urgency allowed for no gentle waking. Older soldiers slept lightly on the whole, and far less than the young ones.

J. M. Merme noted that during the retreat the Emperor stopped two or three times a day to supervise the movements of his rear-guard.

As I was in the 1st Company of the *Chasseurs* of the Guard, I found myself constantly on duty near the Emperor's person, and I had the privilege of lighting a fire for him at each of his halts. I owed this job to the fact that after helping to make the company's bivouac fire, I let those who felt the cold most get close to it. Seeing that I did not lay great store by warming myself, my captain gave me the task I have just mentioned.

This habit of never standing near the fire was noticed by my companions, who said in astonishment: 'This devil of an Egyptian is never cold. He helps us light a fire, but never makes use of it.'

As a result I never had a limb frozen, unlike so many other soldiers whose feet froze. All those who adopted my system came off well.

One day, as I was preparing to make the Emperor's fire, I put my handkerchief over my busby to help keep out the cold a bit. Seeing him approach, I tried to take it off, but he said to me: 'We are not at the Carrousel [Paris] here. It is colder today than usual, so keep the handkerchief on your head.'

Auguste Thirion, senior sergeant of the 2nd Cuirassiers, explains how horses became scarcer from day to day.

It was too cold to kill and cut up those we destined for our rations; our hands, exposed for so long to the cold air, would have refused to perform this service and would have frozen. So we cut a slice from the quarters of horses still on their feet and walking, and the wretched animals gave not the least sign of pain, proving beyond doubt the degree of numbness and insensitivity caused by the extreme cold. Under any other conditions these slices of flesh would have brought on a haemorrhage and death, but this did not occur with 28 degrees of frost. The blood froze instantly, and this congealed blood arrested the flow. We saw some of these poor horses walking for several days with large pieces of flesh cut away from both thighs; there had been a change in the colour of the coagulated blood, which had turned white, or rather yellow, and had become pus.

I had discovered another way of feeding myself. I possessed a small tin casserole which I would not have exchanged for a fortune, because it served to cook whatever I found or bought and induced me to practise the art of butcher. This was my method: when I found a horse near our halting-place, I inserted a knife blade as gently as possible between the ribs, held up my little casserole to catch the blood which flowed from this wound, and then cooked it. I thus found myself with a casserole full of black pudding which nowadays I should consider insipid and unattractive, but which at this period I thought delicious.

Captain Johann von Borcke from Magdeburg, having fought at Jena with the Prussian Army, had then transferred to the Westphalian service and was in 1812 aide-de-camp to General von Ochs. He left Orsha on 20 November.

A dark rumour had spread that two new enemy armies were threatening our line of retreat, after Kutuzov's army had let us out of its clutches and halted behind the Dnieper. Without being pursued, we approached the Berezina, but on the march these rumours steadily gained substance, and the names 'Chichagov' and 'Berezina' passed from mouth to mouth. At the time of our advance four months earlier the river had looked very insignificant to everyone, but now that it seemed possible that the crossing might be fiercely contested, people remembered clearly the long wooden bridge at Borisov and the black marshy bank; and these recollections were enough to make us shudder at the prospect of having to fight our way across against a fresh Russian army. Apart from Napoleon and some of his marshals, there were certainly only a few among the handful of healthy and armed soldiers representing the great French Army whose spirit was inspired by such superhuman courage that it could keep hoping for rescue if the rumours which appeared to seal our fate were confirmed. . . .

Gloomy, silent, and with downcast gaze, this rabble of dying men walked from Orsha to the Berezina like a funeral procession. Preoccupied only with oneself, feeling the seeds of death in one's enfeebled body, and only reminded that one was a human being through one's instinct for self-preservation, one was no longer capable of conversation, of communicating to companions and friends about what was going on and what was of common interest.

We listened with half an ear, answered curtly or not at all, and were without hope or fear. Indifference to everything, to death, even if one had escaped it at that very moment, dominated everybody's dulled spirits. We had sunk to the level of animals. Such was my own condition and that of most of my companions. Only now and then was this insensibility interrupted: the longing for life flickered; a yearning to see home and loved ones stirred, the soul overcame the weakened and brutish body and rose up again when one thought of God and Providence and did not give oneself up as a man.

The Crossing of the Berezina

NAPOLEON'S plan to reach Minsk, join forces with Schwarzenberg and, turning eastwards, to hold the line of the Berezina, was thwarted by the Russian capture of Minsk on 16 November and by the Austrians' failure to prevent Admiral Chichagov's 30,000 troops from moving into position along the river; the Admiral had been shuttling to and fro between Volynia, Grodno, and the Duchy of Warsaw, seldom in contact with the enemy and often deprived of normal communications and, thereby, of news of the Grand Army. In the belief that his Polish cavalry were holding the vital bridge at Borisov, Napoleon ordered the pontoon trains to be destroyed at Orsha, but in fact the bridgehead was lost when Chichagov's men came up on the 21st, surprised the cavalry, crossed the Berezina next day, and then headed east for Loshnitsa, ten miles from Borisov, only to be repulsed by Oudinot's 2nd Corps which had arrived on the scene.

Some of Oudinot's cavalry tried to rush the Borisov bridge, but it was burnt before their eyes, and the prospect of rebuilding it under Russian fire was not to be entertained. Instead the Grand Army must try to reach Vilna by way of the Zembin defile, just west of the river, thus slipping between Chichagov in the south and Wittgenstein's 30,000, who had already reached Chereya, forty miles to the north-east. Accordingly, Napoleon ordered Victor to hold off Wittgenstein so as to allow Ney, Eugène, and Davout to come up through Bobr and to enable Oudinot to throw bridges over the Berezina by Studyanka and Veselovo, through which passed the Zembin road. Normally small, the river was now swollen on account of a thaw, and its banks were marshy to a width of several hundred yards.

Covered by fortified bridgeheads and by forty guns placed on high ground at Studyanka, where peasants said the river was fordable, the French began on 25 November to build one bridge for the cavalry, guns, and vehicles, and a second, two hundred yards upstream, for the infantry. General Eblé's foresight in saving six waggons with tools, equipment, coal, iron material, and field forges, his personal example of zeal, devotion, and endurance, the heroic labours of the pontoniers in chilling water amid floes of

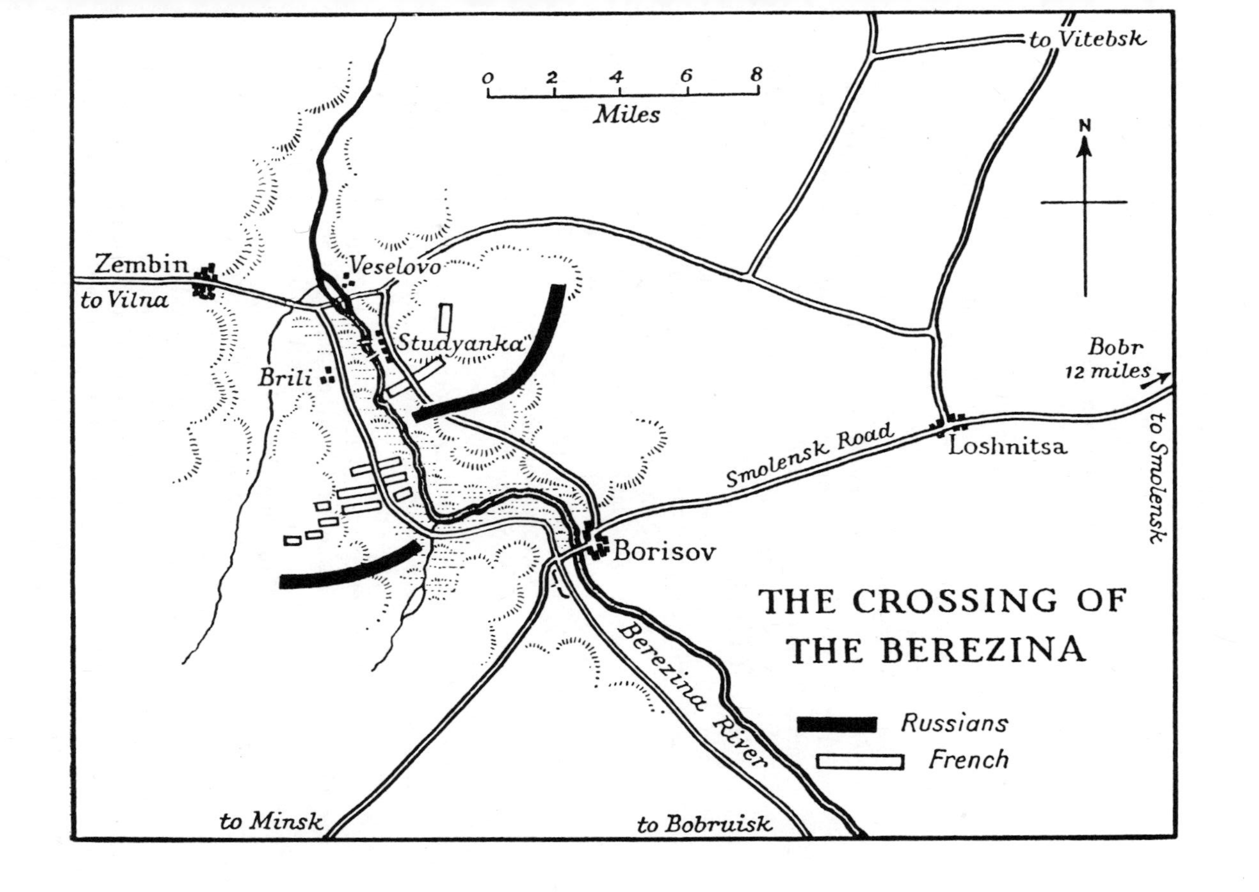
0
2
4
6
8
Miles
N
to Vitebsk
Zembin
to Vilna
Veselovo
Studyanka
Brili
Bobr
12 miles
to Smolensk
Loshnitsa
Smolensk Road
Borisov
THE CROSSING OF
THE BEREZINA
Berezina River
Russians
French
to Minsk
to Bobruisk

ice, and Oudinot's energy and skill at this juncture were to save the army.

The falling-back of Victor's corps to join Oudinot raised the force at Napoleon's disposal to about 40,000, a figure which does not include the thousands of stragglers. This effective remnant of the Grand Army was roughly the size of Kutuzov's main army, approaching from the east but on 26 November still distant at Staroselo, and was all that the Emperor had with which to force a passage of the Berezina while surrounded by superior numbers. Fortunately for him and for those under his command, the feigned march and demonstrations he ordered, coupled with Schwarzenberg's movements beyond Minsk, confused Chichagov into believing that the French would seek to cross the river *south* instead of north of Borisov. Moreover, the Admiral over-estimated Napoleon's strength, assuming that the stragglers were effective fighting troops. So he took his main force southwards, leaving only General Langeron's corps to hold the crossing-place at Borisov and — a far more serious error — placing at Brili opposite Studyanka nothing but a small Cossack detachment.

The French, amazed to find such negligible opposition on the far bank, quickly evicted this detachment facing their all-important bridges. Not until 27 November did the cautious, slow-moving Wittgenstein reach Studyanka, and by this time it was almost too late. Oudinot's corps and the artillery had crossed the previous afternoon. Ney was held up that night by the collapse of three trestles, but Eblé's weary, half-frozen men repaired it twice, and at noon next day Napoleon himself crossed with the Imperial Guard.

On the east bank, still waiting to cross, were the corps of Victor, Davout, and Eugène de Beauharnais, together with a confusion of stragglers, civilians — men, women, and children — miscellaneous detachments, and waggons. Victor deployed his troops about Studyanka to hold off Wittgenstein, but the latter headed south for Borisov instead, and just north of the town surrounded an isolated French division (Partouneaux's), which had been left behind, and compelled over 4,000 men to surrender. It seems that no troops crossed during the night of 27–28 November — a blunder which cost immense losses and produced woeful scenes.

At last, on the 28th, Chichagov, who had hurried back again after his misguided southward march and had then received reinforcements, launched a combined attack on both banks against the Grand Army, now dangerously split in two. To the west Ney and Oudinot repulsed the Russian efforts with heavy casualties, Oudinot being wounded again. To the east, Victor's men held their ground all day against attacks by Wittgenstein, and while the fighting went violently on, many more stragglers and vehicles were able to cross. When, however, the Russians managed to advance at one point and set up guns with which they swept the bridges and their approaches, the scenes among the jostling, panic-stricken mob under bombardment were appalling.

That night indeed, when Victor's troops crossed the river, leaving only a rearguard, they were obliged to cut their way through the throng. Next morning the bridges were set alight, thus thwarting pursuit for at least a day, but trapping on the far bank many thousands of stragglers and pathetic non-combatants, besides about three thousand horses and six hundred vehicles. In this ghastly crossing Napoleon lost approximately 25,000 troops, but twice that number came through — a remarkable feat. Miloradovich reached Borisov that same day, and Kutuzov's army came up on the 30th.

Alexandre-Arnault, General Count de Langeron, gives us a decidedly critical pen portrait of Admiral Pavel Chichagov (1767–1849), who had been brought up in England and was to become a naturalized Englishman in later life.

Chichagov was forty-five years of age. He was not devoid of mental powers, if one can give such a name to a mixture of slang, garrulity, and a very superficial education.

His brain was like a volcano: every minute it produced some new project, and this project, which was usually either absurd or impracticable, had to be executed instantly. He would allow neither argument nor delay in the execution of his whims.

Not one of his ideas was sound. The stiffness of his character and his excessive *amour-propre* prevented him from listening to or taking any advice. With unyielding obstinancy he followed whatever he had conceived in the delirium of his extravagant imagination.

He was no better judge of men than of events, and could never abandon a prejudice.

For three years he had been Russia's Navy Minister[1] and had ruined the Navy. He had no idea about land operations, and his ignorance of our organization and manœuvres soon made him the laughing-stock of his army.

[1] He was Minister from 1802 to 1812.

Chichagov's character accorded perfectly with his mind; he was hard and autocratic, ungrateful and coarse. He had every vice of the heart just as he had every extravagance of the mind. At one time a fanatical admirer of the English, at another time ridiculously enamoured of the French, he had only one constant emotion: hatred and scorn of his own nation, a scorn which he never stopped expressing, even when the cruel circumstances in which Russia found herself had developed the character of her people and soldiers and had won the esteem and admiration of the world.

However, Chichagov had one precious quality: he was honest and disinterested. He carried this virtue to excess both for himself and for others, and he included too many people in the view he held of the corruption both of the century and of his own nation.

It was difficult to understand what had decided the Emperor to entrust an army to this admiral, especially in such critical circumstances. Even had he been endowed by nature with all the talents and genius necessary for commanding land forces, an admiral could never have acquired the basic knowledge and above all the experience required for this service.

Admiral Chichagov and his army crossed the Niemen on 15 November and entered Minsk next day. The Admiral writes:

The governor, the authorities, and some Württemberg troops barely had time to escape. We had no difficulty in appreciating the importance of occupying Minsk. Evidently Napoleon had realized its advantageous position, and had decided to establish a food and ammunition depot in advance, with the eventual intention of installing his headquarters there, spreading his army in Volynia, resting his troops, bringing his formations up to strength with reinforcements from France and Poland, and preparing to resume the offensive or, at least, to await the return of good weather.

In effect we found enormous magazines in Minsk, enough food and ammunition to last an army of 100,000 men for several months. We saw very fine linen intended for twenty-four beds which had been prepared in case Napoleon arrived.

The hospitals contained more than eight thousand sick, lying higgledy-piggledy among corpses which had been there for a week. However, amid this desolation which was undoubtedly caused by the negligence of the Governor of Minsk, the French soldiers, frivolous by nature, and accustomed to hardship and privation, were still able to amuse themselves despite their misery. One saw them in the Minsk hospital heaping up their comrades' corpses and gaily playing cards on this strange table. They also enjoyed dressing the dead in a grotesque fashion, and adorning them with paper hats. They then placed them in the doorways and in the corners of the rooms. These shows entertained them, and they seemed to have no thought but to enjoy the few moments left to them.

We had great difficulty in finding the workmen we needed, in particular farriers to rough-shoe the horses, which by now could move only slowly along roads already covered with ice and snow. For this I employed all the workmen in the town and the Army. There was not a moment to lose if we were to capture Borisov before the enemy had time to assemble his forces there. This point, the main crossing-place for the French Army, was defended by a strong bridgehead built by the Russians and at this time occupied by the enemy.

The civil and ecclesiastical authorities in Minsk who had been unwilling or unable to follow the enemy asked to be presented to me. This was the first time since entering Russian Poland that I found myself outside the Jewish circle, Jews being the only inhabitants we had met in most of the towns. They had eventually attached themselves to Russia because the Russians sometimes paid them, whereas the others gave them nothing and even seized the little money they still had over. We found nobody but Jews to employ as spies or guides, and they were precious to us in this respect, since we were groping our way across a country for which we had no military maps, where the population was hostile to Russia, where we found recruits drilling everywhere in readiness to join the French, and where the peasants, who would only act as guides under duress, always tried to mislead us. As for the Jews they acted with great circumspection. They undertook the espionage, but without ever compromising themselves, and we ran as much risk from being deceived by them as by any other spy. However, protestations of zeal were not lacking, nor the formal resolve to sacrifice their lives for His Majesty's service, which, after the campaign, entitled them to exemption from billeting. But this advantage proved more apparent than real. The first time they wanted to profit by it, they met with a beating.

Count de Langeron describes what took place after Admiral Chichagov arrived at Borisov on 22 November.

All the corps (except Chaplitz's[1] detachment which remained at Brili, near Veselovo, ten versts to our left) assembled on the right bank of the Berezina, to right and left of the bridgehead. We had over 35,000 excellent troops — more than enough to gain the result we hoped for. These 35,000 heroes, veterans of ten campaigns, in good health, well fed, well armed, well equipped, could, if properly employed, overcome the 80,000 ragged, discouraged, and demoralized wretches with whom Napoleon was fleeing from Moscow.

In our position, and given the orders we had received, what should we have done? That question is easy to answer, and the most junior ensign in our Army would have been able to find the solution just as easily as the best of our generals.

We had to stay on the right bank of the Berezina: this bank is high and dominates both river and town. We needed to cut the bridge, establish our numerous guns on the heights, send a strong force of Cossacks in front of Borisov on the route along which the French Army was retreating, so that we should receive warning of its approach and line of march. We should also have sent out bodies of cavalry along the left bank of the river in both directions, prepared a bridge ready to throw across the Berezina at the spot where Count Wittgenstein would arrive, so as to facilitate a junction with him without loss of time. Above all we should have allowed nobody to establish positions in Borisov and remain bivouacked in the bridgehead. Finally, we could have burnt Borisov, though I admit that this useful step would have been very cruel.

The Admiral did none of these things. As he disliked bivouacs, he took up quarters in the best house in Borisov. He allowed, indeed he ordered, all the generals to lodge there too — I was weak

[1] General Chaplitz commanded a division in the Army of the Danube.

enough to do the same. He packed in the whole headquarters, all the Army's baggage, the ambulance, the mobile church, the offices of the general staff, the engineers, and the artillery. He cluttered up this small town to such an extent that not a single room remained unoccupied by a crowd of people, and vehicles blocked every street. And all this took place by our outposts on the road along which we expected the enemy, and which had only a weak line of Cossacks as protection.

Yet we had learnt that Kutuzov had already passed Smolensk and Orsha, and that Napoleon must be two or at most three marches away from us. Nothing could upset the Admiral's calm. It was useless to point out anything to him or to offer advice, without exposing oneself to a very tart rebuff, a scornful silence, or outrageous rudeness.

. . . At one o'clock on 23 November we heard sharp firing — two or three miles from the town. This was our advance-guard which had been attacked by Oudinot's corps. In a moment it was repulsed and dispersed and had to retire to Borisov in complete disorder. The French arrived on their heels. Nobody expected them. We were dining quietly. The carriage and waggon horses were neither harnessed nor bridled. I was the only person who, foreseeing some catastrophe, had my horses harnessed. I had three vehicles: a calash and two little carts. In one were all my office papers and a very large sum of money from the Army's treasury destined for the purchase of the troops' brandy ration. The other contained some provisions. I lost the latter and was very glad not to have to mourn the loss of the former. The two vehicles I saved were riddled with bullets.

By this time bullets were whistling through the streets. Our men — cavalry, infantry, gunners with their guns — were fleeing helter-skelter for the bridge, pursued by the French who were yelling in a really frightening manner. You can imagine the confusion and disorder which now reigned at Headquarters, which had been so rashly placed by the forward posts. Each man ran away, abandoning horses and vehicles, and many of them their dinner too — and this was not unwelcome to the French. The Admiral's meal was already on the table, and was captured, along with his silver plate, his belongings, his clothes, and his portfolio.

We incurred enormous and irreplaceable losses. Our wounded

and sick were left behind with the hospital equipment and they all perished. The rich church was lost. The records of the engineers, which contained all the most valuable plans from the Turkish wars and other maps prepared by our staff officers — there was no other copy in existence — were left in vehicles which fell into French hands. Many officers and servants could not escape and were taken prisoner. The disaster was complete. The Admiral, partly on foot, partly on horseback, managed, just as we did, to reach the heights on the right bank of the Berezina, where our troops were bivouacked.

Count Louis-Victor-Léon de Rochechouart (1788–1858), a French émigré who was a lieutenant in the Russian Imperial Guard, an aide-de-camp to the Tsar, on Admiral Chichagov's staff, records that on 22 November he went to see General de Langeron, who had posted his division in front of the Borisov bridgehead.

That evening the whole army corps joined him and bivouacked on the right bank of the Berezina, separated from the town by an exceptionally long bridge on account of the marshes on the left bank. I returned to sleep in the town.

Next day Admiral Chichagov assembled all the generals for a council of war. He was impatiently awaiting news from the advance-guard which had spent the night at Loshnitsa, six versts away, and which was then to make for Bobr. In the evening I dined with Madame Roshmanov, wife of the senior commissariat officer in our army. I was a close friend of his. . . . In the middle of dinner we saw some Russian hussars belonging to the advance-guard dash up, their horses white with foam. They shouted '*Frantsusyi!*' ['French'] and headed for the bridge. Madame Roshmanov, in a state of great alarm, fortunately insisted on crossing the river at once and setting off for Minsk, despite all my efforts to reassure her. I insisted on having at least some coffee. 'Come and drink it in Minsk,' she replied.

The number of refugees increased from one minute to the next, yet the same soldiers had fought bravely two evenings before. Instead of running to my lodging and ordering my servants to cross to the far bank, I tried to stop the fugitives. A sheer waste of effort. Panic-stricken and drunk with fear, if I may express it thus, they shouted '*Frantsusyi! Frantsusyi!*', being quite unable to say anything else. A few guns, followed by their ammunition waggons, rushed through the town at a gallop, knocking down or crushing everything in their way. One had to follow the torrent, so I headed for the bridge and there found Madame de Lambert,[1] bare-headed. She had managed to halt a few of her husband's hussars and had said to them in Russian: 'Children, are you going to abandon your wounded general?' They dismounted and carried their commander on their shoulders. Four mounted hussars, leading their comrades' horses, headed the procession to clear a path and protect the wounded man until he reached the far end of that interminable bridge.

I took advantage of the escort to cross the Berezina in the middle of the throng, and after risking being crushed or hurled into the river a score of times, I reached General de Langeron's bivouac. There I waited in vain for my horses and carriage. I hadn't even a coat.

The Admiral was just sitting down at table with his officers and had been obliged to leave the meal when it was served and, like me, cross that damned bridge on foot. It was all over in half an hour; that is to say, out of 10,000 men and twelve guns forming the advance-guard, only a thousand men and two guns crossed. The rest were captured or scattered. Fifty French *chasseurs* of Legrand's division,[2] fortified with a stiff brandy ration, had surprised the look-out posts of our advance-guard in front of Loshnitsa. They charged fiercely and swept them as far as the square in this little town, thereby causing a panic which routed the entire corps.

Poor Count Pahlen was unable to muster a hundred men to charge the French *chasseurs*. He had been commanding this division since the previous evening only and, unrecognized by his soldiers, was dragged along against his will by the fleeing mob. He reached our bivouac in an indescribable state of despair.

As soon as the Admiral got to the far bank, fearing at any minute to see the Grand Army arrive on the scene — he did not know its

[1] Major-General Count Lambert, commanding a cavalry corps, had been wounded in the shoulder during the attack on Borisov.

[2] Claude-Juste-Alexandre-Louis Legrand (1762–1815), a veteran of Hohenlinden, Austerlitz, Eylau, Essling, and Wagram, led the 6th Infantry Division in Oudinot's corps.

strength — he had the bridge cut in two places, so making any communication with the other bank impossible.

Grenadier François Pils (1785–1867) had for some years past been attached to Marshal Oudinot, Duke of Reggio, working as personal servant or batman, and seeing action at the battles of Austerlitz, Jena, Friedland, Essling, and Wagram. His memoirs are a valuable record; he was no mean artist, and his son Isidore became a painter of distinction.

The Duke of Reggio spent three-quarters of an hour with the Emperor and then returned to take charge of the works begun by the 2nd Corps for building a bridge between Veselovo and Studyanka. The work was pushed ahead by General Eblé. The bridge-builders had been warned not to talk and the troops of all arms were told to keep out of sight.

As all the preparatory work and the building of the trestles was done behind a hillock, which formed part of the river bank, the enemy look-out posts were unable to watch what our workmen were doing.

. . . The Marshal went outside several times during the night to get away from the smoky atmosphere in the hut. The landscape had a most striking appearance, because the moon lit up the ice-floes of the Berezina and, on the far side of the river, a Cossack post comprising four men only. In the distance we could see a few reddish clouds driven by the wind over the tips of the fir-trees, so to speak. These clouds reflected the camp-fires of the Russian Army.

Between seven and eight o'clock on the morning of the 26th, just as I was opening the door which was fastened by a tourniquet, the Emperor bumped into me and said: 'Is Oudinot there?' The Marshal recognized Napoleon's voice and came hurrying out. His Majesty wore a fur-lined coat and a green velvet cap trimmed with fur which came down over his eyes. The Prince of Neuchâtel [Berthier], who was with him, wore the same costume, but in purple. Oudinot led them to the edge of the Berezina.

The Emperor went a little beyond Studyanka and then studied the area, visited the works, and asked about the state of the 2nd Corps. The Marshal replied that it still had all its artillery and possessed more than fourteen guns captured from the Russians on the banks of the Drissa. He added that all his troops were ready to fight Admiral Chichagov's army, once they had crossed the river. Napoleon rubbed his hands and said: 'Well! You shall be my locksmith to open this passage.'

. . . At eight o'clock in the morning the bridge-builders began placing their trestles at equal distances in the river, which was thick with large floes. The men went into the water up to their shoulders, displaying superb courage. Some dropped dead and disappeared with the current, but the sight of this tragic end did not diminish their comrades' efforts. The Emperor watched these heroes and did not leave the river bank, where he was standing with Marshal Oudinot, Prince Murat, and the other generals, while the Prince of Neuchâtel, seated on the snow, dispatched correspondence and wrote out orders for the Army.

As the Engineers were not numerous enough to cope with such an immense job of work, General Aubry[1] sent for men from several infantry regiments to make fascines on which the roadway of the bridge could be laid.

At about half past nine the Emperor returned to the Marshal's quarters and was served with a cutlet which he ate standing up. When the *maître d'hôtel* handed him the salt-cellar, consisting of a screw of paper, His Majesty said: 'You are well equipped. All you lack is white salt.' The Duke of Reggio then shared what little food he had left with the generals who, for several days past, had been extremely short.

Just before eleven the Emperor was informed that the first bridge was in position. His Majesty at once issued his orders: the first battalion of Albert's[2] brigade was to open the passage. The Marshal went to the head of his first brigade and took command of the advance-guard. Napoleon, who was standing on the bridge-head, his feet on an ice-floe, said to him: 'Don't cross yet, Oudinot. You will get yourself captured!' 'I fear nothing in their midst, Sire,' Oudinot replied, pointing to his soldiers. And he dashed forward beside General Albert, while a *chasseur* led his horse.

[1] Claude-Charles Aubry de la Boucharderie (1773–1813) commanded the artillery in Oudinot's corps until August, when he was given a division.

[2] Joseph-Jean-Baptiste Albert (1771–1822), veteran of Eylau, Essling, and Wagram, commanded the 1st Brigade in the 6th Division.

The scouts had scarcely reached the left bank of the Berezina when carbine shots rang out from various points. The *voltigeurs* deployed as *tirailleurs* and, moving straight ahead, had to cross a marshy stretch before reaching the hill. This they climbed, and the Cossacks were driven one by one from the bushes behind which they had taken cover.

At the point where the crossing was made, the Berezina was three hundred feet wide; its greatest depth was six or seven feet; it flowed slowly and its bottom was muddy. . . .

All the bridging works were built with wood taken from houses demolished in Veselovo during the night of 25 November.

One of the very few Swiss officers to leave a record of the campaign was Captain Louis Bégos, who served in the 2nd Swiss Regiment, part of Oudinot's corps. His post was close to the two bridges which had been nearly completed over the river.

The work done by General Eblé's pontoniers was beyond all praise, especially in view of the blocks of ice which congested the river. One of the bridges was to serve the infantry, the other the artillery and cavalry. On the day we were due to cross to the right bank, the Emperor came to us and spoke sharply to the colonel. 'What is the strength of your regiment?' he asked. The colonel, taken aback by so brusque a demand, did not reply immediately. I saw the Emperor make a gesture of impatience and look irritated. He turned abruptly to me, only a few feet from the colonel, and asked me the same question. I replied without more ado: 'Sire, so many officers, so many men.' He did not answer, and went on his way.

Napoleon was not the great Emperor I had seen at the Tuileries. He looked tired and anxious. I seem to see him still, wearing his famous grey greatcoat. He left us at a gallop and rode through the whole of Oudinot's 2nd Corps. I watched him stop in front of the 1st Swiss Regiment which was in our brigade. My friend Captain Rey was well placed to study him at leisure, and like me he was struck by the Emperor's worried expression. On dismounting he leant against some beams and planks which were to be used in building the bridge. He looked down, and then raised his head with a preoccupied, impatient air. He turned to General Eblé and said: 'It's taking a very long time, General. A very long time.'

'Sire, you can see that my men are up to their necks in water, and the ice is delaying their work. I have no food or brandy to warm them with.'

'That will do,' replied the Emperor. He looked at the ground. A few moments later he began complaining again, and seemed to have forgotten what the General had said.

Captain François Dumonceau records that the 2nd Regiment of the Chevau-légers Lanciers *of the Imperial Guard did not get orders to mount until the afternoon of 27 November, when they rode down to the bridge which had been completed the previous evening.*

Most of our army corps had already crossed, and all the Imperial Guard, of which we were the last to turn up. Only part of their parks and horse teams still remained to follow with us, but the crowd of disbanded troops had arrived and created a block by flocking from all sides, infiltrating everywhere, congesting the ground over a considerable area and refusing to give way to us or to move aside to let us through. Detachments of pontoniers and gendarmerie, posted at the various bridgeheads, struggled hard with the crowd to contain it and control its flow. This disordered multitude persisted in moving forward, and formed a confused tangle of men, horses, and vehicles which increased in numbers all the time almost to suffocation-point, pushing up to the river where several were drowned — thus renewing in all their horror the appalling scenes of the various earlier passages, but this time on a much larger scale in relation to the extent of the ground. . . .

We had to open a way through by brute force. In the end we drew our swords and behaved like madmen, using the flat of the blade to knock aside those who, pushed back by the crowd, hemmed us in as if in a press. In this way we managed to clear a path, and were pursued by a thousand curses.

On reaching the bridge to which we had been directed, we began to dismount and cross one by one, leading our horses so as not to shake the bridge. It had no guard-rail, was almost at water-level, covered by a layer of manure, and was already seriously damaged, dislocated, sagging in places, and unsteady everywhere. Some pontoniers, up to their armpits in the water, were busy repairing it. Among them were a number of Dutchmen who welcomed us and did their best to facilitate our passage by throwing a broken cart into the river, several dead horses, and other debris of all kinds which blocked the bridge.

Once across, we went over the flat marshy ground beside the river, and found it so cut up in several places that we sank into the mud despite the ice. Then we climbed the slopes to the edge of the forest and were posted facing to the left and downstream, so as to support the Young Guard.

Alexandre Bellot de Kergorre, the commissary last quoted as at Mozhaisk in September, was waiting to cross with two friends, a Monsieur Paris and his son, whose hesitancy had already lost them several opportunities of reaching the far bank.

Time was getting on and we still did not leave. Far from clearing, the bridge was becoming more crowded still; and the distant guns, which had been booming all day, were now nearer. I began to reproach myself for being so obliging as not to abandon my companions, and they in turn could not help deploring their blindness.

Shells and cannon-balls fell round us, even inside our bivouac area, though without hurting anyone. All of a sudden their whistling became continuous, so we promptly quitted the spot, leading our horses with us. As it was impossible to get within two hundred yards of the bridge, many people walked upstream in search of a crossing-place. Monsieur Paris wanted to follow their example, but this time I was insistent, and told him that if a bridge had been built where we stood, it meant that there was no other. Consequently we had no option but to cross by it, or be taken prisoner or killed. We bunched together for mutual protection, leading our horses by the bridle. Just before setting out I stuffed a large piece of bread into my pocket, as I could not rely on what the horses carried. . . . For the same reason I put on two furs over my greatcoat, because I knew how important they would be when sleeping out of doors.

We had barely launched ourselves into the crowd when we were scattered like dust in the wind. I found myself carried forward for a moment or two and lost the horse I was leading. I realized the imminent danger I was in, but saw it all quite calmly. I must either swim across the Berezina or else run the risk of being suffocated in my efforts to reach the bridge. The violent north wind and the increasing cold convinced me that if I crossed among the ice-floes I would certainly die, when I reached the far bank, having no change of clothes and no fire to warm myself by. I commended my soul to God, gave a last thought to my family, and resolutely set out to brave all dangers.

Numerous cannon-balls were passing overhead. The enemy was aiming at the crowd, but as usual he aimed too high. Indeed, these projectiles constituted the least danger, and nobody paid any attention. The most appalling danger was the one we were creating for ourselves. To a distance of more than two hundred yards the bridge was ringed by a half-circle of dead or dying horses and several layers of prostrate men. You could not afford a single false step, because once you were down, the man behind stepped on your stomach and you swelled the total of the dying. So however much you were pushed from behind, you had to choose your next stepping-place, as far as possible on the middle of the dying, so that the legs of men who were still moving did not break your own. We were pushed and pulled as in any crowd which is gripped by terror. One had to beware of neighbours who, finding themselves about to fall, hung on and pulled one down with them. No sooner had I stepped up on to this mass of men and horses than one glance showed me that the extreme edge of the river was less crowded and that very few corpses had fallen on the nearest ice. Furthermore, all these people had died from drowning. Accordingly I altered course and headed for the point where these two circumstances reduced the danger, and I eventually reached the bank. My two furs had been torn off me in shreds, and only my greatcoat remained. Three times it had been lifted off my shoulders, but it saved me and I risked my life to hold on to it. Three times I had to stop to slip my arms in again. In the midst of this massacre several people were still dragging a horse, which nearly crushed me. . . . However, I gradually approached the bridge. It was high time, because I felt my strength failing. I had been struggling for two hours and was exhausted. My courage and calm had not deserted me, but if the struggle had lasted another quarter of an hour I should have collapsed. Despite the cold, sweat covered my face after all my efforts.

I was now only two paces from the bridge. I put out my hand and begged those in front to give me a hand. I grasped one of the trestles — but I had forgotten what egoists we were. The final obstacle was a frenzied horse on the ground, and it was while trying to climb over it that I asked vainly for help. In the end Providence came to my aid. A violent shove shot me over the horse, which in an instant was covered by a dozen people trampling on its head and belly. As for me, I found myself propelled between the horse and the bridge. I was safe. The bridge came up to just above my waist. I mustered my remaining strength and managed to climb up. I next found myself twenty yards from the beginning of the bridge. It was covered with people, but we moved forward in orderly fashion, because there were no dead horses or men. We advanced just like a large crowd hurrying across a level piece of ground.

On 30 November Count de Rochechouart found himself at the spot where the French Army had effected its crossing.

Nothing in the world more saddening, more distressing! One saw heaped bodies of men, women, and even children; soldiers of all arms, all nations, choked by the fugitives or hit by Russian grapeshot; horses, carriages, guns, ammunition waggons, abandoned carts. One cannot imagine a more terrifying sight than the appearance of the two broken bridges, and the river frozen right to the bottom. Immense riches lay scattered on this shore of death. Peasants and Cossacks prowled around these piles of dead, removing whatever was most valuable. I found my servant rummaging in the coffers of a carriage. He told me he was trying to restock my wardrobe in respect of shirts, handkerchiefs, stockings, etc., since through his own fault he had let everything be captured.

On the bridge I saw an unfortunate woman sitting; her legs dangled outside the bridge and were caught in the ice. For twenty-four hours she had been clasping a frozen child to her breast. She begged me to save this child, unaware that she was holding out a corpse to me! She herself was unable to die, despite her sufferings, but a Cossack did her this service by firing a pistol in her ear so as to put an end to her appalling agony.

Both sides of the road were piled with dead in all positions, or with men dying of cold, hunger, exhaustion, their uniforms in tatters, and beseeching us to take them prisoner. They listed all their attainments, and we were assailed with cries of: 'Monsieur, take me along with you. I can cook, or I am a valet, or I am a barber. For the love of God, give me a piece of bread and a strip of cloth to cover myself with.' However much we might have wished to help, unfortunately we could do nothing.

General Count de Langeron describes the huge park of vehicles abandoned by the French when Marshal Victor's corps crossed the Berezina.

All the riches of Moscow were collected in this park, and one saw more than ten thousand, including magnificent carriages, berlines, calashes, phaetons, droshkys, etc., taken in the capital, in the houses of noblemen, or in the workshops of harness-makers — trophies which the French had intended to carry to Paris.

All these carriages, waggons, and farm-carts were laden with articles of great value: rich jewellery, superb furs, pearls, diamonds in profusion, sacred goblets from the churches of Moscow, the gilded cross from the Church of St. John the Great, collections of engravings, many books from the superb libraries belonging to Counts Buturlin and Razumovsky, silver dishes, even porcelain. For several days everything was scattered and plundered, yet it was impossible to remove a hundredth part of the treasures abandoned by the enemy. A large part was thrown into the river, and when the spring came the local peasants and the Jews, who never missed such opportunities, rushed from every corner of Poland, fished out the treasures, and made off with an immense haul.

Ten years after the débâcle of the Grand Army, a Prussian officer of Engineers, Major J. L. U. Blesson, visited the various battle-fields of the campaign in order to carry out several historical investigations; he later translated into German Colonel de Chambray's Histoire de l'Expédition de Russie. *Thus, in the summer of 1822, he and his companions inspected the places where the Berezina had been crossed, and Blesson wrote in his report:*

We required no one to show us round, and no explanations in order to find our way. The points where the two bridges had stood were visible from a great distance, and we could even pick out the track along which the wretches struggled forward. Though the banks of the Berezina are so dark, when one goes upstream from Bobruisk to above Borisov, where the river winds through pine forests, the view across the built-over fields of Studyanka, Veselovo, etc., is all the more sharply defined when one steps out of the forests coming from Borisov. Half-way to Studyanka already we spotted — just think of it, ten years after the catastrophe — a mass of leatherware, strips of felt, scraps of cloth, shako covers, etc., strewn on the ground and fields. As one approached the river, these melancholy relics lay thicker and even in heaps, mingled with the bones of human beings and animals, skulls, tin fittings, bandoliers, bridles, and suchlike. Scraps of the bearskins of the Guard had survived. . . .

Where the main bridge had been, an island close to the bank divides the river into two arms. This island owes its origin to the vehicles and bodies which fell off the bridge, and to the corpses which were carried down to this point and then covered with mud and sand. We made our way with difficulty along the bank amid relics of all kinds, and soon reached the second footbridge. Here in particular we came on piles of fittings and mountings, or what remained of them, but there were no mounds of the dead here, since the bodies had been swept further downstream. Below the island three boggy mounds had been formed, and these we found covered with forget-me-not.

The Last Marches and Homecoming

THE passage of the Berezina virtually finished the Grand Army. As it trudged through Zembin towards Smorgon, no body of Russian troops in front impeded its retreat or stood between it and two reserve divisions at Vilna; but the light troops and Cossacks, in alliance with the severe cold of December, sufficed to pursue, harass, and decimate. On 3 December, in the village of Molodechno, Napoleon issued his famous and candid 29th Bulletin, in which he admitted the appalling horrors and losses of the retreat, but laid all the blame upon the weather. Without cavalry, and short of ammunition, the army could not risk a battle, and was compelled to march so as not to be forced into one.

The idea of abandoning his weary, put-upon army had been harboured since learning of Malet's conspiracy, and now became a resolution. On 5 December he announced that he was leaving for Paris to forestall the consternation, or delight, his bulletin would provoke, and to raise without delay a new army of 300,000 men. He must reach France before news of his disastrous failure spread to the capitals of Europe. Moreover, Prussia and Austria must be kept to their promises, otherwise none of his troops would get safely back across the Elbe. He set off that same day with a handful of companions, and, travelling secretly by Vilna, Warsaw, Dresden, and Mainz, reached the Tuileries just before midnight on 18 December.

Command of the remnants of his once immense and imposing army was entrusted to Marshal Murat, King of Naples, whose facial scar from a sabre-wound in Egypt, barely visible in normal conditions, had become very pronounced in the cold. He was not as sound a choice for this unenviable role as Prince Eugène would have been. Indeed, the latter's superiority became evident when he took over command five weeks later. In most units the last vestiges of discipline dissolved. So did plans for halting in Vilna, when Russian cavalry stormed the gates at daybreak and induced Murat to resume the retreat after barely twenty-four hours, leaving the town filled with 24,000 sick and wounded soldiers, a silent host of corpses, and a clamouring host of desperate stragglers. '*Nous sommes foutus . . . filez!*' Murat was heard to say. This was the end. On a long, steep, ice-bound road at Ponari, where the whiteness of snow cloaking the landscape lightened the darkness, Ney did his best, with French reinforcements under the valiant, one-armed General Loison and Wrede's Bavarians, to keep the Cossacks at bay, but on 10 December baggage, treasure, guns, almost every surviving vehicle, and the last trophies from Moscow had to be abandoned.

The reports of Murat to Napoleon were as despondent as those sent by Marshal Berthier, who wrote on the 11th: 'Every human effort is hopeless. One can only resign oneself.' It was the intrepid Ney who, two days later, organized a defence at Kovno, but his efforts to hold the bridge and town with a thousand troops against Platov's Cossacks failed because the Niemen and Vilya were frozen over, so he burnt the bridge and withdrew — the last Frenchman to leave Russian soil.

Out of the half-million soldiers who had fought in Russia, only 20,000 staggered back across the Niemen. About 160,000 horses and a thousand guns were also left behind and lost. Russian losses are reckoned at something over 200,000 men. Kutuzov's main army following Napoleon had left Tarutino with about 97,000 men and by the time it reached Vilna had been reduced by 70,000, of whom 12,000 were dead and the remainder in hospital. The only other remnants of the Grand Army were its two wings: about 40,000 troops under Schwarzenberg and Reynier in the south and 25,000 under Macdonald outside Riga. The former force had retreated from the area of Slonim, between the Pripet Marshes and the upper Niemen, to Belostok and thence into winter quarters. Macdonald's movements will be mentioned presently.

Of the devoted but suffering men whom Napoleon had left at Smorgon, the first reached Königsberg on about 20 December, two days after he himself entered Paris. The other principal collecting-points were Thorn, Marienburg, Marienwerder, and Elbing, though the Poles went south to Warsaw and the Bavarians to Plotsk on the Vistula. The survivors — bearded, masked in dirt, lousy in their motley garbs — looked so dreadful that many hardly dared to cross a threshold, however friendly. Whereas the German soldiers were welcomed in East Prussia, Frenchmen met hostility and insolence, for many inhabitants in towns like Gumbinnen and Insterburg sought opportunities to avenge the post-Jena occupation, with its excesses and oppression.

Oppressive now were the amputations, the frost-bite, the typhus, the melancholy. One aide-de-camp had lost seventeen horses in the campaign. A commissary forfeited three fingers on each hand. A captain had four toes drop off when he unwrapped the protective rags. Out of 1,100 men, the 7th Hussars could muster 120 in Gumbinnen, of whom only twenty were mounted.

The Battle of Malo-Yaroslavets, from the painting by Guesse

The Crossing of the Berezina, from a lithograph by V. Adam

The Crossing of the Berezina, from a drawing by an unknown artist in the Musée de l'Armée, Paris

The Young Guard had been 8,000 strong on leaving Moscow, but at Vilna totalled a bare 400. Of the 3,000 soldiers in de Fezensac's 4th Regiment who had campaigned in Russia, only 200 regained the Vistula, and a further 100 came home many months later from captivity. Fifteen hundred Westphalians out of 24,000 returned to Thorn. The 6th Regiment of *Tirailleurs* of the Guard had left Smolensk already reduced to 31 officers and 300 other ranks. Of these only 14 officers and 10 men stood with the colours on 19 December. Of the rest, 13 had been killed, 56 wounded men had fallen into Russian hands, 24 had died from exposure, and 214 had been left behind, ill or frost-bitten, and were presumed prisoners.

Grim statistics issued later by the Russian Ministry of the Interior showed that in the Moscow area, apart from hundreds of bodies carted away before the frosts came, peasants disposed of 49,574 corpses and 27,849 horses up till 3 February 1813. In and around Smolensk the human bodies numbered 71,753, while dead horses totalled over 50,000. The corresponding figures for the Vilna region until the end of February were 72,205 and 4,407; for Minsk over a shorter period 18,709 and 2,764; and for Kaluga 1,027 and 5,584. Beside the Berezina the Russians found 13,106 corpses and more than double that number of horses. The totals — 226,374 human dead and 119,370 horses — cannot but appal; and the Russian losses have to be added to this toll of slaughter. Yet within a few months Napoleon could remark to Metternich: 'A man such as I am is not much concerned over the lives of a million men.'

* * *

Marshal Macdonald, outside Riga and in Courland with his corps of 25,000 men, who included some 18,000 Prussians under General Yorck as well as Poles and Germans, did not receive orders to withdraw until 18 December. Despite this late start, he conducted a skilful retreat, broke through the Cossacks, crossed the Niemen at Tilsit, and waited there to assist the withdrawal of Yorck, who was coming behind. He was astounded to learn, on the last day of 1812, that in response to overtures by the Russian General Diebitch, commanding Wittgenstein's weak advance-guard which had intercepted the Prussians' line of march, Yorck had, on the previous day, concluded a convention at Tauroggen with the Russians instead of brushing them aside with his superior force. He had taken this step on his own initiative and authority. The Prussian corps was to be unmolested until orders arrived from King Frederick William. If the latter then required his troops to reunite with the French Army, the corps was not to resume hostilities against Russia for two months from the date of the convention. Meanwhile the Prussian corps was to remain neutral and hold the district between Memel and Tilsit, which was also to be considered neutral.

Yorck's defection, tantamount to treason against both his sovereign and Napoleon, was applauded as patriotic and noble by the Prussian people (four and a half million of them) but repudiated at first by their King, who sent orders for the arrest of Yorck. The General claimed that he had acted to avoid sacrificing the greater part of his troops, with all their baggage and artillery, and as 'a true Prussian, a patriot who sought only the welfare of his country'. As for Marshal Macdonald, he retreated as far as Libau, but coming under strong attack had to go on to Königsberg. What remained of the Grand Army pulled back first behind the Oder and then west of the Elbe, leaving strong garrisons in Stettin, Danzig, and the main fortresses of Prussia.

When the people of East Prussia rose spontaneously to greet the advancing Russian troops — men like Stein had persuaded the Tsar not to be content with expelling the French from Russian soil but to carry the war into central Europe — and when, at Königsberg, the East Prussian Provincial Assembly placed its forces at the disposal of Napoleon's opponents, King Frederick William could hold back no longer. At the end of February he and Alexander signed the Treaty of Kalish, both promising not to lay down arms until Prussia had regained the territories she had possessed before Jena in 1806. By a subsequent declaration, any princes or peoples in Germany who did not join the Allies would lose their independence when a settlement was eventually made. On 4 March 1813 the French evacuated Berlin; then the Tsar joined the King at Breslau in Silesia, whither the latter had moved from Potsdam; and on 16 March Prussia declared war on France. A new campaign was about to open — a campaign which would involve Austria as well and, after the Allied victory at Leipzig in October, would send Napoleon back over the Rhine to defend French soil for a change.

General Rapp relates that when they reached Smorgon, Napoleon sent for him.

He carefully closed the doors of his room and said: 'Well, Rapp, I am leaving tonight for Paris. My presence there is necessary for France and even for this unfortunate army. I am entrusting command of it to the King of Naples.' I was not expecting this confidence, because I admit frankly that I had not been let into the secret of his journey

'Sire,' I replied, 'your departure will have an unpleasant effect on the troops. They are not expecting it.'

'My return is essential. I must watch Austria and contain Prussia.'

'I do not know what the Austrians will do; their sovereign is your father-in-law. But as for the Prussians, you will not hold them back. Our disasters are too great for that, and they will take advantage of the fact.'

Napoleon was pacing up and down, his hands behind his back. He remained silent for a moment and then went on: 'When they hear that I am in Paris, when they see me at the head of the nation and of 120,000 troops whom I shall organize, they will think twice before declaring war on me.'

Armand de Caulaincourt, Grand Equerry, accompanied Napoleon on the fortnight's journey to Paris, and in his memoirs gives an account of their arrival in Kovno at five o'clock on the morning of 7 December.

The courier had arranged for a fire to be lit in a sort of inn kept by an Italian scullion who had set himself up there since the Army went through. The meal he served seemed excellent because it was hot. Good bread, fowl, a table, chairs, a table-cloth — all these were novelties for us. Only the Emperor had been well served during the retreat, that is to say, he had always had linen, white bread, his Chambertin, good oil, beef or mutton, rice, and beans or lentils, his favourite vegetables. The Grand Marshal [Duroc] and Count Lobau joined us.

I never remember such cold as we suffered from between Vilna and Kovno. The thermometer had passed twenty degrees. Although the Emperor was wrapped in wool and covered with a good fur, with his legs in fur boots and then inside a bearskin bag, he complained so much that I had to cover him with half my bearskin rug. Our breath froze on our lips, our eyebrows, and round our eyelids. All the cloth on the carriage, and particularly the hood where our breath rose, was white and hard. When we reached Kovno, the Emperor was shivering; one would have thought he had an attack of the ague.

Butkevicius, the Lithuanian priest, relates in his memoirs that from the middle of November onwards retreating French and Polish troops, including Poniatowski's 5th Corps, passed through Seniai. Rumours circulated, and false alarms about Cossack incursions. Then all went quiet again.

But on 8 December, during a chemistry lesson at school, one of our teachers came in and asked the priest who was taking the class: 'Have you ever seen Napoleon, and can you remember what he looks like? There is someone here with Marshal [General] Caulaincourt who resembles him.'

The priest replied that he had seen Napoleon from a distance in 1806 at Warsaw,[1] but he pointed to me and said that I must be able to recognize Napoleon as I had had occasion to see him at Wilkowiski.

So we both went to the inn. Napoleon was pacing to and fro in the saloon, and at the same time trying to get near to the fire, but the landlady kept bumping into him as she passed the kitchen-range where she was cooking a meal for the travellers. The Emperor wore the uniform of a *chasseur*, and on top a short jacket lined with ermine. Instead of his usual little hat he was wearing an ermine cap lined with green velvet. I had no difficulty in recognizing him. My teacher told me not to alert those present, because Napoleon was doubtless travelling incognito. The room was full of people, but he seemed quite unaware of them. Sometimes when near the fire he would go up to the landlady and whisper: 'Ah, the beautiful *polonaise*!'

Suddenly we saw an officer of the Guard come in, wearing full dress. After saluting the Emperor he addressed him with the word '*Sire*'. Napoleon replied: 'But where did you learn that you had to call me *Sire?*' Then the officer, pointing to the Legion of Honour he wore on his breast, stated that he had had the honour of receiving it from the Emperor after the battle of Wagram [July 1809]. Napoleon recovered his equanimity and said: 'If that is so, then I have no need to conceal my name any longer. Go and fetch the sub-prefect, as I need him.'

When he went out, the officer ordered everybody to uncover out of respect for the Emperor's presence, and Napoleon, who was

[1] He was there from 19 to 23 December.

touched by this attention, thanked him, adding that he did not wish to disturb anyone. The landlady no longer kept him away from the fire, and he was very soon restored to a good humour. He talked with the women. One of them in particular, the wife of a justice of the peace, took his fancy by her beauty and youth, and he paid her compliments, tapping her on the shoulders, face, or ears.

Hortense de Beauharnais (1783–1837), wife of Napoleon's brother Louis and former Queen of Holland, had been extremely anxious about her brother Eugène in Russia, and on hearing that the Emperor had returned to Paris she hurried to the Tuileries.

He seemed to me exhausted, preoccupied, but not downcast. I have often seen him display petulance over some trifle: a door either open or shut, a room well or ill lit. Yet he never showed better self-control than in moments of misfortune or difficulty.

I inquired anxiously whether the Army's disasters had been as severe as his bulletin reported. He replied with a touch of suppressed pain: 'I have told the whole truth.' 'But we have not been the only ones to suffer!' I exclaimed. 'Surely our enemies have suffered huge losses too?'

'No doubt,' he replied. 'But that does not console me.'

After Napoleon's departure from the Army, Count de Ségur found himself transferred to Murat's headquarters, and he states that 6 December was one of the coldest and most murderous days of the entire retreat.

On the following day, either because of disorder around Murat or of personal preoccupation, I lost all trace of the King's lodging. As this fatal day was drawing to a close, I felt exhausted by the effort of walking a dozen leagues on glistening ice and weighed down by the seventy-five pounds weight of my weapons, my uniform, and two enormous furs; so I tried to hoist myself back into the saddle. But almost immediately my horse collapsed on top of me so heavily that I was trapped underneath. Several hundred men passed by without my being able to persuade one of them to set me free. The most compassionate moved a little to one side, others stepped over my head, but most of them trampled me underfoot. Eventually a *gendarme d'élite* picked me up.

I had gone all day with nothing to eat, and I spent that night — the coldest of any — without food, in a hut open to the wind, surrounded by corpses and huddled near a dying fire.

The flames could not get a grip on a huge fir trunk which had been dragged into this shelter; one end protruded out to the door, the other out of the window. An elderly Engineer general came and shared this melancholy shelter. Right in front of me he devoured some remnants of food without offering me any and I could not bring myself to ask him for a small share of the paltry meal to which he was reduced.

This room abutted on to a huge barn which was still standing, and during that bitterly cold night between four and five hundred men took refuge inside. At least three quarters of them froze to death, even though they had lain one on top of another round several fires. The dying had clambered over the dead in their efforts to approach a fire, and so it went on.

When, before daybreak, I tried to grope my way out of this dark tomb, my feet kicked into the first comers. Astonished by their taciturn impassivity, I stopped, but having tripped over another obstacle on to my hands, I felt the stiff limbs and frozen faces and these explained the silence. After looking in vain for a way out, I had to climb painfully over these various heaps of corpses. The highest was near the door, and was so high that it entirely hid the exit from this barn.

That same day I reached the gates of Vilna, weak with hunger and half frozen. I was fortunate to be ahead of the column and got in easily, whereas an hour later I should have been compelled to join the crowd which thronged the defile and perished there.

Colonel Lubin Griois describes the costume he wore throughout the retreat: it was in tatters long before the end.

Fortunately I had, during the two previous months, adopted the habit of wearing a flannel waistcoat next to my skin. I wore it all the way to Königsberg, and God knows the state it was in! A waistcoat of red cashmere, a light linen dress-coat, over that a plain frock-coat, linen trousers buttoning at the side and worn without pants, very tight Suvorov boots, and cotton socks — such were my ordinary clothes. This light costume, though admirably suited to the autumn weather, was quite inadequate against the cold we experienced. However, it was impossible to change it, and a bearskin I had obtained did not replace the coat stolen from me at the Berezina crossing. The fur, which did excellent service in bivouacs at night, was much too heavy to be worn on the march. I was obliged to leave it on my horse, but necessity made me turn it to advantage. Out of several strips of fur I had made a sort of stole, fastened at the ends to a string which I fastened round my neck. When I was walking I put my hands inside, for lack of gloves, and turned it into a kind of muff. When I was on horseback it changed its function, because I then placed it in the stirrups to the benefit of my feet, which felt the cold more than my hands did. With another strip of fur I made a chin-strap which covered the lower part of my face and was tied behind my head.

It was in this peculiar rig, with my head barely protected by a battered hat, with my skin chapped by the cold and blackened by smoke, my hair sprinkled with hoar-frost and my moustache bristling with icicles, that I covered two or three hundred leagues from Moscow to Königsberg, and among the crowd along the route I was one of the few whose costume still preserved some vestiges of uniform. Most of our unfortunate companions were like phantoms in carnival masks.

If any items of military wear survived, they were not visible, being covered by the warmer garments that everyone tried to procure. Some, content at keeping their greatcoat, had transformed this into a sort of hooded mantle fastened in round the waist with a cord. Others made use of a woollen blanket or petticoats for the same purpose. Several wore round their shoulders women's cloaks made of valuable furs, souvenirs of Moscow which had originally been intended as gifts for a sister or a mistress. Nothing was more commonplace than to see a soldier, his face dark and repellent, wrapped in a coat of pink or blue satin trimmed with swan or blue fox which camp-fires had scorched and splashes of grease had soiled. Most men had their heads wrapped in dirty handkerchiefs tucked under what remained of a forage-cap, and ragged bits of linen, blanket, or fur did duty for worn-out shoes. It was not only the private soldier who was compelled to disguise himself in this way. Most of the officers, colonels, and generals wore equally ridiculous and miserable costumes.

Early in December Lieutenant J. L. Henckens, from Holland, was temporarily commanding what remained of the 6th Regiment of Chasseurs à cheval.

As for my health, I had an iron constitution. I managed to keep warm by rubbing myself with a great deal of snow, a commodity to be found in profusion. Whenever we found any food I did not eat greedily, and despite our misery I ate only small quantities of horsemeat, seasoned with powder instead of salt, since horsemeat is insipid and weighs heavily in the bowels. Furthermore, I cooked the pieces I took on the point of my sabre, turning my head away from the fire so as not to run the risk of getting gangrene, which I dreaded more than anything else. How many men I have seen whose nose and ears were turning dark blue as a result of passing suddenly from a warm place into the cold air, and who later on lost part of their extremities.

Beyond Smorgon I decided to slit my breeches. This was scarcely proper and had snags, but I had already seen so many poor devils who, after performing their natural functions, were unable to pull up and fasten their breeches, while their companions either could not or would not help them, that my decision was soon made, and several others followed suit.

On 7 December we have Major von Lossberg writing home to his wife from east of Vilna to describe a night he spent in a farm building with a dozen members of the Old Guard.

We found fodder for the horses and a little food; the latter we divided scrupulously, and we shared a meal mash, which was handed to me in my casserole on a small side-table by the N.C.O. of the Guard. He described to me the death of a French officer of the line, and the following serves as record not only because of its originality but also because it epitomizes the degree of our common suffering. A French infantryman, who took this officer to be dead and considered himself as his heir, was in the process of stripping off his clothing so as to cover his own nakedness when the officer, who was not yet dead, summoned up all his strength and groaned out, barely audible, the words: '*Camarade, je ne suis pas encore mort!*' This caused the soldier to stand respectfully to one side and reply: '*Eh bien, mon officer! J'attendrai encore quelques moments!*'

However witty this reply may sound (particularly if one tells this to someone at home), I thought it proper at the time, when we were still so far from the Niemen, to keep this to myself, because I had with me several officers who would have seen in that incident confirmation of their opinion that it was quite impossible to reach even this river, which for a long time they had not regarded as the limit of their suffering. I did this all the more readily because this story indicated that the infantryman had kept within the bounds of discipline *vis-à-vis* the dying man.

Wilhelm, Count von Hochberg, afterwards Margrave of Baden, has left us a grim account of the scenes he witnessed in the second week of December and of the relations between the French and their allies.

Often Frenchmen would run after a Baden soldier to pick up the little bits of biscuit which he dropped. At the Berezina and also in Vilna the biscuits which had arrived from the Grand Duchy had been issued to the Baden troops.

Vehicles, horses, and men mingled on the road. Whenever this was wide, the ammunition waggons, post-chaises, ordinary waggons, and sleighs travelled three abreast, but when a defile was reached, each wanted to go first and the result was great confusion. Those horses which had not been shod slipped and fell frequently on the ice. When we crossed a bridge — usually these had no parapet — the sleigh on which a wounded officer was travelling would be thrown down on to the ice. Pity was at a discount. Everyone wanted to get past, and quickly too. If the word '*Cosaque*' — that terrifying word — was heard, then confusion reached its peak and the scene became indescribable. People shouted, ran, and pushed their animals or their teams of horses.

Towards evening, and often far into the night, this crowd would leave the road in search of shelter in one of the nearby villages. Every house, every barn, every stable was filled with men and horses. If one could not get inside a house, one was quite happy to find some protection behind it from the biting north wind.

One of the severest privations was the lack of water, for everything was frozen; often I was so thirsty that I could hardly wait for the moment when snow had melted on the fire in a can. People willingly paid six francs for a bad loaf baked on the embers, and forty to fifty francs for a Russian loaf would be paid to the petty traders who brought it from some distance and in this way did a profitable business. I wanted to buy a sugar loaf off a soldier, but he replied that he would only exchange it for a round loaf. I saw one French general receive one of these loaves in exchange for some candles.

No German dared warm himself by any fire which had been lit by the French. Our regimental doctor, Hauer by name, who had lost his way, had to pay six francs for the privilege of approaching a French fire. The hatred between the two nations was displayed again in heightened form, and yet what would the French have achieved in this campaign without their allies? You had only to hear the Bavarians, Württembergers, and Westphalians on the subject.

Count de Rochechouart, describing the Russian pursuit south-east of Vilna in the second week of December, comments on the treatment of prisoners.

On our way through the wretched town of Oshmyanyi we saw about a hundred French officers who had been captured and were packed into the local gaol, behind barred windows. These poor fellows were in shirtsleeves, having been stripped of their coats, trousers, etc., by the Cossacks. On seeing us, these wretches shouted through the bars, asking for food and warmth, and reinforcing their heart-rending cries with expressive gestures. Such sad spectacles were so frequent that I was very surprised to see my companions go up to the gaol windows and distribute the remnants of our food and a few clothes, and then go to the *starosta* — a Slav name given to the mayor or village headman. They required him to light the stove in the prison, and they even left money for the purchase of clothing, bread, and meat for the prisoners, threatening the *starosta* with dire punishment if their orders were not obeyed.

I asked Wlodeck the reason for this extraordinary interest, and he replied: 'They are freemasons. They made signs of distress, and as we ourselves are freemasons, we had to help our brothers, since we were in a position to do so.'

6 December finds General Wilson writing in his diary, at Dobrieka, thirty-five versts from Minsk:

The weather is cold in the extreme, above eighteen degrees of cold this day; and there is not a bottle of wine with the Army. If one accidentally appears, the price given for the worst quality is twenty-four shillings English currency; a pound of white bread costs three shillings; and everything else is in proportion. These prices, with the misery of our habitations, certainly make Newgate at once a preferable residence. . . .

And from Minsk: Yesterday, in a dreadfully cold day, I came here on horseback without any accident, though my horse were not rough-shod. Many persons were less fortunate, and various accidents, as I hear, occurred in the different columns, some of a serious nature.

I was much pleased to find Minsk an excellent town, which had not been plundered, and which afforded various supplies, at a dear rate, but still supplies. . . . Although I got a tolerably good quarter, alas! I could find no wood for the stoves and that night and this morning I was in splendid misery, and longed for my cabins with cockroaches, earwigs, children, scents, &c. It was near ten o'clock before I could get a fire lighted in a chimney and the air was afterwards so severe that water froze at the distance of three feet from a wood blaze that in England would have scorched intolerably at twelve feet.

My dragoons[1] are all chilled to the bones and I am obliged to procure them here sheepskin coats. However, when in the air, I defied the cold, for I even took off the greatcoat that I had been accustomed to wear in order that it might be repaired, and walked about, with the thermometer at nineteen degrees, in my jacket

[1] In Sicily, on his way to Russia, Wilson's establishment had been increased by a corporal and four men of the 20th Light Dragoons, which he had commanded at the Cape of Good Hope early in 1806.

without any waistcoat. The vanity of the act, I believe, kept me warm, for I was not so cold as I had frequently been before in less frost and with more covering.

Colonel Antoine-Marcelin Marbot, commanding the 23rd Regiment of Chasseurs à cheval, *relates how, several days' march east of Vilna, the intense cold killed off many of his horses and prevented the others from being ridden, so all his horsemen went on foot.*

I should like to have been able to do the same, but my wound made this impossible, so I took a sledge and had one of my horses harnessed to it. Seeing this new vehicle gave me the idea of using this method to save my numerous sick, and as in Russia there is no dwelling so poor that it does not contain a sledge, I soon had a hundred of them, and each, pulled by a troop horse, saved two men. This means of transport seemed so effective to General Castex[1] that he gave me permission to put all my other horsemen on sledges. As Colonel Monginot of the 24th *Chasseurs* had received a similar authorization, all that remained of our brigade harnessed its horses and formed a caravan which marched in excellent order.

You will doubtless think that in moving like this we were paralysing our means of defence, but don't be deceived, because on ice we were much stronger with the sledges, which can go anywhere and whose shafts support the horses, than would have been the case had we remained in the saddle on horses which fell at every step.

The road was strewn with abandoned muskets, so our *chasseurs* took two each and also an ample supply of cartridges. Consequently, when the Cossacks ventured to approach, they were received with the liveliest musketry and drew off again promptly. Besides, our men could fight on foot if necessary. Then in the evening we formed a great square with the sledges, and lit our fires in the centre. Marshal Ney and General Maison[2] often came and

[1] Bertrand-Pierre, Baron Castex (1771–1842), commanded the brigade of light cavalry composed of the 23rd and 24th *Chasseurs*.

[2] Nicolas Maison (1771–1840) commanded the 8th Infantry Division, but since Marshal Oudinot had been wounded he had taken command of the 2nd Corps. Maison became a Marshal of France in 1829.

spent the night with us there in security, since the enemy pursued us with Cossacks only. No doubt this was the first time a rearguard had been formed with sledges, but the frost made any other method impracticable and this one succeeded.

Colonel Josef Szymanowski, a Pole, describes yet another facet of the disorder which prevailed in the French Army.

Not far from Vilna the horses pulling the Imperial waggon laden with casks of gold refused to go any further. Immediately the escort commander and chief paymaster decided that it would be better to break open the barrels full of gold and distribute the contents, giving anybody as much as he could carry away, rather than to leave the lot for the enemy, who was close behind. The bung was removed from several casks, and the soldiers of the escort prepared to stuff their pockets with gold; but all of a sudden the Cossacks arrived and, being more greedy for money than for prisoners, they began to help our men to pick the gold out of the casks. They too filled the pockets of their wide breeches. It must have been a strange and amusing sight to see a French grenadier side by side with a Cossack and together emptying the waggon of the Imperial treasure.

When I reached Vilna with a handful of men I found Wegierski, the Paymaster-General of the Polish Army, in the same predicament. Thanks to a lack of shod horses, he did not know what to do with the Army's treasure-chest. Hearing that I was on my way through the town with what remained of the 2nd Regiment, he begged me to take as much money as I wanted for my officers, non-commissioned officers, and men, on condition that I gave him a receipt. The N.C.O.s and men did not have to be asked twice, but very few of the officers would agree to take more than two months' pay, and I did the same as far as I can remember. What happened to the rest of the money in the chest? I do not know.

General Dirk van Hogendorp, a Dutchman by birth, had been appointed Governor of Vilna and was responsible for organizing Lithuania. At the approach of the retreating Grand Army he made the best arrangements he could.

The head of the unfortunate column — those who had enough strength left to get in front of the rest — began to enter Vilna. Vain efforts were made to draw their attention to the placards printed in large letters and posted up to show the soldiers of each army corps to which monastery they were to go, and where they would find soup, meat, bread, and warm lodging. Vilna contained a number of large monasteries belonging to different religious orders, and I had persuaded the monks to move into a single monastery so as to be out of harm's way when the army arrived in a state of disorder. This placed at my disposal some huge buildings, where I had food kept constantly prepared.

However, everyone, generals and soldiers alike, forced his way into the first likely-looking house, and hunted for the best-heated room, lay down there, and had food brought to him. The strongest men turned out the weakest. The generals and officers, if they still exercised any measure of authority, compelled the soldiers to make way for them, even to the extent of a room or a bed. The town would inevitably have gone up in flames but for the fact that all the houses were built of stone. No doubt it would also have been plundered if the men had had more energy, but they were exhausted. Besides, there were plenty of provisions, and these were issued without ceremony to the first comers.

I went to meet the King of Naples and the Prince of Neuchâtel, who were on foot because of the intense cold. Murat was huddled in huge and superb furs. A very tall fur hat added to his already large stature, making him rather like a walking colossus. Berthier, his small frame weighed down with heavy clothing, made a strange contrast beside him.

The King of Naples told me that to avoid too great a crush in Vilna he had ordered the dismounted cavalry to go off to the left to two remount depots. . . . But the cavalry had already passed the side-roads leading to the towns in question, so the dismounted horsemen mingled with the others, and so eager were they all to get inside Vilna that the gate became congested, and they trampled on one another in their efforts to force a way through. It proved impossible to restore order, even with the battalion I had under arms.

When the King of Naples and the Prince of Neuchâtel eventually reached the centre of the town they asked my advice about ways of stopping this appalling chaos. They wanted me to assemble all the marshals and generals at the Prince's lodging for a conference. But how was I going to find each of them in whichever billet he chanced to be, willy-nilly? However, I had a circular order printed and taken round to every house and posted up at every street-corner, inviting the marshals and generals to assemble next morning at the Chief of Staff's house. There must have been at least a hundred generals in Vilna, but so great was the depression and, indeed, the demoralization that barely ten of them responded to the invitation. They no longer paid any heed to orders, and general officers refused to listen to the aides-de-camp sent to them by the Chief of Staff.

Baron Désiré Chlapowski, a Polish officer, was commanding a squadron in the 1st Regiment of Lancers of the Imperial Guard. He emphasizes the demoralization which reigned among the soldiers from the Confederation of the Rhine.

The best proof of this was my encounter with General Wrede, commanding the Bavarians, on the day after we reached Vilna. There were more than twenty degrees of frost, and it was the iciest day of the campaign. In the morning I went to Murat's headquarters in the Castle. I met a man who was wearing a civilian coat, a sort of turban on his head, a sword, and no gloves. In addition, he was running, followed by about fifteen soldiers armed with muskets and presenting their bayonets as if about to charge. Seeing me and recognizing my *czapka*[1] and uniform, he shouted: 'Where is Headquarters? They are arresting men in the streets, and the Imperial Guard have not left their quarters!!!'

I looked closely at the speaker's face which was swathed in handkerchiefs, and from the sound of his voice recognized General Wrede, whom I had often seen in 1809. I replied quietly: 'I am on my way to Murat's headquarters, and if the General will permit, I

[1] Polish helmet worn by lancers, uhlans, etc.

will guide him there. But we can go without any fuss, since the town gates are guarded by infantry, guards have been posted all over the place, and I assure you that no Cossacks are in town yet.'

'General,' I added, 'sheath your sword or you will alarm King Murat.'

The Countess de Choiseul-Gouffier relates that Vilna was in a state of tumult on the day the French prepared to evacuate the town.

The King of Naples was kind enough to assure me, through his secretary, that the town would not be defended and that I had nothing to fear. The King left that evening. The soldiers were lighting fires in the streets to keep themselves warm. The Town Hall Square resembed a Teniers painting.[1] One could see a thousand men scattered among the flames and leaping sparks, and also the Town Hall with its colonnade which still bore some festival decorations: Napoleon's cipher appeared to be covered with a veil as one looked at it through the clouds of smoke rising to the sky. The night effects had a Rembrandt touch about them.

In the University courtyards opposite the Castle the Emperor's carriages were being burnt all night, as well as a pile of other things — tents, camp-beds, etc., etc. — instead of leaving them to the inhabitants as some compensation for the losses the town had incurred. One young academician wanted to buy from a sentry a magnificent mathematical case made in gold and bearing the imperial arms, but the soldier pushed the case into the flames with the point of his bayonet.

. . . Next morning I was woken with the news that the Cossacks were in Vilna. I got up, went to the window, and saw the *last* Frenchmen disappearing from the square.

A detachment of *chasseurs* halted in front of the house. We still did not know whether they were Russian or French, but soon afterwards we saw them arrest an officer and a grenadier of the French Guard, though without harming them. At eleven o'clock we heard shouts of '*Hourra!*' and I recognized, from their pointed caps, their long lances, my old acquaintances, the Cossacks, who

[1] David Teniers the Younger (1610–90), a native of Antwerp, painted fairs, country life, village inns, etc.

The Retreat from Russia, from a drawing by an unknown artist in the Musée de l'Armée, Paris

The Retreat, from the painting by Nicolas Charlet

galloped through the streets and even out as far as the hills near the town, pursuing the wretched remnants of the French Army.

Many more prisoners and a great deal of booty were taken. The Jews behaved barbarously, and handed over the weakened, defenceless French to the Russians. The women were no less cruel and massacred these poor soldiers by hitting them with the heels of their slippers. Blood and water flowed under the carriage gateways.

I tried to go out on foot (my father had taken his horses), and this walk made me very depressed. A few feet away a Frenchman was knocked down and robbed. I sent my servant to his help, but in vain. I saw terrifying corpses in the streets, seated on the ground, leaning against walls, preserved by the cold, their limbs shrunken and stiff in the position in which Death had overtaken them. They had died of hunger, of pain, and without physical or spiritual help. One dared not look at these poor creatures, and when one accidentally met these pitiful objects one averted one's eyes involuntarily.

Xavier de Maistre, author of Voyage autour de ma chambre *and, in 1825, of* La Jeune Sibérienne, *was serving in the Russian Army. He wrote to his brother Joseph on 21 December from Vilna.*

I can give you no idea of the route I have covered. The corpses of Frenchmen obstruct the road which, from Moscow to the frontier (about eight hundred versts), looks like one continuous battlefield. When one approaches any villages, which are usually burnt, the spectacle becomes even more terrible. There the bodies are heaped, and in several places where the wretches had gathered in houses, they were burnt to death inside without having the strength to get out. I have seen houses in which more than fifty corpses lay together, and among them three or four men were still alive, stripped to their shirts in fifteen degrees of frost. One of them said to me: 'Sir, get me out of here or else kill me. My name is Normand de Flageac, I am an officer like you.' I had no means of saving him. He was given some clothes, but we could not take him away, and had to leave him in this dreadful place. A certain Count Barzetti of Turin said he was a relative of mine and begged for help.

I immediately sent him my horse and a Cossack to fetch him in, but the prisoners' depot had gone. I do not know what happened to it, though I sent out search-parties in all directions. On every side and along every track one comes across these wretched men who still drag themselves along, dying of hunger or cold. They are so numerous that one cannot always pick them up in time, and most of them die on their way to the depots. I never saw one of them without thinking of the infernal man who led them to this surfeit of misfortune.

The Tsar travelled from St. Petersburg on 18 December and reached Vilna three days later. He spent an evening with the Countess de Choiseul-Gouffier and her lady companion.

The Tsar wished to know what impression Napoleon had made on me. I said that his outward appearance did not tally with my preconceived idea of his genius — Alexander said that he had gained the same impression — and that His Majesty's presence inspired more fear in me.

'Oh!' replied Alexander in a tone of mild reproach. 'How can I possibly inspire fear in you?'

'Yes, Sire, a fear of displeasing you.'

'Have you noticed Napoleon's eyes?' Alexander asked later. 'Light-grey eyes which gaze at you so piercingly that you cannot withstand them?'

The Tsar talked about the campaign with great moderation and impartiality. . . . As a really enlightened prince, filled with humanity, he explained to me Napoleon's faults, and spoke of his pride which was so fatal for Europe.

'What a career he has ruined!' he said. 'Having gained so much glory, he could bestow peace on Europe, and he has not done so! The spell is broken.'

The Tsar repeated this word several times in the course of the evening, which proved that he himself had come under that spell.

On 26 December Major-General Sir Robert Wilson wrote in his diary:

Yesterday was the Emperor's birthday.

Parade, a confidential conference with the Emperor, mess, and twenty-five degrees of frost, were the incidents of the morning. The Marshal [Kutuzov] gave a great state dinner to the Emperor afterwards, on the occasion of his receiving the Order of St. George of the First Class.

[*Some details of this 'confidential conference' appear in Wilson's* Narrative.]

On the morning of the 26th December Alexander sent for the English General [Wilson], and after a few appropriations to the festival, said: 'General, I have called you into my cabinet to make a painful confession; but I rely on your honour and prudence. I wished to have avoided it, but I could not bear to appear inconsistent in your estimate of my proceedings; which I must be thought if my motives were not explained. . . .

'You have always told me the *truth* — truth I could not obtain through any other channel.

'I know that the Marshal has done nothing he ought to have done — nothing against the enemy that he could avoid; all his successes have been *forced* upon him. He has been playing some of his old Turkish tricks, but the nobility of Moscow support him, and insist on his presiding over the national glory of this war. In half an hour I must therefore (and he paused for a minute) decorate this man with the great Order of St. George, and by so doing commit a trespass on its institution; for it is the highest honour, and hitherto the purest, of the empire. But I will not ask you to be present — I should feel too humiliated if you were; but I have no choice — I must submit to a controlling necessity. I will, however, not again leave my army, and there shall be no opportunity given for additional misdirection by the Marshal.

'He is an old man, and therefore I would have you show him suitable courtesies, and not refuse them when offered on his part.

'I wish to put an end to every appearance of ill will, and to take from this day a new departure, which I mean to make one of gratitude to Providence and of grace to all.'

Wilson noted in his journal for 30 December:

Sickness has made very serious progress in this city. In fifteen days nine thousand prisoners have died, and in one eighteen hours seven hundred. The mortality has extended of course to the inhabitants. The physicians have ordered straw to be burnt before every house, but the pestilential atmosphere is not to be corrected by such palliatives; and as if fate resolved to spread the contagion to the utmost, there has been a thaw for the last twenty-four hours.

In the spring Vilna must be a complete charnel-house. All the carcases which are removed from the streets and hospitals are laid at a short distance from the town in great masses; and then such parts as the wolves have not devoured during the winter will throw pestiferous miasmata back upon the city, which, from its position, is always shrouded in vapour. I rode yesterday round the town to look at the camp which the enemy proposed to trace, and in all directions I saw mountains of human bodies, and carcases of beasts. Disgusting as the sight was, I could not help occasionally stopping to contemplate the attitudes in which those who had been frozen had died. The greater part happened to have been writhing with some agony at the instant their hearts' blood congealed; some were raised upon their hands with their heads bent back and their eyes uplifted, as if still imploring aid from the passers-by.

[*He added further details in his* Narrative.]

The hospital of St. Bazile presented the most awful and hideous sight: seven thousand five hundred bodies were piled like pigs of lead over one another in the corridors; carcases were strewn about in every part; and all the broken windows and walls were stuffed with feet, legs, arms, hands, trunks and heads to fit the apertures, and keep out the air from the yet living.[1]

The putrefaction of the thawing flesh, where the parts touched and the process of decomposition was in action, emitted the most cadaverous smell.

Nevertheless in each of these pestilential and icy répertoires

[1] General de Langeron noted: 'One of my aides noticed two convalescent soldiers playing piquet. They were using as a card-table the frozen back of one of their comrades who had frozen to death. They called this their marble table-top.'

three or four grenadiers of the Guard were posted, inhaling the pestilential effluvia.

On the English General [Wilson] making the Emperor acquainted with this inconsiderate 'employment of his finest troops', he went himself to the convent and inspected the chambers, speaking the kindest words to the unfortunate inmates, and giving the requisite directions for their treatment. The Grand Duke followed his example, but caught the epidemy, from which he with difficulty recovered.

Another description of Vilna comes from the pen of Ernst Moritz Arndt, the German patriot and poet, who arrived there on 11 January 1813 with Baron von Stein, the Prussian statesman who had been in Russia as political adviser to the Tsar.

The town looked to me like some Tartar hell. Everywhere frightful dirt and smells; greasy Jews; some unfortunate prisoners, most of them wounded or convalescent, crept miserably around; every street was wreathed in acrid smoke and steam, because people had set fire to all sorts of inflammable materials, even dung-heaps, in front of each house, in order to disperse the pestilential air from the many hospitals and infection-centres, and these heaps smoked day and night. I noticed here and there French cockades lying in the streets, dirty plumes, torn hats, and shakos which, humbled in the dust and trodden underfoot as they now were, reminded one of how five months earlier the French had strutted insolently through Vilna with them. I went out of the gate and for a few ghastly hours wandered through the outskirts of the town in the direction of Vilkomir and Kovno. What horrors! Those insignia which I had seen in the town now lay thicker on the ground, and everywhere naked corpses, dead horses, oxen, dogs — faithful and unfortunate companions in this appalling misery. Many houses were entirely desolate, without floors, windows, and stoves, and many of them mere burnt shells. Among these dreadful memorials of destruction a few shadowy prisoners and convalescents crawled about; and a poor abandoned horse stood freezing and hunched in the ruins, pathetically nibbling a few stray tufts of hay.

When I returned to the town I met a fine young man to whom I spoke and put several questions. He came from Brabant and was senior surgeon in a hospital for French prisoners, who were lodged in a religious establishment. I accompanied him as far as the entrance-hall of distress, saw the whole churchyard of the convent full of corpses, and turned back. He told me he had between fifty and eighty deaths every day out of two thousand patients in the hospital. This would soon reduce his work.

As I approached the town gate I met fifty or sixty sledges, all laden with bodies which had been removed from the hospitals and public places. They were driven as one drives firewood and were stiff with the frost and as withered as palings, and would provide a poor meal for the worms and fishes, because many of the bodies were thrown into holes which had been hacked in the ice.

A sergeant from Lippe named Dornheim has left us a poignant glimpse of Kovno on 13 December.

A largish group of soldiers had lit a fire in the centre of the market-place and the flames were licking up as high as the houses. Round this fire part of the group crouched in the snow; the others remained standing. In the midst of this gathering of troops we saw a Westphalian colonel who was filling a small earthenware pot with snow and placed it on the fire. He had shaken into it a portion of ground coffee; the snow turned into water and soon began to boil in the little pot. He was about to take this off and drink down the stimulating brew when a crowd of soldiers pushed so close to the fire that the poor colonel fell on his face and upset the coffee-pot. 'Oh my God! Not that too!' he cried. These few words, spoken in tones of extreme anguish, aroused feelings of pity and sympathy in many of us, but most of the soldiers laughed over the mishap, and were of the opinion that the colonel needed no coffee to drink, as they were not drinking any either.

One of the most faithful and diligent letter-writers of the retreat was Major von Lossberg, who was always concerned to spare his wife undue anxiety by getting news to her if humanly possible. On 15 December he wrote from Schierwind, in eastern Prussia.

A great crowd of the local people besieged me with the question: 'Are the Russians following close behind?', although they did not appear at all worried at the prospect. However, they all showed me the most sincere sympathy.

... To find oneself once more in a warm room among friendly people in a house (yes, in a town) where everyone speaks German, after a march, or rather a wander, of forty-nine days in such a country at this season and in the climate and circumstances that prevailed — this is an everlasting joy. But how much store I set by the fact that I can tell you, my dear wife, and all the others who are interested in me, that Providence preserved my life. I am in perfect health and have definite prospects of being with you soon! Yes, that is the truth!

The Army was unable to hold out any longer in Russia. The Emperor has transferred it to peaceful winter quarters. On 28 October we began our retreat from Mozhaisk, have fought successfully from time to time, and have arrived this far. . . . I should have liked to have written to you during this period, as I could have spared you many fruitless worries. But not a single field-post went back.

Johann has shown himself a faithful servant throughout. Through a mishap which surprised him, I lost a great deal of particular value to me, because they were things which would have reminded me of the dreadful time I have lived through and because I had so many little things for you, my good wife! These last items, which he knew about, have upset him the most, although I have assured him that the preservation of my life and his is the main thing and that you will be just as good to him as before when you hear from me that he has shown me an exceptional devotion during this dangerous period. . . .

There will be no post out from here for five days, so I shall have to take this letter with me.

[*Four days later he wrote again from Insterburg.*]

On the road here from Schierwind I went through the little town of Pillekallen and found lodging for the night in various villages, where, as a German, I was always well received. But things were not so good for any non-German who had to go through this area on his own. In one village where some French stragglers had arrived, the people wanted to turn them out of the best houses, and a crowd of young peasants prepared to do just this, but I prevented them by remaining in a small inn where my room was never free of inquisitive locals who wished to ask a question and who barely concealed their hatred of the French.

. . . In Insterburg all military coming out of Russia are told by the local authorities where they must go next. Thorn has been designated as the assembly-point for the 8th Army Corps, so I shall make my way there in the next few days.

One who came through the retreat was Count Mathieu Dumas, the Intendant-General.

At long last we were out of that cursed country — Russia. The Cossacks no longer pursued us with such zeal. As we advanced across Prussian territory we found better lodgings and resources. The first place we could draw breath was Wilkowiski, and then Gumbinnen, where I stopped at a doctor's house as I had done when I first passed through the town. We had just been served with some excellent coffee when I saw a man wearing a brown coat come in. He had a long beard. His face was black and seemed to be burnt. His eyes were red and glistening. 'Here I am at last!' he said. 'What, General Dumas! Don't you recognize me?'

'No. Who are you?'

'I am the rearguard of the Grand Army, Marshal Ney. I fired the last shot on the bridge at Kovno. I threw the last of our weapons into the Niemen, and I have come as far as this through the woods.'

I leave to your imagination with what respectful eagerness we welcomed the hero of the retreat from Russia.

Captain Louis Bro spent rather a gloomy Christmas at Königsberg, where Murat had assembled much of the surviving cavalry.

1 January 1813 was far from gay. Snow fell heavily from eight o'clock in the morning until four in the afternoon. At about midday the passing-bell tolled from the cathedral to announce the funeral of a wealthy citizen. It seemed to me that this was the knell sounding for our comrades in arms who, so many of them, lay buried

beyond the Niemen. Some *chasseur* officers, after paying Murat a visit, gathered in a tavern, and here they heard two local inhabitants affirm that the famous Napoleon had left fifty thousand Frenchmen in the snows of Russia and that his reign was almost over. The students gave us insolent looks and hummed the tune of one of the poet Körner's[1] war-songs which preached German insurrection against us. Had it not been for strict orders from the King of Naples to avoid any quarrels, we should have tweaked these Prussians' ears for them. Even so, we persuaded them to voice their hopes more quietly, and most of them obeyed.

Jean-Roch Coignet, formerly a sergeant in the Guard and since July a lieutenant on the staff at Imperial Headquarters, eventually reached Königsberg, and with two companions found board and lodging with a Prussian, who also provided for the horses.

The poor beasts had not eaten any hay or oats since Vilna. How pleased they were to be able to munch at a bundle of hay! And how happy we were to lie down on straw in a warm room! I sent for a doctor and a bootmaker to look at my left foot, which had frostbite. The doctor had to be consulted before I could have a boot made. It was decided that I should have one lined with rabbit-skin and should leave my foot imprisoned in it, having once slit open the boot in order to dress the foot.

'Make the boot tonight,' I said, 'and I will give you twenty francs.' 'You shall have it at eight o'clock tomorrow morning.' So I kept my boots. Next day the doctor and bootmaker arrived. The latter slit my boot and revealed the foot of a new-born babe: no toe-nails, no skin, but otherwise in perfect condition. 'You will be all right,' the doctor told me.

He called in the landlord and his wife. 'Come and have a look. A chicken's foot. I need some linen to wrap it with.' They gladly produced some fine white linen, and my foot was put back into my boot and well laced.

'How much do I owe you?' I asked the doctor. 'I've been

[1] Karl Theodor Körner, born in Dresden in 1791, was a dramatist and patriotic poet. His songs were published in 1814 under the title *Leier und Schwert*, a year after his death in battle.

paid,' he said. 'Such a service is not for payment.' 'But surely. . . .' 'No buts, if you please.'

I held out my hand to him. 'I will tell you one way of curing yourself,' he added. 'Your foot will be sensitive to the cold and heat, so do not expose it to the air. It must stay just as it is, but when the next strawberry season comes round, you should mash a plateful of two or three pounds, make a poultice, and bind it round your foot. Keep doing this as long as the strawberry season lasts, and you will have no pain.'

'Thank you, doctor. And Mr. Bootmaker, here are twenty francs.' 'Certainly not, sir. My expenses only, if you please.' 'How much then?' I asked. 'Ten francs.' 'But you two have been conspiring together.' 'Well,' said my two companions, 'let's drink a rum punch.' 'No,' they said. 'Time is precious, and we must get back. Good-bye, brave Frenchman.'

I followed the doctor's instructions and never felt any inconvenience from my injury. But it cost me twelve francs' worth of strawberries.

One who day by day watched the remnants of the Grand Army trickle into Berlin was Ludwig Rellstab, who was then a thirteen-year-old schoolboy.

One saw no guns, no cavalry, only suffering men crippled by frightful wounds, men with hands, arms, or feet either missing or else completely destroyed by frost-bite. That the hand of God could strike so terribly — one trembled to believe one's own eyes.

. . . As far as I was concerned, I heard the first news of what had happened from my friend E. Magnus, on the way home from school at midday. I shall never forget either the emotions which filled me or the place where he told me — outside the State Bank. At first I had doubts and took the matter quite casually, but when my friend angrily reproached me for my indifference and blurted out the words 'I cried for joy when I heard it', I believed him, and this kindled a flame of jubilant enthusiasm which swelled inside me. I flew home. They had already heard the news there. My father had come home with it from the Werkmeister Museum, an institution in the Jägerstrasse where one could read journals and new publications and which at the time formed a kind of political stock-exchange where every item of news was collected.

Everybody was overjoyed. At last, at long last eyes glistened again with tears of hope and of gratitude to Him who controls the destinies of nations and individuals.

. . . Eventually the remnants of the Grand Army arrived, as I have said earlier. The sight of these unfortunate people was ghastly, and even our happiness at events as a whole had to give way at such moments to the impression aroused by their unspeakable suffering which these innocent individuals had endured and were still enduring as victims of their leader's insatiable greed.

Hatred gave way to pity. When the farm-carts filled with straw, on which lay these terribly disfigured wretches, had to stop somewhere on account of a traffic block in a narrow street, I often saw how the householders hurried out with refreshments, clothing, warm drinks, so as to fortify the half-frozen victims with soup, coffee, or whatever else was available, or else to help them with money. The stench from these carts was frightful. The festering and maybe gangrenous wounds gave off a really pestilential vapour which in the cold air carried further and was felt all the more unpleasantly.

All who witnessed such scenes shuddered. But the ruling hand of God was perceived in these pictures of horror, and anger mounted still higher against the man who was guilty of all this misery in his unprecedented presumption. . . . In the schools teachers discussed the fateful event, pointing out the consequences for the Fatherland. We were, it is true, still under French domination, but their power was no longer so great. They suffered a great deal, even from individuals, and they seemed pleased when they did not have everybody against them.

It is certainly not praiseworthy to mock a helpless enemy, yet I cannot exculpate us boys, least of all myself, of that offence. I frequently used my smattering of French to reproach the soldiers who were billeted on us or whom I met elsewhere with the fate of their army in Russia and to describe the horrors which had overtaken the proud conquerors, for so long invincible. All this was to be deplored, yet in the mood of the moment quite understandable. And we were given a public example. The unspeakable misery of the Grand Army, which we had watched with horror in its individual fragments and which admittedly should have aroused nothing but human sympathy for human suffering, did not escape the bitterest derision. In every print shop, indeed out in the streets in the open-air picture galleries which were usual at that period, and where bad engravings and other pictures were strung up on house walls, one saw caricatures and representations of the army's fate in Russia.

One showed a troop of soldiers in a dreadful state. A marshal on a starved horse which was nothing but skin and bones rode in front, followed by officers and soldiers all with frost-bitten noses and ears and wrapped in strange garments: Jew's furs, women's dresses, or cobbled rags, with military uniforms and badges showing through the holes. The procession of hungry men had stopped beside a horse lying in the snow, and were greedily slicing off the disgusting food with their swords. Despite the efforts at comic representation, the group looked dreadful, and above hovered a hungry eagle, holding in its beak a piece of paper on which was written: '*Ça ira! Ça ira!*'

Another survivor was Second Lieutenant Christian von Martens, who returned to his native Württemberg in the suite of his uncle, Count von Scheler.

At midday [21 January] we entered Heilbronn, where I was formerly garrisoned. I went in at the same gate through which the splendid Crown Prince Regiment had joyfully marched to war, but now I had no waving plume on my helmet and no gleaming sash; I was the only representative of this regiment, and had frozen limbs and a melancholy countenance and feeling. We stopped at the Sun Inn, where the landlord received us in the friendliest and most unselfish way. The champagne-glasses were all emptied in drinking toasts to everyone who was fortunate enough to see the Fatherland again, but also to the memory of those who could not share this good fortune.

At ten o'clock that night we went through the King's Gate at Stuttgart,[1] and soon afterwards stopped our vehicles outside Count von Scheler's home. How can I describe the delight with which wife and children welcomed back the father they adored,

[1] Some thirty miles south of Heilbronn.

who burst into tears of joy. The happiness of seeing each other again after so many days of fear and anxiety was too rapturous. My good aunt was overcome with happiness and collapsed on the steps. I was a silent witness to this touching scene, and the family's joy was so great that I passed unnoticed. Deeply moved, I went away so as not to interrupt these moments of happiness.

Most regiments arrived back in their garrison towns a mere shadow of their former selves, both in strength and appearance. Second Lieutenant Muralt describes how the 5th Bavarian Chevau-légers *returned. It was not untypical.*

About a year after we had marched out, we came back to Dillingen[1] on the Danube, but *quantum mutati ab illis.* We had gone forth to war with between 600 and 700 horses, the men had been in good heart and fine shape, the officers superbly mounted, in glittering uniforms, full of courage and vitality. What a transformation had occurred! Piled up on twelve to fifteen waggons, we made our entry. Half a dozen gaunt and wretched hacks which trotted beside the trace-horses was all we brought back, and I believe these had all been bought in Poland on the way home. The number of men totalled around fifty, mostly officers and N.C.O.s, and few of these were fully restored to health.

Let Colonel de Fezensac have the final word on the end of one fell campaign and the stirrings of another amid mourning and forebodings.

The short time I spent in Paris that winter left me with sad and lasting memories. I found my family, my friends, and society in general terror-stricken. The famous 29th Bulletin had informed France abruptly[2] that the Grand Army had been destroyed. The Emperor was invincible no longer. While we were dying in Russia, another army was perishing in Spain, and in Paris an obscure

[1] Between Ulm and Augsburg, near the battlefield of Blenheim.

[2] Published in *Le Moniteur universel,* official newspaper of the French Government, on 17 December, a day ahead of Napoleon's arrival in Paris.

conspirator had tried to seize power. The campaign of 1813 was about to open, but in what circumstances! The defection of Prussia was no longer in doubt, the Austrian alliance was at the very least shaky, and the exhaustion of France increased in proportion as the list of her enemies grew longer. The stories told by officers who had survived the retreat contributed to intensify people's fear. Paris, used as she had been to songs of victory during the previous fifteen years, was learning day by day and with pained surprise the details of some fresh public or private calamity. The amusements of the carnival stopped. Everyone stayed at home, preoccupied with present misfortunes and anxiety for the future. In the midst of this general consternation people were shocked to see the Emperor entertaining at the Tuileries. This was an insult to the public grief, and revealed a cruel insensitivity to the host of victims. I shall always remember one of those dismal balls, at which I felt as if I were dancing on tombs.

Key to the Sources of Extracts

The Grand Army Prepares

Rambaud, 200 [Antonina]
Fantin des Odoards, 293
Bourgoing, 69–70
Peyrusse, 59–60
Bigarré, 297–8
Schlosser, 67–69
Dumonceau, ii. 17–18
Noël, 167
Suckow, 137–8
Kügelgen, 105–7
Richter, 18
Metternich, i. 122
Rambuteau, 86–87
Bro, 101–2
Brandt, 232–3
Girod de l'Ain, 236–7
Roguet, iv. 452
Schrafel, 46–47
Butkevicius, 898–9
Dumonceau, ii. 37–38
Saint-Chamans, 212–13
Suckow, 150
Butkevicius, 902

Across the Niemen

Rosselet, 191–5
Caulaincourt, i. 343–4
Henckens, 114–15
Compans, 153–4
Oginski, 150–5
Löwenstern, W., i. 189–90
Choiseul-Gouffier, 92–95
Soltyk, 35–38
Fantin des Odoards, 308–9
Jomini, 71–72
Castellane, i. 112
Coignet, 295–6
Adam, 155–7
Bourgoing, 87
Suckow, 156–7
Wider Napoleon!, ii. 118
Rotenhan, 9–10
Rehtwitsch, i. 246 [Scheler]
Fabry, iii, 216–17 [Deroy]
Wedel, 53–55
Rossetti, 217–19
Roos, 34–35
Adam, 159–60
Suckow, 174
Adam, 166–8
Bourgoing, 97–8
Faré, 260–1, 264–5
Fezensac, 220–2
Roos, 54–56, 46–47

Russia Reacts

Staël, 270, 279
Arndt, 163
Mikhailowitch, i. 99–101 [Bagration]
Nesselrode, iv. 68–69
Nesselrode, iv. 70
Wilson, *Brief Remarks*, 1–49
Porter, 131–4
Wilson, *Brief Remarks*, 27–39
Fabry, iii. 343–4 [Vassilievich]
Troyat, i. 102 [Pushin]
Löwenstern, W., i. 206–8
Löwenstern, W., i. 218–79
Löwenstern, W., i. 377–8 [Barclay]
Garin, 7, 8 [Rostopchin]

Smolensk to Borodino

Löwenstern, E., 109–11
Wedel, 65–67
Lyautey, 493
Martens, Chr., i. 98–100
Martens, C., 151–5
Caulaincourt, i. 394–6
Rossetti, 232–3
Larrey, iv. 30–31
Mikhailowitch, i. 101–3 [Bagration]
Brandt, 260–2
Rotenhan, 23–24
Dupuy, 175–7
Bertin, 25–26
Oudinot, 161–2
Schrafel, 50–54
Comeau, 453–7
Brandt, 268–9
Lossberg, 146
Girod de l'Ain, 252–4
Caulaincourt, i. 409–11
Mouravieff, 361–2 [Alexander I]
Wilson, *Narrative*, 130–1
Bennigsen, 133–4
Clausewitz, 110–12

The Battle of Borodino

Rotenhan, 25–27
Biot, 31–33
Rapp, 200–2
Lejeune, ii. 205–6
Fain, *Mémoires*, 39–40
Fain, *Manuscrit*, ii. 18–19
Wider Napoleon!, ii. 132
Girod de l'Ain, 255
Schreckenstein, 60–63
Bausset, ii. 81–82
Roos, 74–75
François, 791–3
Planat de la Faye, 82–83
Bréaut des Marlots, 17–19
Rapp, 206–7
Dumas, iii. 440
Bertin, 87–88 [Soltyk]
Lejeune, ii. 216–18
Wolzogen, 145–8
Griois, ii. 41–42
Meerheimb, 294–8
Fezensac, 240–1
Fain, *Manuscrit*, ii. 44–46
Bellot de Kergorre, 59–64

Moscow

Narichkine, 139, 141–2
Fusil, 228–9
Garin, 26 [Soimonov]
Löwenstern, W., i. 279–80
Narichkine, 161–2 [Rostopchin]
Württemberg, 98–100
Garin, 20 [Muravyev]
Bennigsen, iii. 94–5
Garin, 24 [Shcherbinin]
Rehtwitsch, i. 301 [Württemberg]
Bertin, 120–3 [Boris-Galitsin]
Löwenstern, W., i. 282–4
Narichkine, 175–6 [Rostopchin]
Garin, 31 [Glinka]
Garin, 22–23 [Yermolov]
Wedel, 96–98
Rambaud, 204 [Pokhorsky]
Ysarn de Villefort, 2–4
Garin, 27–28 [Karfachevsky]
Soltyk, 267–70
Brandt, 285–6
Herzen, 11–14
Wider Napoleon!, ii. 151–3
Bausset, ii. 91, 94–95
Vionnet, 50–51
Boulart, 259–60
Ysarn de Villefort, 15–20
Fusil, 230–3
Labaume, 228–9
Castellane, i. 155–6
Garin, 53–54 [Sysoyev]
Rambaud, 222 [Grigorievna]
Garin, 66 [Karfachevsky]
Kurz, 95–96
Vionnet, 42–43
Im Kampf um Freiheit, 139–40 [Klinkhardt]
Fezensac, 245–6
Lettres interceptées, 61 [Parguez]
Garin, 48 [Sokolsky]
Rambaud, 213 [Antonina]
Rambaud, 210 [Alekseev]
Rambaud, 211–12 [a nun]
Surugue, 34–35
Bourgoing, 134
Castellane, i. 161–2, 164–5
Bausset, 99–102
Roos, 113–14
Soltyk, 314–15
Fantin des Odoards, 339–41
Lettres interceptées, 111–12 [Bacler d'Albe]
Narichkine, 193–4 [Rostopchin]
de Maistre, i. 193–5
Wilson, *Private Diary*, i. 193–4
Garin, 90 [Davidov]

Retreat to the Dnieper

Kurz, 125–6
Lejeune, ii. 234–5
Roguet, iv. 497
Aubry, 167–70
Griois, ii. 77–82
Wilson, *Narrative*, 221–9
Löwenstern, i. 294–6
Dedem van der Gelder, 280–1
Lagneau, 219–21
Griois, ii, 107–9
Wilson, *Private Diary*, i. 213–16
Wilson, *Narrative*, 255–60
Langeron, 89–93
Bourgogne, 54–55, 61
Lettres interceptées, 269–70 [Beyle]
Pastoret, 472
Lossberg, 253–6
Compans, 231
Caulaincourt, ii. 154–5
Bourgogne, 106, 99–100
Württemberg, 171–2
Boyen, ii. 252
Larrey, iv. 125, 132–4
Thirion, 229–31
Lecointe de Laveau, 143–6
Roos, 179–80, 182
Bertin, 283–4 [Merme]
Thirion, 238–9
Borcke, 206–8

The Crossing of the Berezina

Langeron, 1–3
Tchitchagoff, 134–7
Langeron, 50–54
Rochechouart, 187–90
Pils, 140–5
Soldats suisses, 189–90 [Bégos]
Dumonceau, ii. 221–2
Bellot de Kergorre, 88–91
Rochechouart, 195–6
Langeron, 71–72
Förster, 688–9 [Blesson]

The Last Marches and Homecoming

Rapp, 250–1
Caulaincourt, ii. 209
Butkevicius, 909–10
Hortense, ii. 152
Ségur, *Mémoires*, 23–24
Griois, ii. 174–6
Henckens, 166–7
Lossberg, 303–4
Hochberg, 198–202
Rochechouart, 200–1
Wilson, *Narrative*, 354
Marbot, iii. 222–3
Szymanowski, 56–57
Hogendorp, 335–8
Chlapowski, 299–300
Choiseul-Gouffier, 136–9
de Maistre, i. 296–7
Choiseul-Gouffier, 150, 153
Wilson, *Private Diary*, i. 256–7
Wilson, *Narrative*, 356–7
Wilson, *Private Diary*, i.
Wilson, *Narrative*, 354–5
Arndt, 173–4
Holzhausen, ii. 175 [Dornheim]
Lossberg, 328–31
Dumas, iii. 484–5
Bro, 126
Coignet, 343–5
Rellstab, 163–8
Martens, Chr., i. 258–9
Holzhausen, ii. 200 [Muralt]
Fezensac, 355–6

Bibliography

Published Sources

N.B. The place of publication is Paris unless stated otherwise.

Adam, Albrecht, *Aus dem Leben eines Schlachtenmalers.* Selbstbiographie nebst einem Anhange herausgegeben von Dr. H. Holland (Stuttgart, 1886).

Arndt, Ernst Moritz, *Erinnerungen aus dem äusseren Leben* (Leipzig, 1840).

Aubry, Capitaine Thomas-Joseph, *Souvenirs du 12e Chasseurs, 1799–1815* (1889).

Bausset, Louis-François-Joseph, Baron de, *Mémoires anecdotiques sur l'intérieur du palais et sur quelques événements de l'Empire depuis 1805 jusqu'au 1er mai 1814* (4 vols., 1827).

Bellot de Kergorre, Alexandre, *Un Commissaire des Guerres pendant le premier Empire.* Journal de Bellot de Kergorre publié par le vicomte de Grouchy (1899).

Bennigsen, General Count Levin August Theophil, *Mémoires du Général Bennigsen.* Tome III, *Campagne de 1812 et de 1813 et Annexes* (1908).

Bertin, Georges, *La Campagne de 1812 d'après des témoins oculaires* (1895).

Bigarré, Auguste, *Mémoires du Général Bigarré, Aide-de-Camp du Roi Joseph, 1775–1813* (no date).

Biot, Hubert-Charles, *Campagnes et Garnisons. Souvenirs anecdotiques et militaires du Colonel Biot, aide-de-camp du Général Pajol,* avec une introduction et des notes par le comte Fleury (1901).

Borcke, Johann von, *Kriegerleben des Johann von Borcke, weiland kgl. preuss. Oberstlieutenants, 1806–1815.* Nach dessen Aufzeichnungen bearbeitet von V. Leszczynski (Berlin, 1888).

Boulart, Jean-François, *Mémoires militaires du Général Baron Boulart sur les Guerres de la République et de l'Empire* (no date).

Bourgogne, Jean-Baptiste-François, *Mémoires du Sergent Bourgogne (1812–1815),* publiés d'après le manuscrit original par Paul Corrin et Maurice Henault (new ed., 1909; 1st ed., 1896).

Bourgoing, Paul de, *Souvenirs militaires du Baron de Bourgoing, 1791–1815* (1897).

Boyen, L. H. C. von, *Erinnerungen aus dem Leben des General-Feldmarschalls Hermann von Boyen* (3 vols., Leipzig, 1889).

Brandt, Heinrich von, *Souvenirs d'un Officier polonais. Scènes de la vie militaire en Espagne et en Russie (1808–1812)*. Ed. Baron Ernouf (1877).

Bréaut des Marlots, Jean, *Lettre d'un capitaine de cuirassiers sur la campagne de Russie*, publiée par M.-J.-A. Léher (Poitiers, 1885).

Bro, Louis, *Mémoires du Général Bro (1796–1844)*, publiés par son petit-fils le Baron Henry Bro de Comères (1914).

Butkevicius, 'Napoléon en Lithuanie 1812' (d'après des documents inédits). A translation of the recollections of Butkevicius by René Martel, *La Revue de Paris*, 15 août 1932.

Castellane, Boniface de, *Journal du Maréchal Castellane* (5 vols., 1896).

Caulaincourt, Armand de, *Mémoires du Général de Caulaincourt, Duc de Vicence, Grand Écuyer de l'Empereur*. Introduction et notes de Jean Hanoteau (3 vols., 1933).

Chlapowski, Général Désiré, *Mémoires sur les Guerres de Napoléon, 1806–1813*. Publiés par ses Fils. Traduits par MM. Jan V. Chelminski et le commandant A. Malibran (1908).

Choiseul-Gouffier, Countess de, *Mémoires historiques sur l'Empereur Alexandre et la Cour de Russie*, publiés par Mme. la Csse. de Choiseul-Gouffier, née Comtesse de Tisenhaus (1829).

Clausewitz, Karl von, *La Campagne de 1812 en Russie*. Traduit de l'allemand par M. Begouën (1900).

Coignet, Jean-Roch, *Les Cahiers du capitaine Coignet (1799–1815)*, publiés par Loredan Larchey d'après le manuscrit original (1883).

Combe, *Mémoires du Colonel Combe sur les campagnes de Russie 1812, de Saxe 1813, de France 1814 et 1815* (1853).

Comeau de Charry, Sébastien-Joseph, Baron de, *Souvenirs des Guerres d'Allemagne pendant la Révolution et l'Empire* (1900).

Compans, Jean-Dominique, *Le Général Compans (1769–1845)*, d'après ses notes de campagne et sa correspondance de 1812 à 1813, par son petit-fils M. Ternaux-Compans (1912).

Dedem van der Gelder, Baron Antoine-Baudouin-Gisbert van, *Mémoires du Général Baron de Dedem de Gelder, 1774–1825* (1900).

Dumas, Mathieu, *Souvenirs du Lieutenant-général Comte Mathieu Dumas de 1770 à 1836*, publiés par son fils (3 vols., 1839).

Dumonceau, François, *Mémoires du Général Comte François Dumonceau*, publiés d'après le manuscrit original par Jean Puraye (3 vols., Bruxelles, 1958–63).

Dupuy, Victor, *Souvenirs militaires de Victor Dupuy, chef d'escadrons de hussards, 1794–1816* (1892).

Fabry, Lieutenant G., *Campagne de Russie (1812)*. Publié sous la Direction de la Section historique de l'État-major de l'Armée (5 vols., 1901–3).

Fain, *Mémoires du Baron Fain, Première Secrétaire de Cabinet de l'Empereur*, publiés par ses arrière-petits-fils (1908).

Fain, *Manuscrit de Mil Huit Cent Douze, contenant le précis des événements de cette année, pour servir à l'histoire de l'Empereur Napoléon;* par le Baron Fain, son Secrétaire-Archiviste à cette époque (2 vols., 1827).

Fantin des Odoards, Louis-Florimond, *Journal du Général Fantin des Odoards. Étapes d'un officier de la Grande Armée, 1800–1830* (1895).

Faré, Charles-Armand, *Lettres d'un jeune Officier à sa Mère, 1803 à 1814* (1889).

Fezensac, M. de Duc de, *Souvenirs militaires de 1804 à 1814* (1863).

Förster, Friedrich, *Preussen und Deutschland unter der Fremdherrschaft, 1807–1813* (Berlin, no date).

François, Charles, *Journal du Capitaine François* (dit le Dromadaire d'Égypte), *1793–1830* (2 vols., 1903–4).

Fusil, Madame Louise, *Souvenirs d'une Femme sur la Retraite de Russie* (new ed., 1910; 1st ed., 2 vols., 1841).

Garin, F. A., *Izgnanye Napoleona iz Moskvy* ['The Expulsion of Napoleon from Moscow' — an anthology of eyewitness accounts] (Moscow, 1938).

Girod de l'Ain, Général Baron, *Dix Ans de mes Souvenirs militaires, de 1805 à 1815* (1873).

Griois, Lubin, *Mémoires du Général Griois, 1792–1822* (2 vols., 1909).

Henckens, Lieutenant J. L., *Mémoires se rapportant à son service militaire au 6ème Régiment de Chasseurs à cheval français de février 1803 à août 1816*. Publiés par son fils E. F. C. A. Henckens (La Haye, 1910).

Herzen, *Erinnerungen von Alexander Herzen*, aus dem Russischen übertragen, herausgegeben und eingeleitet von Dr. Otto Buck (2 vols., Berlin, 1907).

Hochberg, Wilhelm, Graf von, *La Campagne de 1812. Mémoires du Margrave de Bade*. Traduction, Introduction et Notes par Arthur Chuquet (1912).

Hogendorp, *Mémoires du Général Dirk van Hogendorp*, publiés par son petit-fils (La Haye, 1887).

Holzhausen, Paul, *Die Deutschen in Russland, 1812. Leben und Leiden auf der Moskauer Heerfahrt* (2 vols. in one, Berlin, 1912).

Hortense, *Mémoires de la Reine Hortense*, publiés par le Prince Napoléon, avec Notes de Jean Hanoteau (3 vols., 1927).

Im Kampf um Freiheit und Vaterland, 1806–15. Herausgegeben vom Leipziger Lehrerverein (Leipzig, 1912).

Jomini, Baron Henri de, *Précis politique et militaire des campagnes de 1812 à 1814 extrait des souvenirs inédits du Général Jomini, avec une notice biographique*. Publiés par F. Lecomte, colonel fédéral suisse (2 vols., 1886).

Kügelgen, Wilhelm von, *Jugenderinnerungen eines alten Mannes* (Ebenhausen bei München, new. ed., 1907).

Kurz (?), Hauptmann von, *Der Feldzug von 1812. Denkwürdigkeiten eines württembergischen Offiziers.* Herausgegeben von Horst Kohl (Leipzig, new ed., no date; 1st ed., Esslingen, 1838).

Labaume, Eugène, *Relation circonstanciée de la Campagne de Russie en 1812* (4th ed., 1815).

Lagneau, L.-V., *Journal d'un Chirurgien de la Grande Armée, 1803–1813.* Edited by Eugène Tattet (1913).

Langeron, L. A.-A., Comte de, *Mémoires de Langeron, Général d'infanterie dans l'armée russe. Campagnes de 1812, 1813, 1814.* Publiés d'après le manuscrit original pour la Société d'histoire contemporaine par L.-G. F. (1902).

Larrey, Dominique-Jean, *Mémoires de Chirurgie militaire, et campagnes du Baron D.-J. Larrey* (4 vols., 1817).

Lecointe de Laveau, G., *Moscou avant et après l'Incendie* . . . par G. L. D. L., témoin oculaire (1814).

Lejeune, Louis-François, *Mémoires du Général Lejeune*, publiés par M. Germain Bapst (2 vols., 1895–6).

Lettres interceptées par les Russes durant la campagne de 1812, publiées d'après les pièces communiquées par S. E. M. Gorainow, Directeur des Archives de l'État et des Affaires étrangères de Russie et annotées par Léon Hennet et le Commandant E. Martin (1913).

Lignières, Marie-Henry, Comte de, *Souvenirs de la Grande Armée et de la Vieille Garde Impériale* (1933).

Lossberg, General Lieutenant Friedrich Wilhelm von, *Briefe in die Heimath geschrieben während des Feldzuges 1812 in Russland* (Cassel, 1844).

Löwenstern, Eduard von, *Mit Graf Pahlens Reiterei gegen Napoleon. Denkwürdigkeiten des russischen Generals Eduard von Löwenstern (1790–1827).* Herausgegeben von Baron Georges Wrangell (Berlin, 1910).

Löwenstern, Woldemar Hermann, Baron von, *Mémoires du Général-Major Russe Baron de Löwenstern (1776–1858).* Publiés d'après le manuscrit original et annotés par M.-H. Weil (2 vols., 1903).

Lyautey, Hubert, 'Lettres d'un Lieutenant de la Grande Armée', publiées par Pierre Lyautey (*La Revue des Deux Mondes*, 12 décembre 1962).

Maistre, Joseph de, *Correspondance diplomatique de Joseph de Maistre, 1811–1817*, recueillie et publiée par Albert Blanc (2 vols., 1860).

Marbot, Antoine-Marcelin, *Mémoires du Général Baron de Marbot* (3 vols., 26th ed., 1891).

Martens, Carl von, *Denkwürdigkeiten aus dem Leben eines alten Offiziers. Ein Beitrag zur Geschichte der letzten vierzig Jahre* (Dresden and Leipzig, 1848).

Martens, Christian Septimus von, *Vor fünfzig Jahren. Tagebuch meines Feldzuges in Russland, 1812* (2 vols. in one, Stuttgart and Oehringen, 1862).

Meerheimb, Franz Ludwig August von, *Erlebnisse eines Veteranen der grossen Armee während des Feldzuges in Russland, 1812*, herausgegeben von dessen Sohn Richard von Meerheimb (Dresden, 1860).

Metternich, Klemens Wenzel Lothar, Prince von, *Mémoires, Documents et écrits divers laissés par le Prince de Metternich.* Publiés par son fils (2 vols., 1880).

Mikhailowitch, Grand-Duc Nicolas, *L'Empereur Alexandre Ier. Essai d'étude historique* (2 vols., St.-Pétersbourg, 1912).

Mouravieff, Boris, *L'Alliance Russo-Turque au milieu des guerres napoléoniennes* (Neuchâtel, 1954).

Napoléon, *Correspondance de Napoléon Ier*, publiée par ordre de l'Empereur Napoléon III (vol. 24, 1868).

Narichkine, *1812. Le Comte Rostopchine et son Temps.* Par Madame Narichkine, née Comtesse Rostopchine (St.-Pétersbourg, 1912).

Nesselrode, *Lettres et Papiers du Chancelier Comte de Nesselrode, 1760–1850.* Extraits de ses Archives, publiés et annotés par le Comte A. de Nesselrode (vol. 4, 1905).

Noël, Colonel Jean-Nicolas-Auguste, *Souvenirs militaires d'un Officier du premier Empire (1795–1832)* (1895).

Oginski, Michel, *Mémoires de Michel Oginski sur la Pologne et les Polonais, depuis 1788 jusqu'à la fin de 1815* (4 vols., 1826–7).

Olivier, Daria, *L'Incendie de Moscou (15 septembre 1812)* (1964).

Oudinot, *Le Maréchal Oudinot, Duc de Reggio, d'après les Souvenirs inédits de la Maréchale*, par Gaston Stiegler (1894).

Pastoret, Amédée de, 'De Witebsk à la Bérésina', *La Revue de Paris*, mars-avril 1902.

Peyrusse, Guillaume, *Lettres inédites du Baron Guillaume Peyrusse, écrites à son frère André pendant les Campagnes de l'Empire de 1809 à 1814* (1894).

Pils, François, *Journal de Marche du Grenadier Pils (1804–1814)*, recueilli et annoté par M. Raoul de Cisterne (1895).

Planat de la Faye, Nicolas Louis, *Vie de Planat de la Faye, aide-de-camp des Généraux Lariboisière et Drouot, officier d'ordonnance de Napoléon Ier.* Souvenirs, Lettres et Dictées recueillis et annotés par sa veuve (1895).

Porter, Robert Ker, *Travelling Sketches in Russia and Sweden* (London, 1808).

Potocka, *Mémoires de la Comtesse Potocka (1794–1820)*, publiés par Casimir Stryienski (1897).

Rambaud, Alfred Nicolas, 'La Grande Armée à Moscou. Récits de témoins oculaires russes.' D'après l'ouvrage publié par T. Tolytchef, *Revue des Deux Mondes*, 1 juillet 1873.

Rambuteau, *Mémoires du Comte de Rambuteau*, publiés par son petit-fils (1905).

Rapp, Jean, *Mémoires du Général Rapp, aide-de-camp de Napoléon*, écrits par lui-même (2nd ed., 1823).

Rehtwisch, Theodor, *1812–1815. Geschichte der Freiheitskriege* (2 vols.; 2nd ed., no date; 1st ed., Berlin, 1908).

Rellstab, Ludwig, *Aus meinem Leben* (2 vols., Berlin, 1861).

Richter, Adrian Ludwig, *Lebenserinnerungen eines deutschen Malers*, herausgegeben von Heinrich Richter (Frankfurt-am-Main, 1885).

Rochechouart, Louis-Victor-Léon, Général Comte de, *Souvenirs sur la Révolution, l'Empire et la Restauration*, publiés par son fils (1889).

Röder, Franz, *Der Kriegszug Napoleons gegen Russland im Jahre 1812*. Nach den besten Quellen und seinen eignen Tagebüchern dargestellt nach der Zeitfolge der Begebenheiten (Leipzig, 1848).

Roguet, *Mémoires militaires du Lieutenant-Général Comte Roguet* (4 vols., 1862–5).

Roos, Ritter H. U. L. von, *Ein Jahr aus meinem Leben oder Reise von den westlichen Ufern der Donau an die Nara, südlich von Moskva, und zurück an die Beresina, mit der grossen Armee Napoleons, im Jahre 1812* (St. Petersburg, 1832).

Rosselet, Abraham, *Souvenirs de Abraham Rosselet, lieutenant-colonel en retraite au service de la France*. Publiés par R. de Steiger (Neuchâtel, 1857).

Rossetti, Marie-Joseph, 'Journal du Général Rossetti. La Campagne de Russie', *La Revue de France*, 15 mars 1932–1 mars 1933.

Rotenhan, *Denkwürdigkeiten eines württembergischen Offiziers aus dem Feldzuge im Jahre 1812*. Veröffentlicht durch Freiherrn von Rotenhan (3rd ed., München, 1900; 1st ed., Berlin, 1892).

Saint-Chamans, Alfred-Armand-Robert, *Mémoires du Général Comte de Saint-Chamans, ancien aide-de-camp du Maréchal Soult, 1802–1832* (1896).

Schlosser, Ludwig Wilhelm Gottlob, *Erlebnisse eines sachsischen Landpredigers in den Kriegsjahren von 1806 bis 1815* (Leipzig, 1846).

Schrafel, Joseph, *Merkwürdige Schicksale des ehemaligen Feldwebels im königl. bayer. 5ten Linien-Infanterie-Regiment, Joseph Schrafel, vorzüglich im russischen Feldzuge und in der Gefangenschaft, in den Jahren 1812 bis 1814, von ihm selbst beschrieben* (Nürnberg, 1834).

Schreckenstein, General Freiherr Roth von, *Die Kavallerie in der Schlacht an der Moskwa am 7. September 1812* (Münster, 1858).

Ségur, Général Comte de, *Histoire de Napoléon et de la Grande Armée pendant l'Année 1812* (2 vols., 9th ed., 1826).

Ségur, *Du Rhin à Fontainebleau. Mémoires du Général Comte de Ségur (aide-de-camp de Napoléon)* (new ed., no date).

Soldats suisses au service étranger. Includes 'Souvenirs des campagnes de Lieutenant-Colonel Louis Bégos' (Genève, 1909).

Soltyk, Comte Roman, *Napoléon en 1812. Mémoires historiques et militaires sur la Campagne de Russie* (1836).

Staël, *Oeuvres complètes de Mme. la Baronne de Staël.* Tome XV, *Dix Années d'Exil* (1821).

Suckow, Karl von, *Aus meinem Soldatenleben* (Stuttgart, 1862); French translation: *D'Iéna à Moscou. Fragments de ma vie* (1901).

Surugue, l'Abbé Adrien, *Un Témoin de la Campagne de Russie*. By Léon Mirot (1914).

Szymanowski, Général Joseph, *Mémoires, 1806–1814*. Traduits du polonais par Bohdane Ockinczye (1900).

Tarlé, Eugène, *Napoleon's Invasion of Russia, 1812*. Translated from the Russian by G. M. (London, 1942).

Tchitchagoff, *Mémoires de l'Amiral Tchitchagoff (1767–1849)*, avec une notice biographique d'après des documents authentiques (Leipzig, 1862).

Thirion, Auguste (de Metz), *Souvenirs militaires, 1807–18* (1892).

Toll, *Denkwürdigkeiten des russischen Generals von der Toll.* Herausgegeben von Theodor von Bernhardi (2 vols., Leipzig, 1856).

Troyat, Henri, *Pouchkine* (1946).

Vandal, Albert, *Napoléon et Alexandre Ier. L'Alliance russe sous le premier Empire* (3 vols., 6th ed., 1911).

Vionnet de Maringoné, Lieutenant-Général Louis-Joseph, *Campagnes de Russie et de Saxe (1812–1813). Souvenirs d'un ex-Commandant des Grenadiers de la Vieille Garde. Fragments de Mémoires inédits* (1899).

Wedel, Carl Anton Wilhelm, Graf von, *Geschichte eines Offiziers im Kriege gegen Russland, 1812, in russischer Gefangenschaft 1813 bis 1814, im Feldzuge gegen Napoleon 1815. Lebenserinnerungen* (Berlin, 1897).

Wider Napoleon! Ein deutsches Reiterleben, 1806–1815. Herausgegeben von Friedrich M. Kircheisen (2 vols., Stuttgart, 1911; 1st ed., 1861).

Wilson, Sir Robert, *Brief Remarks on the Character and Composition of the Russian Army, and a Sketch of the Campaigns in Poland in the Years 1806 and 1807* (London, 1810).

Wilson, General Sir Robert, *Narrative of Events during the Invasion of Russia by Napoleon Bonaparte, and the Retreat of the French Army, 1812*. Edited by his Nephew and Son-in-law, the Rev. Herbert Randolph (London, 1860).

Wilson, General Sir Robert, *Private Diary of Travels, Personal Services, and Public Events, during Mission and Employment with the European Armies in the Campaigns of 1812, 1813, 1814, from the Invasion of*

Russia to the Capture of Paris. Edited by the Rev. Herbert Randolph (2 vols., London, 1861).

Wilson, General Sir Robert, *General Wilson's Journal, 1812–1814*. Edited by Antony Brett-James (London, 1964).

Wolzogen, *Memoiren des königl. preuss. Generals Ludwig Freiherrn von Wolzogen (1807–14 in russischen Diensten)* (Leipzig, 1851).

Württemberg, *Erinnerungen aus dem Feldzuge des Jahres 1812 in Russland von dem Herzog Eugen von Württemberg* (Breslau, 1846).

Ysarn de Villefort, François Joseph d', *Relation du Séjour des Français à Moscou et de l'Incendie de cette Ville en 1812, par un habitant de Moscou* (Bruxelles, 1871).

Index of Persons

(Bold figures indicate authorship of an extract)